VICTORY
A.C. GREEN

WITH J.C. WEBSTER

CREATION HOUSE
BOOKS ABOUT SPIRIT-LED LIVING
ORLANDO, FLORIDA

Creation House
Strang Communications Company
600 Rinehart Road
Lake Mary, FL 32746
Fax: (407) 869-6051

Dedication

To the world's greatest parents,
A.C. and Leola, for your unmovable love and support
and for always being there to give direction about
any decision, big or small.

I dedicate this book to you because of the impact
of the true quality, character and principles that you've
enforced in me from 2' to 6'9".
You've helped me understand God's love
in so many things you've said and done.
Thanks for being my role models and heroes.

Junior

Special Thanks

For this book that you now hold in your hand I must give special thanks to my brothers and sister — Lee, Steve and Faye — for being the ones who kept me going both on and off the courts. Especially you, Lee and Steve, with your constant one-on-one challenges which I'm sure will never end.

To all my nieces and nephews who believe there is only one star in the NBA — thanks for your constant phone calls to say, "There's nothing you can't do, Uncle Junior."

To my spiritual family, Pastor and Sister Irving, Rod and Karen Bragato — if it weren't for your burden for youth I probably wouldn't be in the position to write this book today. To Pastor David and Joan — thank you for believing in God's call on my life in my early Christian days.

To Pastor Phil and Karen, Tom and Dave, for the example of God's grace and faith that you live by. I take it with me daily, and it makes it fun to be a Christian.

To Greg and Helen Ball — you've been so influential in my development into manhood. I appreciate your friendship.

To Lee and the Johnson family, for letting me invade your home and be part of your family. Administrative judge Lee Johnson, you're an example of persistence toward a goal and one of the best friends yogurt can buy. And thanks to my other lifelong friends who keep me strong — Rice, Roger, Darryl, Eric, Dennis, Darrell, Big Dave, Barry, John.

To Tootie and the administration office at OSU, to E.O.P. and to coaches Lanny, Steve and Jimmy and, of course, Ralph — I thank you all for your commitment to excellence.

To my high school coaches, Coach Vertees, Coach Pennington and Coach Gray, for teaching me NBA-style basketball — run and gun!

To all my teammates from the Lakers — real "Showtime" is what we accomplished in the 1980s, champion-style. Thanks for the memories and the friendships. Thanks also to all the Laker wives for the extra plate at dinner for the single guys on the team.

To Dr. Buss and Jerry West, for taking a chance on a skinny, backwoods kid from Oregon. Thank you for believing in me and instilling qualities of manhood in my life. To my Laker coaches, Pat Riley, Bill Bertka, Randy, Chet, Larry and Mike, for demanding nothing but the best, even with the earthquakes.

To my Suns family — thank you, Jerry Colangelo, for your commitment to winning and for allowing me to be part of the Phoenix Suns family. To the fellas — we've got work to do, so let's have fun doing it. Thanks for fouling me all the time in practice. To Coach Westphal, Lionel and Scotty — thanks for accepting nothing but the best, even with all the distractions, 80 degrees plus.

To my staff at the A.C. Green Programs for Youth, for never letting me forget my vision and goals.

And to my homies and families in P.O. — the Washingtons, the Stewarts, my cousins and Uncle Tut and family — and to the Greens everywhere else for being there, wherever you are.

To my editor and the outstanding team at Creation House, for your encouragement and talent that made this book possible.

Last, to J.C.W., for your constant effort to see this book live up to its potential. You taught me so much. I only apologize that you had to interview so many people.

CONTENTS

Introduction

WARM UP
AND STRETCH

I WAS TAUGHT to be a well-mannered youngster. I was coached to be a championship-level basketball player. I was inspired to be a good Christian. But when I finally gave God my life completely and let go, He developed me into something bigger and better than anything I was ever taught, coached or inspired to become. He will do the same for you.

As a kid I had no idea of what my life could become. I dreamed of being a winner, so I tried hard to win at the little playground sports we played. As I grew, I naturally leaned toward basketball. But when Jesus Christ became my best friend, my Lord, my Coach with a capital C, I found the larger purpose for my life and went on to pursue it as well as professional sports.

Basketball is my talent, but the gift God gave me is much larger than that. God uses my talent as a platform from which I can achieve my greater purpose. My goal is to influence others to fulfill their potential by pursuing their dreams in accordance with their gifts and talents. Young or old, male or female — you can achieve your purpose in life. A limitless God can make you a champion.

Generally, a champion is someone who reaches a victory. A teammate of mine who won several championships defined being a champion as being acknowledged above all peers and competition as the undisputed "number one." But I don't define *championship* based on competition or accolades. To me, champions are people who achieve their true purpose in life, who reach victory in many areas.

True champions measure themselves by a higher standard. Nobody's perfect. If we try to become champions by competing against imperfect people or measuring up to someone else's imperfect victories, we measure ourselves against imperfection. By accepting their weaknesses or failures, we keep ourselves from reaching our full potential. The only perfect man who ever walked this earth is Jesus Christ, God's Son. The champions I'm talking about compare themselves to Him and try to live up to the goals He sets. The best part is that He helps them do it. We don't need to compare ourselves with others or compete against them. To be true champions, we can measure ourselves against Him alone and compete against any force that would keep us from being like Him.

The more we become like Christ, the more goals we'll reach. He wants us to win, so He leads us into championship living. We win inwardly when we measure up, to the best of our ability, to the standard He sets for us. It may take years for others to see our championship qualities and acknowledge them. But eventually the inner peace, character, strength, obedience and other championship qualities God places within us will show up.

People may say to you: "You're holding a good standard."

"You're a man of integrity."

"You're a woman with morals."

Acknowledgment from peers is always secondary, however. We don't need to depend on their acceptance and praise. It is greater to be accepted by Christ and have the inner satisfaction that we've done our best. True champions are praised not just for their outer performance, but also for their inner substance, which is the real measure of total victory. The accolades in the spirit are greater than those in the flesh.

As much as I love basketball and work hard to excel in it, I have to say that the greatest victories are not scored on basketball courts or playing fields. Winning on the court is great, but it leaves many players miserable in other areas of their lives. People who don't discover or achieve their true purpose live in misery regardless of what athletic victories they rack up. A true champion achieves his or her life purpose as designed by God.

You and I were born with certain talents and traits, strengths and weaknesses. Your characteristics fit together to give you — and you alone — the unique ability to accomplish a specific purpose. Your first important step on the road to victory is to find that purpose. When you find it, you throw yourself into it. You don't hold back, live in fear, apologize or hide from your purpose. You pursue it wholeheartedly, and God helps you fulfill it.

Victories won't come after every battle, either. We won't win every game. But even losses can become victories if we learn from our mistakes. True champions understand and accept that. When we fail, we get up and try again.

"If you don't quit, you won't lose," Evander Holyfield said after regaining his heavyweight boxing title from Riddick Bowe in 1993. That's a champion.

Abraham Lincoln lost more elections than he won, but he still became a great U.S. president. That's a champion.

"Champions are not those who never fail, but those who never quit," Ed Cole teaches.

If we fight enough battles, we can eventually win the war.

The stories I tell in the following chapters are not just there for laughs or entertainment. Each story is an experience that shows a principle of life. Principles are laws, like throwing a ball up and knowing it will come down because of the law of gravity. That's a principle. What goes up must come down — through the hoop, we hope.

In the same way, the principles you find on the following pages are like laws that, if you obey them, will lead you to be a winner in life. Use them in whatever way they apply to your life. They will help build the internal character needed to sustain championship living, and they will advance you toward your goals.

Look at this as a little one-on-one basketball. It's just you and me. Out on a court all alone. No one around. I'm showing you the moves, teaching you the plays that will guarantee victory. The question is, do you really want it? Are you content to sit on the sidelines, or do you have the courage to get into the game?

To make it a little easier, I have highlighted the principles, and in the back of the book are some deeper questions that go with them. That means you can use this book as a study guide for either personal devotions or group study.

So, whether you're 12, 20 or 120, get ready for the challenge of your life. We're talking about a championship here. Where the stakes are higher, the costs are higher. The winner's circle is sweet, but it's reserved only for those who reach victory!

1

DREAMS AND GOD'S GRACE

I WAS A typical kid who loved his parents and didn't like getting in trouble but didn't really like following the rules, either. As children we get free room and board and usually a free education, and, in return, we do stupid things that could kill us. It's only by God's grace that most of us survive our childhood, much less pursue and achieve a goal in life.

I did my childhood duty well and narrowly escaped death when I was about eight. My cousin Willie was visiting on a bright, warm Sunday afternoon in midsummer. My mom and dad, Leola and A.C., were gone for a few hours, so we thought we could get away with running through the house. My parents' home was a two-story, gray clapboard house in Portland, Oregon. We lived in a nice, quiet neighborhood where poplars, maples, lindens and other trees shaded the street and where neighbors could hear each other's screen doors squeak open and slam shut with a clang. My sister, Vanessa Faye, was in charge of watching us that day. Faye, as we call her, is the oldest, five years older than I am. Then comes Lee, four years older, and Steve, a year older. I'm the baby.

"Hey, Junior," Willie said, using my family name, "wanna play tag?"

"Yeah!" I answered. He chased me, and I ran from him screaming.

"Watch out!" I hollered as I threw open the front door and ran through the house.

"You're it!" he said as he tagged me. I chased him out the back door, quickly dragged a chair to prop open the door, then raced around to the front again.

We had a concrete front porch that stood about three feet high and extended almost the entire length of the house. It served as the favorite hangout for parents on warm summer evenings. They would drag chairs out of the house to talk the night away while we kids played kick ball in the street. I loved that porch. It was great for hide-and-seek because no one could see you if you crouched right around the corner. If home base was close by, you were almost assured of never getting tagged "it." I loved to balance myself on the brick railing that ran the perimeter, and I loved to jump off that railing as far out into the yard as I could. I often missed the lawn and landed right in my mother's flower beds, which I always paid for on the seat of my pants.

When the weather warmed in the spring, I had two favorite sounds: the school bell signaling the end of the day and the music of the neighborhood ice cream truck. When I heard the truck coming, I'd run out the big front door and scream for the others as I leaped from the top of the stairs to the walkway and dashed out the gate to the street. Our front door was glass, made of small window panes from top to bottom that were framed by wood. Directly across from the door, four painted concrete stairs led down to the walkway. I loved not only to jump off the porch, but also to jump from the walkway up onto the porch, scaling those stairs in a single leap. As soon as I mastered that maneuver when I was about seven, I never took the steps again.

Willie and I dashed again through the house — out the back door, around the side, hurdling onto the porch, then through the open front door and back through the house again. Furniture rocked. The floor shook.

"Gotcha!" I screamed.

"Gotcha back! You're it!" he shouted.

"Stop running in the house!" Faye shrieked. She tried to stop us each time we raced from front to back, but we didn't hear or see her — if we did, we didn't pay attention. Finally she got tough. As soon as we cleared the back door on our next round, she moved the chair, closed the door and ran to the front to shut that door, too. At that exact moment, Willie jumped the porch, with me hot on his heels, and squeezed through the crack as the door closed.

I was right behind him and could not stop. I threw out my arm to keep from slamming my face into the door. The glass panes shattered on impact, leaving a triangular piece jutting up from the woodwork. My left arm went through the glass, and that triangle acted like a sharpened blade, slashing my arm open from wrist to armpit. I collapsed.

"Junior!" Faye screamed.

"Oh, no!" Willie said. "Junior, get up! Stop faking it!"

I looked at my arm laid open in front of me.

"Oh, please, someone stop the bleeding!" I said.

"Quit playing!" Willie insisted with wide eyes.

"Will, what did I do to myself?"

Faye brought towels to sop up the blood. Four towels soaked through as she walked me across the street to our neighbor's house. By then Willie was somber. Seeing the blood, he was thinking, DOA. Mrs. Welch was a nurse, but all she could do was wrap my arm in a sheet while Faye called our parents.

Mom and Dad were near enough to get to the house quickly.

"Is my baby OK?" Mom asked Mrs. Welch anxiously.

"Come on," Dad said. "Let's get him in the car."

He turned to the other kids who by now were gathered on Mrs. Welch's porch, and he felt my life was hanging in the balance. "Were you horseplaying in the house?" he asked. No one said a word. "Wait here."

In no time Dad got us to the nearest emergency ward, which wasn't equipped for that serious an injury. The staff transferred me to another hospital, but they feared I was going to die because I had lost so much blood. Finally I was in surgery, with Mom and Dad in the waiting room.

"He's lost so much blood," the doctors told them. "It looks like another pint would have killed him. You got him here just in time."

Dad paced the floor, and Mom wrung her hands and prayed until the doctors came back an hour later. "He's going to be OK," they announced. "His arteries were cut, and the gashes were deep, but the nerves are intact. It looks like he'll have full use of his arm after it heals."

"Oh, my baby!" Mom said.

When Dad got home, the other kids heard his opinions about running in the house. They felt a little of the pain I felt, too, only they got it on their backsides. I'm sure the only daylight Willie saw for a week after that was outside the kitchen window, as he stood at the sink washing dishes. His parents told him to do extra chores while they decided what his *real* punishment would be. The anxiety was probably as bad as the love pats he eventually got.

Meantime, the next thing I knew, I was lying in a bed eating bad-tasting dry eggs and looking at a big bandage covering my arm. The bandage had the smell of a sickly clean antiseptic that only a hospital would use. When my parents came in and told me I'd be all right, I thought I had just lucked out. Years later I realized God's grace had protected me from an enemy who tried to destroy me that day. God had a purpose for me that a little boy from Portland would never have dreamed possible.

Grace means to get something you don't deserve or not to get something bad that you do deserve. Most of us deserve to die for any number of crazy things we have done. But God's grace keeps us. His grace gives us life instead of death, opportunities instead of dead ends.

PRINCIPLE #1
See how God's grace protects you. Realize that God's grace has kept you for a purpose that only you can accomplish.

I was in the hospital for a couple of days. I hated the food, so I lived off orange juice and a lot of attention until I was released. At first, people brought me gifts. Being the youngest of four, I always competed for everything — attention, food, being allowed to play with the big kids, clothes, respect. Now, all at once, my brothers and sister were nice to me. It was like the movie *Home Alone.* Suddenly, everyone liked me. They catered to me. They sat in my hospital room and talked to me — real, civil conversation. I thought, Yeah! This is all right! and I milked it for all I could.

When they took off my bandages, my arm was lined with dozens of stitches. Little black threads stuck out everywhere, as if my mom or some other seamstress had gone crazy on me. The wound healed in scabs that looked like a bad case of real orderly chicken pox. Surprisingly, my arm never hurt, perhaps because my big brothers had increased my level of pain tolerance by wrestling and roughing me up so often. To this day I don't feel injuries that much, but I can hardly stomach needles. In the 1993-94 basketball season, I had to have stitches in the back of my head in the middle of a playoff game because Otis Thorpe's smile collided with my head. For the first time I was alert through a whole surgical procedure. The doctor used the longest needle I ever saw. If I hadn't had to go right back out and play, I'd have asked them to put me under.

When I finally got home from the hospital, recess time was over. Faye, Lee and Steve smiled on the outside, but they were mad. "We got whippings!" Lee said when Mom and Dad left the room.

"You got us in trouble!" Steve said.

Faye felt personally responsible for the accident, but she still maintains that I was the guilty party. "He should have got lit up like the rest of us," Faye will tell you today.

Their kindness definitely stopped at the hospital door. It was payback time in a big way.

"Bring me a glass of water, Junior," Faye would order.

"Change the channel on the television," Lee demanded.

"Give me that!" Steve said about something I cherished.

"Let me go first," Lee said with an elbow if I was in front of him in line.

As for running in the house, you'd think I would have quit. But once I was back on my feet, I held my left arm steady with my right, and I was off to the races again. Some things were just hard for me to learn. I did figure out, however, that, in our house, being hospitalized was the only way you could avoid discipline. Mom and Dad were loving, unselfish, devoted parents, but "Spare the rod and spoil the child" was a principle they lived out.

Mom and Dad had what you could call an earthy, street knowledge of life based on experience and common sense. They didn't concern themselves much with national events or global news, but they knew how to raise a family.

Dad was born to the Green family of Ballinger, Texas, and inherited the family resemblance, as well as an accent I can't understand when we visit my relatives there. Fortunately, he's lost a lot of it, but he can still clip a sentence or word off in nothing flat. His voice is the most imitated voice I've ever heard. All my childhood friends do Papa Green impressions.

Mom was born Leola Thompson in Wagner, Oklahoma. Soon after she married Dad, they moved to El Centro, California, where Dad's family had settled. Mom's family is large. Dad's family is immense. On Dad's side we have relatives everywhere from Washington State, down through California and over to Texas. After having three kids, Mom and Dad left El Centro to be near Mom's father, who had moved to Oregon. I was born in Portland on October 4, 1963.

My folks were hard workers and always lived in nice neighborhoods where everyone worked just as hard, usually both parents in the family. My dad loves cars. He was a car detailer and salesman at a Ford dealership until he had an injury when I was a teenager. It left him permanently disabled, though not handicapped. He has always found more than enough work to occupy his time. His work ethic definitely inspired me, and it became a private joke I shared with Magic Johnson years later. Mom worked for thirteen years as a fabric processor at Jantzen sportswear, then changed careers when they dismantled her division.

In the summertime our Portland cousins came over to our house, or we went to theirs every day. Sometimes my family took vacations by car to California and Arizona to see Grandma Jesse and our other cousins. I remember one trip we took in style, driving Dad's 1965 Pontiac Bonneville — wow! We had a great time. The kids ran around at rest stops, laughing and carrying on.

But our eyes were always focused squarely on family, not on the larger world. When I got to Oregon State University years later, I was a city boy who acted more like a country hick. When the team traveled, I was all eyes. I had my first airplane ride the summer before I graduated from high school, and that plane may as well have been the space shuttle. It was all new to me.

I appreciate the way my parents raised me. I'm especially glad that our family always ate together. On winter mornings I could smell the cream of wheat cooking in the kitchen, and I'd spring out of bed and run down for a huge helping. That was the happening breakfast for me. In summer we all had our favorite cereals, which Mom bought in the jumbo, economy sizes. I have to admit I liked the sugary kinds.

In the evenings the favorite food for Dad and my brothers was fish. We lived in fish country, where weekend trips to the ocean or rivers were common, but I never got the desire or the taste for it. When I smelled fish cooking, I'd start saving myself for the weekends and Mom's traditional soul food. She made collard greens, black-eyed peas, ham hocks, smoked neck bone, hot water cornbread and fried okra, along with biscuits to die for. The entire Laker team later fought over those biscuits and for seconds at Mom's table, just as we did growing up.

In the summertime Mom followed up dinner with sweet-smelling watermelon. We'd sit around as a family, and the kids would kick each other under the table, trying to get the other person to laugh. Steve was the charismatic one. He always tried to get me and Lee in trouble. Friends dropped by to join us — some invited, most not. In our neighborhood, somehow every mother knew what foods the neighbor children liked best, and it was common for them to send over a helping or to invite us in.

Mom always knew my biggest weakness, though. "You hurry and get your chores done," she'd say. "And do them right, because if you do, I'm going to make you Hamburger Helper."

My mouth would start watering right then. Hamburger Helper was my absolute favorite meal, right up through college. If she hadn't offered it for a while, I'd be waiting when she got home from work. "Mom, can we please have some Hamburger Helper tonight?"

Mom and Dad dished out discipline, but they heaped on love, too. Even though they worked long hours, they were generous with their time and whatever material wealth they could give us. Dad couldn't buy us everything, but when he did purchase something, he always bought quality. He taught us to respect quality, and he expected us to be responsible for our possessions.

"Here's your bike, all ready to ride," he said as he tightened the last screw when the bike was new or after an overhaul. "Now you ride it carefully, take good care of it and don't skid those tires!"

The cardinal rule with Dad was "Skid your tires — put away the bike." Even if there were skid marks on the street in front of our house, we would have to put our bikes up. All our friends knew that, and they'd get even for squabbles we had by skidding in front of our house to set us up.

All the neighborhood kids loved good bikes. "Look what I got!" I said triumphantly to Lee and Steve when Dad bought me an orange Craig. I was out the gate on it in a flash.

"Is that a new bike, Junior?" the neighbors asked.

"It sure is," I said proudly. It wasn't a ten-speed or a mountain bike. It was built sort of like a modern-day dirt bike. They don't make bikes like that anymore — literally.

"Come on — let's race," Lee said one day. He always liked to get me to do things he could beat me at, since he was bigger. "You go that way, and I'll go this way," he said, "and we'll see who gets home the fastest."

I was younger, not dumber. We both headed for the same short-cut to beat each other.

"Look out!" I shouted as his bike bore down on mine, but it was too late.

His smile was the first to connect with the back of my head. I walked my bike home with blood gushing out of my skull. But for all the blood it turned out to be minor. Lee is sure that in the playoff game where I was injured, he saw me say, "Oh, no, not again!"

Dad took great care of his vehicles. Even if he was driving an old truck, it was perfect, never beat up. Lee picked up that trait from him and started modifying his bikes, so of course Steve and I copied him. We added eight-inch-wide sissy bars that stood about two feet above the seat so we could lean back against them like chopper riders. That was the style at the time. You weren't cool if your bike didn't have a sissy bar and a generator for the light. We must have been the coolest brothers on the block.

One time we held one of our famous wheelie contests, seeing who could go for a whole block on his back tire.

"Watch this!" I said as I lifted the front of my trusty orange Craig into the air. Instantly I knew from the feel of my bike that this was a run for the world championship.

"Go! Go! Go!" everyone screamed as they chased me down the block.

I was going, going, going. Finally my tire came down, as if in slow motion, like an airplane landing. Then it fell the last few inches and slammed to the ground, and my bike frame cracked in half. Both bars beneath the seat that led to the handlebars broke right in two.

"Wow, look what I did!" I said, staring at the two halves of my bike.

"What a ride! You hold the record, Junior!" someone said.

We all laughed and looked at my bike, but reality was slowly setting in. This was my only bike.

"Yeah, that's pretty funny," I said. "I broke my bike."

I laughed as long as I could, standing on that corner. But inside, the exhilaration of the moment was completely swallowed up by the dread of having to go home and show Daddy. Good old Elmer's glue had helped me out of a lot of scrapes, but even Elmer couldn't help me now.

Lee, Steve and I finally headed for home. I put my bike in the garage and carefully arranged the pieces to make them look whole before I faced Dad. But one of my brothers got in the house first and hinted at what had happened.

"I had an accident," I said nonchalantly when I saw Dad inside. "Not too bad. I think it can be fixed."

"Where's the bike, Junior?" Dad asked me.

"I brought it home," I said, maintaining my casual tone, trying to think of what Perry Mason would do.

"*Brought* it or *rode* it?" Dad asked.

"It's in the garage," I answered evasively, but it was all over for me. Dad was on his way to the garage in a flash.

"How'd you break your bike in two?" he asked incredulously, holding the two pieces in his hands. I had to admit — it was a minor miracle. Kids dent, bend, nick and scrape bikes, but they don't usually break them right in two.

"You're going to have to wait until your birthday to get another one, Junior," he said grimly. I didn't see a bike again for a month or more, which seemed like centuries in kid years. I probably looked out the same kind of kitchen window Willie looked out while washing dishes, but going without a bike was the worst punishment I could have had.

Dad didn't lord things over us abusively. He simply taught us to be responsible in a very practical way. He knew how much I missed having a bike, so he finally relented and bought me a bike before my birthday.

The neighborhood was a stable world. A thoroughfare at the bottom of the hill on the north end separated us from shipping yards and train tracks, where train whistles blew routinely like background music to our lives. The kids were entrepreneurs, creating corporations together to sell lemonade and juices at corner stands or mowing lawns for two dollars. In bad weather the young kids would stay indoors and play games around the fireplace. The bigger kids played outdoors almost year-round — rain, snow or shine. The smells of rain-sogged wood outdoors and burning oak indoors are still the smells of home to me. In the summer, if we didn't want to play, we could join the adults on the porch to hear vivid stories about the "good ol' days." On those summer nights Dad would turn up his music in the living room so we could hear it out on the porch.

Dad loved the blues and early rock and roll. Every evening he would come home and put on his favorite albums. Wilson Pickett and Otis Redding were his speed, while Mom listened to Al Green and Tom Jones. They both loved Little Richard. Dad thought so much of Little Richard that he named his oldest son after him. Lee's driver's license still reads "Little Lee Green." In 1992 Steve and I took Dad to a Little Richard concert in Los Angeles, and we all went backstage to meet the man. Steve and I were quickly forgotten as Dad and Little Richard started swapping stories.

"Remember when you played such-and-such place?"

"Yeah, and ol' what's-his-name was with me."

"Yeah, well, I was there!"

"Yeah?"

"Yeah!" Dad was just one giant smile, like a basketball junkie who got to meet Michael Jordan.

My parents didn't allow us to go outside our neighborhood much. Even within the neighborhood our friends were screened.

We didn't do many sleep-overs unless our parents knew the other kid's family well and knew they weren't drinkers or partiers. Faye never got to sleep over at a girl's house if she had a lot of brothers, which showed my parents had foresight as well as wisdom.

When it came to obedience, Mom and Dad were not the only ones we had to answer to. "What do you think you're doing?" a neighbor would cry out when she saw us terrorizing a little neighbor kid. "Get over here and let me show you how that feels."

A whipping and a tongue lashing might follow, but that wasn't the end of it. As we rode our bikes slowly home, she was on the phone. "Mrs. Green," she would say, "I've just caught Junior and his friends over here picking on little so-and-so."

We'd go home and get it all over again. For discipline, every place in that neighborhood was "home." The Bible says that people keep sinning if they don't get swift judgment. Well, swift judgment was the name of the game in our neighborhood. That helped me later on when I learned about sin — to act on it swiftly. Don't let sin set in.

With such tight-knit surroundings, we pretty much did as we were told. But when we were caught misbehaving, we were masters at blame-shifting.

"It wasn't me," Faye said.

"Not me," Lee said.

"Me neither," Steve said.

I was left all alone in the courthouse. I never got to see the jury. I was set up, accused, tried and hung all at once. Finally I got smart and started sitting on the porch to wait for Dad to get home from work so I could be the first to tell — and I'd tell it my way. That's how I became the chief of police around our house.

What we called discipline then, many would call child abuse now. My family, friends and I are all products of the inner city, but our neighborhood has still not suffered from blight and urban decay as many others have. I believe it's because people passed down through the years that same discipline, along with common sense, respect and an understanding of the value of human life. Discipline preserved the neighborhood in the same way discipline preserves people.

When we're young, discipline is inflicted upon us like a thick, deep, engraved mark that is etched, traced and retraced on us. When we grow up, compromise will slowly erase that line until all we have left is a faint chalk line, a hint of wrongdoing, where the deep groove of conviction used to be. Where once we feared telling a small fib, we become able to tell huge lies without a worry. At one time, decisions were made for us about going to school, facing consequences and striving to do our best. But when we grow up, we have to motivate ourselves to do those things on our own, from within.

You must have discipline to reach a championship level in life.

In professional basketball, if a player has talent and ability but doesn't have discipline, he washes out. Anyone can do something once, but not well. Maybe after a lot of tries, someone can do something perfectly a time or two. But to do something perfectly every time requires constant practice, and practice requires discipline. Coach Pat Riley always worked our Laker teams to the point of fatigue at practice. His reasoning was that we had to be able to shoot and execute plays as well at the end of a game, when we were tired, as we did at the beginning, when we were fresh. Discipline made us a championship team. Discipline will take what you master or acquire and keep it for you.

Discipline is a key in the arsenal of championship weaponry.

PRINCIPLE #2
**Discipline will preserve you. Accept discipline
from others and develop self-discipline.
Start your arsenal of championship
weaponry with discipline.**

My family lived in the same neighborhood my whole life except for when I was in grades four through six, when we moved twice. First we moved to St. Johns in North Portland, then to Gresham, a suburb of Portland. When Dad was injured, we moved back to the old neighborhood and dug deep roots on N.E. Morgan Street. I entered junior high when we returned.

Typical of boys our age, Lee, Steve and I, along with our friends, were fascinated by anything that moved. We loved to make home-built go-carts with old plywood. We nailed two-by-fours to a piece of plywood, then nailed on some wheels. The best were from those three-wheeler Big Wheels that little kids ride. We'd string ropes from the front two-by-four to steer — a little. An unspoken rule was that we always had two riders. We pulled each other around until we got going, then headed straight for a corner to see if we could make it. We never did, but the crashes were as spectacular and satisfying as if we'd made the corner.

About that same time Dad bought us a motor bike. A kid named Jeffrey Washington moved into the neighborhood right after that, just two doors down from my best friend, Ricky Stewart. The day he was moving in, I rounded the corner on our yellow bike just as his dad was rolling his off the U-Haul truck. His was exactly like ours but blue. Jeffrey, Ricky and I were the same age, and from that moment on, we were the best of friends.

All the neighborhood kids stayed busy doing things ourselves rather than watching other people do things on television. We wanted to have the fun ourselves. But one thing we always watched was boxing. Lee, Steve and I would join Dad in the living room to watch the pros duke it out. When Dad was in El Centro years before, he had been an amateur boxer with the opportunity to go professional. He still loved it. One time Dad took me to stand in line for two and a half hours to get Floyd Patterson's autograph when he was in Portland.

"My dad was a boxer," I told the neighbor kids proudly. "He's tougher than Muhammad Ali!"

"Is not!"

"Is so! He's bigger than Floyd Patterson, too. I know. I saw him in person."

I embellished every story and believed everything I said. To me, Dad was the greatest boxer of all time.

"I can prove how great he is," I'd say. "Here's his professional robe."

Dad's robe hung in the laundry room. It was silky green, with gold lettering emblazoned across the back: "A.C. Green, El Centro, California." When I was in the mood to pretend, to act like something bigger and better than I was, I'd get it off the hanger. The cool, fresh-smelling silk would swallow me, especially those giant sleeves. I'd parade around, imagining that I was in a boxing ring with the announcer calling out, "A.C. Green versus Muhammad Ali!"

"Let me show you how he punched," I would tell friends who were small enough to beat up. Then I'd fulfill the fantasy by taking advantage of them.

Lee and Steve didn't want to wear the robe as much as I did, but when they wanted it, the real fights took place.

"Give me that," Lee said, pulling it off my shoulders.

"Give it to *me*," Steve said, yanking on it.

Next thing we knew, Dad's boxing robe had a hole here and a rip there. We didn't understand the value of sacred treasures back then. We made that holy robe a *holey* robe.

Those dreams of winning were an important step to becoming a real winner later on. People who lose their dreams of winning stop trying. The Bible says we become what we think.

Wearing Dad's robe was my first real taste of victory, the first time I ever felt I wanted to win no matter what — to be on top, to become a champion, to be number one. I especially identified with that robe since my name was on the back. I wanted to live up to it.

Every child dreams of winning — before events and attitudes have the opportunity to steal those dreams. Having a dream of victory is the first step to achieving victory. Everyone can become a champion, but it has to start with a desire not to settle for anything less.

PRINCIPLE #3

Don't settle for anything less than victory. Admit that you desire to win, to be a champion. That's the first, small step toward achieving victory. If your desire has been trampled down, ask God to revive it and make it strong again.

My name has often confused people because A.C. doesn't stand for anything. Even though I'm the youngest, I'm named after my dad. I'm a "Junior," so that's what my family calls me. Lee was the oldest boy, but he never cared that he didn't get Dad's name. After all, I'm the one who has to explain all his life that A.C. doesn't stand for anything. Mom says I got Dad's name because when I was born, I looked exactly like him. She gazed down at me and said, "This is A.C.," and it stuck. Of course, dozens of other Greens looked like him as well, but I got the name.

I wasn't the most popular kid in school or on my street when I was younger. If people have to dress for success, I shouldn't have amounted to anything. My family still laughs at memories of my striped pants. My school didn't require uniforms, but my personal taste dictated wearing striped pants. I was the guy who, long after the fashions changed, still wore leisure suits, polyester, and plat-form shoes. I always pulled my pants up to keep them on, high-water style. And I made strange combinations like wearing plaids with stripes.

"Junior, look at you," Faye would say.

"What?"

"Your pants and your shirt," she said.

"Hey, they've both got red in them, so what's the difference?"

For years Mom stuck to the philosophy that her children could pick out their own clothes and test themselves as individuals. But she finally asked one time, "Junior, have you ever heard of a color scheme?"

"No, Mom," I answered. From then on, she chose my clothes.

If I accidentally wore something stylish, I still had to fight the Great Clothing War with Steve. Steve was cool and sharp. And he had a rule never to wear the same clothes I did. Even though we were only a year apart and most parents buy similar clothes for their kids, Mom couldn't buy us anything alike. Sometimes when she couldn't help it she might buy both of us navy blue trousers. Steve went crazy over that. He always got ready first if we were going somewhere and waited in the front seat of the car as the rest of us came out of the house. I was always the slowest to get ready, so I came out last. If I had on the same colors he was wearing, like the navy trousers, he went into fits.

"No, no, no — he can't wear that!" he'd scream. "I've got that on! He has my pants on."

Steve wouldn't even give me hand-me-downs. He threw old clothes in the garbage rather than let me have something he had worn. I learned how to dress at some point during junior high school and finally became one of the "cool kids." But it wasn't until college that I matured and found out what "cool" really meant.

2

FOLLOW
THE LEADER

ALMOST EVERY BOY'S fantasy is to become a professional athlete of some sort, and I was no different. Down at the park, as I reached for the slam dunk, I'd say, "I'm Dr. J." Or I'd try a hook shot as I yelled, "I'm Kareem Abdul-Jabbar." Or I'd say, "Get ready — it's a Magic Johnson pass."

Amazingly I ended up playing with or against every one of those guys. I have found that most professional athletes feel shocked when the television screen all of a sudden turns into real life, when a dream becomes a reality.

Dad didn't watch a lot of sports outside of boxing unless you count horse-riding in Westerns — Dad loves his shoot-em-ups. I picked up what was happening in sports from friends, who picked it up from others like their brothers, uncles and fathers. Since there wasn't much opportunity to do anything destructive in our neighborhood, except to beat up our own bodies, everyone played sports. Girls got together and played with dolls, had slumber parties and did each other's hair. Boys got together and massacred each other in baseball, football, basketball, tennis and kick ball. In my backyard we annihilated each other in swimming, too. My family had the neighborhood pool. Dad played softball with us kids and threw the baseball to us, and he rarely missed one of our games when we played in organized leagues, but he never pushed any of us. It was my peers who got me into sports, and peer pressure pushed me into competition.

Until high school I was the same height as other kids my age, and baseball was my dominant sport. We played double-or-nothing sandlot baseball, where we had to get a double or we were out. We also played on organized teams, starting young with T-ball. I made it to the All-Stars in Little League and was the home run champ in my division one year. I was one of my school's top home-run hitters when I got to junior high, which is more than I could say for my academics.

I didn't love schoolwork, but I did love Woodlawn Junior High School, a red brick building with tall windows and white trim. It was the daytime home of every preadolescent kid in the neighborhood.

I still go back to visit the students about once a year. Last year they made me a big birthday card, and everyone signed it. It meant a lot to me.

I got baseball completely out of my system by the time I left Woodlawn for high school. Kareem Abdul-Jabbar always dreamed of the baseball career he never had, and Michael Jordan left basketball to start one. That's not for me. I caused a lot of pain to a lot of baseballs, but when the balls started to get even, I decided to hang it up. In Little League, Coach Archie Jamison taught me to play shortstop by sacrificing any available body part to make the stop. It seemed I was always getting hit by the baseball, so when I left

Woodlawn, I decided to leave the pain behind. Ironically I left the pain of an occasional ball to the leg for the daily pain of elbows to the head and knees to the thighs, not to mention teeth to the head.

Before my earliest memories, my brothers introduced me to basketball. I can't remember not playing. When we lived in St. Johns, Lee used to torment me.

"I'll let you shoot this time," he would promise. It was hard enough for me just to get the ball up to the rim, but he'd swat it away.

"It's not fair," I'd wail after several attempts, and then I'd storm off for home, frustrated beyond anger.

He was a giant, and I was a little kid. I guess he prepared me for opponents like Mark Eaton and Manute Bol. At 7'4" and 7'6", they were two of the most frustrating players I've ever gone up against. (At the time of this writing, Bol is still playing in the NBA, but Eaton has retired.) You could forget your basic layup when one of them was on the court. Their long arms can reach in from outside the key and swat those balls down like King Kong swatting airplanes.

I was much more evenly matched with my friends Ricky and Jeffrey. We played every sport together, like street football. In summer we'd play late into the night, pushing our luck to stay out a little longer.

"Would you boys get in here? Come in the house!" Corey Stewart hollered.

"Junior! It's time for bed," my mom called from a few doors down.

"OK, next touchdown wins," we'd say as we faced each other on our imaginary line of scrimmage.

You name it — we played it. One of Ricky's habits was so annoying it became hilarious neighborhood folklore, and we never let him live it down. He was the only guy in the neighborhood who had a good basketball. Back then most of us used a rubber kick ball that we called a "rubber duck." We could leave those balls outside at night, and no one would take them. But Ricky had an elite outdoor suede basketball that everyone coveted. None of us will ever forget that incredible ball. It smelled of rich leather and felt like the fuzz on the perfect peach. We could almost palm it.

That was the ball we always took down to the park to play. But if Ricky was in a close game, he would suddenly grab his ball and go home. It always happened at crunch time, like with the score tied at fifteen points each when we were playing to sixteen. If he didn't get a foul in his favor, or if he lost, everyone knew what was coming.

"I'm taking my ball and going home," he'd say as he stomped away with that awesome ball tucked under his arm.

"Ricky, come on! Come back here!" we'd call after him. But it never helped. He always left us standing there.

To this day, when Ricky comes back to the neighborhood to visit, everyone teases him about that, especially Steve. "What are you going to do, Ricky — take your ball and go home?" he says.

When I start harassing him, he has his comeback ready: "I'm going to tell your coach what I used to do to you on Saturdays." He still believes he can beat me at anything. "He's going to give me your spot," he says.

We always went next door to Mrs. Brannon's basket to shoot when we couldn't go to the park. Her son, Michael, regaled us with stories about his high school coach, Coach Gray, the ultra-famous, winningest coach in the state of Oregon. I was always awestruck when he talked about this legend as a personal friend.

Back then I was too young to see beyond the cuffs of my high-water pants, but my parents got the vision for my destiny while watching me play basketball with the neighbors. God was working in them, giving them an idea of what was happening and what could possibly occur down the road. They saw that underneath those checks and stripes, those sibling fights and silly pranks, lay a pool of bubbling potential. They saw the big picture.

You need to see the big picture in your life. Someone else may have to tell you about it. For me, it was Mom and Dad. So often we get caught up in the activities of daily living and don't realize what God is doing or where He's taking us. Spending time away from the pressures of life can help you get a glimpse of the larger panorama of your life and help you find your place.

PRINCIPLE #4
Get the big picture of life. Spend time in prayer,
talking with someone you respect or just getting
away from it all to look at the possibilities God
has for you.

My friends and I watched professional basketball players on television making incredible moves in front of millions of people, running on beautiful courts, wearing cool uniforms. It looked great — but I never knew they were getting paid! I don't even know if my parents realized that someone could make his living playing a schoolyard game. Still they encouraged me.

"Stick with it, Junior," they said. They didn't push, just encouraged. I never thought about quitting basketball because it was fun, so their encouragement was a mystery to me.

Until fourth grade, kids usually do what their parents lead them into. In fourth through eighth grades, kids usually do what their peers lead them into. In high school, things finally start separating out, and a person starts becoming more of an individual; yet peer pressure is at an all-time high. For me, peer pressure defined my whole life right up through the last day of high school.

One Saturday Ricky, Jeffrey, another guy and I played basketball while we were still going to Woodlawn. We took a breather and sat down on the curb, hot, dirty and sweaty.

"Where are you going to high school?" one of us said. Strict boundaries weren't observed, and no one abused the public school system, so we had some choice in where we went.

"I'm going to Adams," the other guy said.

"I'm going to Jackson," Jeffrey said.

"I'm going to Benson," Ricky said.

So I said, "OK, I'm going to Benson, too." Done. No thinking. Just copying. My life was like that, totally dictated by what my friends did.

Pretty soon Ricky and I headed off for Benson together, riding the number eight bus down tree-lined 15th Avenue to the Lloyd Center bus stop. We crossed the street, cut across the park, crossed another street and were at Benson Polytechnic School. On one side of the street sat a Cadillac dealership which, beyond my dreams, I would one day come to know. On the other, Benson rose from the pavement, a huge, prestigious, red brick structure covering about four square blocks of downtown Portland.

An enormous front lawn, complete with a fountain on the street level, slopes upward from the sidewalk toward the mammoth entrance. Wide concrete steps lead to three sets of double front doors that are framed by gigantic concrete columns. Huge windows in sculpted concrete frames with white wood trim stretch two rows deep on each side of the doors. Stepping into the tiled lobby, the first thing a visitor sees is a picture of Simon Benson, the namesake, who lived in a previous century. It is an institution in the fullest sense of the word. We called it the brick White House.

The students from Benson were known as the brainiacs, the smart kids. To stay in school, Ricky and I knew we'd have to keep our grades up. I tried out for basketball just because most of my friends tried out, and I made the freshman squad. My coach, Bill Virtees, and a lot of great teachers encouraged me to keep up with my studies as well as my sports. I wasn't thrilled to do either, but I worked at it a little just to keep people off my back. In my sophomore year Hugh Pennington became my coach. He was serious about encouraging me, and for the next three years he continued to help me on my defensive skills after practices.

I made the junior varsity team and started practicing with the team after school. We also played what we called "rat ball" in the gym before the 8:20 opening bell and during lunch. Fully dressed in our school clothes, we would go at it, playing full-court games and smelling as sweet as a professional basketball team throughout the rest of the day. I may have never excelled in my studies or on the court except for what happened one day during such a workout.

Coach Dick Gray, whom my neighbor Mike Brannon had played for, enjoyed basketball so much that he came to school early and sat through lunches in the gym just to watch us compete. He looked like a distinguished, elder statesman with gray hair — balding a little on top — and glasses. He was still in good physical shape even though it was his thirtieth year of coaching at Benson. He hadn't won a state championship in seven years, and he had an intense desire to win another. He became my physical education teacher during my sophomore year, but he didn't notice me much. When I met him, I felt like I was meeting a legend. I watched him from a distance, intrigued by being so close to such a famous person.

One day right after we had played in the gym, Coach Gray came up to me and laid his hand briefly on my shoulder. "You stick with it. You might have some potential," he said.

To a frail, insecure, fifteen-year-old this was like a reprieve to a death-row inmate. I could possibly have potential — *wow!* Something inside clicked. From then on, I wanted to please him. Suddenly I was no longer in basketball to follow my friends; I was there to follow Coach Gray. I was desperate to make the varsity basketball squad. I was no longer at Benson to follow Ricky Stewart. I was there to follow Dick Gray. I wanted to learn, to excel, to become a champion. I had a goal — to make the varsity team, to play Coach Gray's kind of game, to learn from him. I had found a leader.

Finding a leader is one of the most important steps in becoming a champion. Whether you're old or young, you need to find a leader and make a decision to follow him or her. High school peer pressure is notoriously strong. But there is equally strong peer pressure on the grown man who thinks he needs to be driving a new car because everyone else has one. There's also equally strong peer pressure on professional ballplayers who think they need to go out club-hopping because other guys on the team are doing it. And there's equally strong peer pressure on church board members who think they've got to build a new sanctuary because their sister church across town built one. Peer pressure can be used in a specific, positive way, but we're not talking about that yet. Either you're going to follow your peers, which is generally negative and stagnant, or you're going to follow a leader.

Peers don't make good leaders. They're at the same part of the road as you and haven't experienced what is up ahead. They're called peers because they are the same as you. It's impossible for them to lead you further. If you look to them as leaders, they will become misleaders.

PRINCIPLE #5
Find a leader; then follow that leader. Look for someone who is reaching some goals. Remember: peers don't make good leaders.

Your leader should be someone who has achieved a goal you want to achieve, as well as someone you can trust. Whoever becomes another's leader and leads him toward his God-given destiny is a real hero, an unsung hero. If you're ready and willing to follow, God will bring a leader your way.

The heroes and role models of high school students, particularly teachers and coaches, affect so many lives. When Coach Gray stepped into my life, he came at the most impressionable, vulnerable time of my life. He had the power to confirm what my parents were saying or to steer me in a totally different direction. I gave him and his opinion that much weight. Fortunately for me, he was a great influence, someone God planted in my path. He encouraged me, worked me hard and challenged me to excel. He was the first to teach me not to accept mediocrity. When things come easy to a person, when the talent or the intelligence is naturally there, that person has a great temptation to slide along and not really excel. Coach Gray brought me up short whenever I tried to coast. He made me excel in the classroom and on the court.

I was a common sight my first year at Benson — a 5'10" freshman who played basketball in the neighborhood. I returned for my second year a different person. That summer I had needed a cast on my leg because I had a problem with my joints from growing so fast. My brothers had always been taller. When I started my sophomore year, I matched Steve at 6'3". By my junior year I was Lee's height, 6'7", and had learned to watch my head going through doorways. They stopped growing, but when I got to college, I was 6'8-1/2" and grew to just over 6'9" after I joined the NBA.

Even with my cast on during that fast-growth summer, I stayed active. The best thing for growing bodies is activity. It works out a lot of problems before they start. I didn't know back then that a person can lose coordination. My constant sports activities kept my coordination so I was never clumsy.

My high school years were full. In the summers I had jobs. I worked one summer for the Oregon Forest Service under the supervision of rangers, out in the woods. We cut timber, dragged trees where they told us and laid walking paths and hiking trails. It was hard work, but fun. I had to get up at 4:00 A.M., get dressed, make my own lunch for the first time (my mom had always done that), grab my overalls and boots, catch the 4:30 bus to Benson and catch the vans out to Estacada, a neighboring city. I remember that finding steel-toed boots in a size fifteen was a challenge.

I also worked in the Nike warehouse for two summers. That was a fun job, and I made great friends. I worked in shipping and receiving, often sending out shoes to professional athletes. I didn't know all of them, but occasionally I'd see a name I recognized, like football quarterback Dan Fouts and basketball forward

Maurice Lucas, who had played for the Portland Trail Blazers championship team in 1979. (I certainly never expected that one day I'd be on their list. One of the friends I met at Nike packed a pair of shoes for me recently and inserted a note saying, "Hi, how are you doing?" I laughed at the irony.) Nike allowed me to work as much overtime as I wanted, so I always went in an hour early and left an hour late. They paid well, six bucks an hour, and I was finally able to save some money for college.

Through the school year I had studies, practices, games and other jobs. For a while I worked after school on the cafeteria cleaning crew. I swept and mopped the floor and cleaned the tables. I had to be there at 3:45, so I didn't have much time to play basketball after school. The responsibility of that job made me feel more a part of Benson.

"Hey, stop that. I have to clean this place up!" I said if someone started making a mess during lunch. I was proud of my clean cafeteria.

Evenings after school and practice were always the same. I got home, did homework, ate dinner and played sports until dark, even later when the park lights were on.

We couldn't stay out too late on school nights, but I didn't want to anyway because I never missed Ed Whelan on the 11:00 news. Ed was the local CBS sportscaster who was from our neighborhood. He always told jokes on his broadcast, and all of us loved him. I've followed his career, and he, in turn, followed mine. When he announces sports, he still calls me "A.C. Junior." He tells me now that he knew I'd become a pro because he used to see me when I was "a little ol' kid with a big ol' head and big ol' feet that used to walk by my house every morning going to school."

Most guys in our neighborhood continued playing sports, and everyone who didn't play watched. High school games were almost always sellouts. Mom would get off work and be over at the school by 4:00, when my junior varsity games started. When I made the varsity team and games were later, most of my family became regulars.

Having my family support me, in my desires as well as financially and emotionally, helped me stick with the goals that Coach Gray challenged me to make. Supportive people are part of every one of my successes. Building that good, strong network of support people and quality friends is another key to becoming a champion. There are no Lone Rangers at the top. At the time, I didn't know how to choose good friends. I was drifting along with the crowd, but God's grace continued to protect me.

In my sophomore year I teamed up with Lee Johnson, who became and has remained my best friend. Lee played football and baseball for Benson while I was playing basketball, so we never played anything together officially. Instead we've fought each other for bragging rights in everything. We have competed at baseball, football, basketball, tennis, swimming, golf, pool, bowling — just about anything you can go head-to-head in.

We still compete in our ongoing Mark Spitz swimming contest — that's how far back it goes. Lee was in my backyard recently at midnight still trying to beat me. When we were kids, his brother Jay would come over to our house and race me and Steve, the Johnsons versus the Greens. The Johnsons were always slower. He'll contest that — something about my body length giving me an unfair advantage — but take it from me, the Green brothers are the fastest swimmers on Morgan Street.

Because Benson was a technical high school, we had to declare a major and learn a trade while we were there. Lee and I, feeling like pretty tough guys, chose machine shop. We learned to use machinery to work a piece of metal into a screwdriver, a wrench or other interesting parts. And we used our creativity to make some interesting kinds of pipes.

I've never been in a machine shop since, but Lee has. He worked at one for about two months after high school until he said, "No, I can't do this for the rest of my life!" The next thing I knew he was at Oregon State with me, and we roomed together for four years. When I went on to the Lakers, he went to the University of Texas law school, and he's an administrative judge in Texas today. There's always been that competition between us, and we still go head-to-head every time we get together.

Ricky Stewart, on the other hand, turned out to be sort of a brain. He got an award for having a grade point average over 3.5 for two straight years, went to the University of Oregon and now works as a veterinarian in Southern California.

In my junior year, the varsity basketball team was really coming together, but arch-rival Grant beat us in the play-offs, so we didn't make it to the sixteen-team state tournament. Benson's rivalry with Grant is a Portland tradition. We were like the Lakers and the Celtics, the Cowboys and the Redskins or the Hatfields and the McCoys. When we played, it was almost for blood. We couldn't stand one another. One of my neighborhood friends, Terrel Cage, played for them. He and I had played together for years, but during basketball season, our friendship vanished, just the way it happens in the pros.

In the summer before my senior year, I played at the Basketball Congress Invitational, which was a national meet in Birmingham. I went with some Oregon players whom I had just met, and I flew on an airplane for the first time.

"Think you'll end up in the pros?" one of the kids asked one evening as we walked toward our dorm in the dark.

"Yeah, maybe," I said, too embarrassed to admit that I had never thought of it.

"That's what I'm going for," he said.

What looked like lightning above my head made me flinch, but it went away.

"I am, too," another kid said.

I saw more "lightning" near my head and got distracted. At the time I was still getting used to the gnats there in Birmingham. Gnats usually hover together at about six feet, so it's not unusual for tall guys like me to put our faces into a swarm of them. But this was different. This looked like bugs that lit up! I started boxing at the air.

"What's that chasing me?" I cried out, as I ran a few yards.

"Fireflies," one of the guys said.

"What's that?" I asked.

"You know, lightning bugs," said another.

Just then I saw another light up, and I ran all the way to the safety of the dorm. I could hear the guys laughing behind me.

"You've never heard of fireflies?" one of them asked when he walked in. "They're bugs that light up at night."

"There are no bugs that light up!" I said, still rattled. "You're crazy."

Even though I was the hotshot basketball player, I realized right then that there was a lot about the world I still didn't know.

In my senior year Coach Gray started us right off toward a championship season. "If you run the ball, no one can beat you," he told us, and we believed him. We practiced a little defense, and he taught us some good moves, but mostly we just aimed to outscore other teams.

"Play basketball! Run! Have fun!" he said as we took the court for our first game.

He instilled such a fun-loving, confident attitude in us. We had athletes who were real marksmen, like Sam Morton and Greg West. When we kept up our shooting percentage during practices, we believed we really were unbeatable. I was the center, wearing number forty-five, and my role was not to score but to rebound. Even so, I was usually double- or triple-teamed whenever I got the ball. They wouldn't play me one-on-one; most teams played zone.

"The only points you're going to score are off the offensive boards," Coach Gray said, forcing me to work on rebounds. Every night after practice, assistant coach Pennington drilled me on rebounds, rebounds, rebounds.

Before the year began, most colleges and scouts were watching Dean Derrah, an All-State player at Hillsboro High, which had been one of the top high school teams for three straight years. He made a verbal commitment to Oregon State University before they ever looked my way. Coach Gray had a few coaches calling about me, but they were from places like Piedmont Community College, not big schools with major basketball programs. We were a team of unknowns, basically, and we came up against Hillsboro early in the regular season. They had another All-State player on their squad besides Derrah — John Immel. Even with Derrah and Immel, Coach Gray had us so pumped that we really thought we were going to win. Instead we lost by a few points in the final seconds.

"You can learn from your loss and work it into a victory, or you can cry over it," Coach Gray told us. We were so upset about losing to Hillsboro that we wanted to destroy every team from then on.

When we came up against arch-rival Grant, I don't know where the fire marshal was because the gym was packed, including the aisles. No one could move except vertically, and we had the crowd on their feet most of the game. Tracy Bailey's father was our loudest fan. Even in those packed gyms with what seemed like the entire city of Portland screaming at the same time, we could hear Mr. Bailey above the rest. He was a six-foot-tall truck driver with a higher pitch to his voice than you'd expect and the vocal chords of a newborn baby on an airplane. When a call went against Tracy he got crazy.

"Ref, are you blind," he hollered at the referees. "Where did you get your license? You get it from a Cracker Jack box?"

Benson led Grant from the start. At one point we were up by ten when I stole the ball from an opponent at about three-quarters of the court. I dribbled the breakaway from the outside and drove toward the basket. On the opposite side, a would-be Grant hero was angling to cut me off before I reached it. I got to the top of the key, wide on the sideline, and he cut me off five feet from the bucket.

During the drive I made up my mind that if I could get the ball near the paint, I was going to dunk it. My teammate Greg West, at just 5'8", could also dunk the ball, so we called him "Doc" for Dr. J. But this was my turn.

I dribbled once more, then palmed the ball with my right hand the way I used to see Dr. J. do it on television. I reached way back behind my head as I jumped. The defender stayed with me, jumping in front of me to block my shot. When he sprang up, our bodies collided, but I reached over him and dunked the ball on the way back down. Then I turned and ran back up the court. I intended to continue play, but instead I ran right into my teammates, who hugged me and slapped high fives. Then I looked over and saw Faye, Lee and Steve in front of a crowd that was going crazy.

"Atta way, boy," Mr. Bailey hollered. "You show 'em!"

Benson supporters stood, mouths open, veins popping out of their necks, screaming. The Grant crowd sat down, shielding their eyes with their hands and saying, "No, oooh, ouch." It was great fun, a sweet moment. My body was still numb with goose bumps the next day, and my forearm was very, very sore.

We beat Grant and rolled the rest of the year. We averaged over ninety points a game in thirty-two-minute games. Because we were destroying teams in our division, coaches got desperate. When we played at Wilson High School, their coach told his players to hold the ball. We didn't play with a shot clock back then, so they were able to slow the ball down to keep us from scoring. At the end of the third quarter the score was only 17-9, and their own fans started booing them. When the fourth quarter started, their coach gave in and told his team to go out and play.

We scored fifty-six points in one quarter and won 73-19. That might be the biggest margin I've ever won by in my life.

We went on to the play-offs and killed Grant in the first round. Then we won every game in the state tournament, taking us to just one win away from the championship. By now we were ranked the number-one team and were favored to win, but the challenger for our last and final game was number two, Hillsboro. Whoever won the game took home the state championship and a lot of pride.

When the game started, I got two early buckets, and we were up 10-4 in three minutes. That forced them to run, to play our game. We were up by ten points at halftime, and we stayed pretty much in control of the game from then on. With 2:56 left in the fourth quarter, we led by fourteen points. The standing-room-only crowd of around twelve thousand in Memorial Coliseum was almost out of control. A high school crowd doesn't just make noise; it deafens people. A lunatic version of "Battle of the Bands" whipped them into a frenzy as both pep bands played their school fight songs furiously, at a tempo that the trumpet players still probably haven't recovered from.

"We're number one! We're number one!" the Benson crowd chanted. They hugged each other and waved toward the bench to get their favorite player's attention, which we gladly gave to them. Nervous ushers and guards brought the yellow rope around the court to hold people off. With all that going on, I got totally distracted.

"We won!" we said to each other on the sidelines when we saw the yellow rope.

Within forty-five seconds of our reaching that fourteen-point lead, Hillsboro had cut the lead in half, to just seven. Suddenly, our team was scared. We lost the edge. We had already started celebrating, and now we were too nervous even to shoot the ball. We lost concentration, and with it went our confidence. We were tired, too.

"Suck it up!" Coach Gray screamed over the ruckus.

"Keep playing, boys!" Mr. Bailey hollered a few decibels over the crowd.

With one and a half minutes to play, Sam Morton raced in for a breakaway, and we were up by ten. But it wasn't enough to give us back our momentum. With a minute left to play, we were only ahead by six. They scored, and we were up by four. Greg "Doc" West dunked one to put us up by six again. Then Greg got fouled.

"Best call I've seen all day," Mr. Bailey yelled.

Greg made the free throw that put us up by seven. The crowd started to chant.

"Ten, nine, eight...."

Dean Derrah hit a shot from the baseline, another Hillsboro player scored, and suddenly we were only up by three points.

"Seven, six, five, four...."

John Immel stole the ball from us and scored again, bringing Hillsboro within one point.

"Three, two, one!"

People screamed so loud we could hardly hear the buzzer. Somehow the clock ran out, and we squeaked past them 74-73.

"We did it!" someone near me cried with relief.

"We're number one," I screamed, and then I scrambled to find my family in the crowd that broke the yellow ropes and filled the court. I looked frantically around until, suddenly, big arms grabbed me, my legs came off the ground, and I was airborne, aloft on the shoulders of my brothers and friends.

"He did it!" Lee Johnson screamed.

"We won!" my brother Lee hollered.

I leaned back, "TECH 45" emblazoned across my chest. I stretched both arms out with my fingers pointing toward the roof signaling number one. People jostled the guys carrying me and reached up at me.

"A.C., you did it!" they yelled.

I thought, This is a Kodak moment! Enjoy this. Freeze this.

My family could not have been happier if they themselves had played the game to win the championship. As far as I was concerned, they did win it. I looked over, and Coach Gray's family was smothering him, too. He struggled through the mob to shake hands with Hillsboro's coach.

Then came the presentation of the trophy.

"These kids worked hard all year," Coach Gray said. "We've come a long way since our early loss to Hillsboro. Now we can say we really did beat every team on the way here. With a record of 26 and 1, I'm just real proud of them."

I was happiest for Coach Gray, and I'm sure I shared that feeling with all of Portland. It was his fourth state championship in nine tries over a thirty-year career. Ten years before our win he'd beaten Grant in the final game. Ten years *after* our win he beat them again, that time winning the championship by just two points. He finally retired a few years ago, and I was privileged to return to Benson to honor him. Some of his players went on to compete in college, and two of us so far, Richard Washington and I, have gone on to the pros.

Men often talk about their "glory years" in high school, after they've gone on to pursue other careers, and I'm no different. High school basketball was basketball at its most fun. It was competitive. We played for the sheer joy of the game and for tasting victory. I've never seen people get so riled up as we did during those years. The only thing I could compare it to is the Lakers' world championships — it was every bit as good.

That year I learned a very important lesson: Never quit, *especially* when you're ahead. Never stop playing until you're past the finish line. If you don't quit, you won't lose. Winners are just people who won't give up until they win.

PRINCIPLE #6
Never quit, *especially* when you're ahead. Never stop playing until you're past the finish line. If you don't quit, you won't lose.

I was the tallest guy on the team and could have broken scoring records, but Coach Gray wouldn't let me. Even with the brakes on, twice that year I scored thirty-nine points and in the season finale against Wilson I scored forty. I averaged twenty-seven points per game. As a team we scored more than a hundred points in seven games and averaged over ninety. I was voted the *Oregonian's* 1981 All-Metro area player of the year, and I joined Dean Derrah on the All-Metro team.

Coach Gray wouldn't allow me to be a hotshot scorer because he was more interested in the final stat — number one. He knew the only way we could reach that championship level was for us to become team players. In basketball and in life everyone starts out with a what's-in-it-for-me attitude. Children are selfish. That natural selfishness has to be broken to be a winner. You have to realize you can't do it all by yourself. You need the team. Coach

Gray made me pass the ball and play unselfishly. Regardless of individual stats, we, the team, reached the top. We went all the way.

By the time I left Benson, Coach Gray had inspired the desire within me not to become a typical basketball player. That was my identity in high school — I was just a basketball player. Actually I was a sports-minded, egotistical maniac. God had to deliver me from that later. But Coach Gray planted seeds inside me that caused me to work harder, to become something more, so people couldn't say to me, "You're just this" or "just that." The inspiration didn't take root then. It blossomed in me later.

PRINCIPLE #7
Learn to live unselfishly. Realize that you can't do it all by yourself. You need the team.

That summer was spectacular. The whole world was beautiful to me. Tall stands of wildflowers filled every vacant space in the neighborhood with blue, purple, yellow, pink and red flowers that stood knee-high. The sky was often cloudy, but it seemed to clear every afternoon so the sun rays could shine just on me. I went to Pennsylvania to play in the Dapper Dan Classic with the top U.S. prep players. Then I played the state All-Metro game at home. I was on the All-American team. Everything was going right for me.

I got a summer job at Silver Eagle, a shipping company, and learned how to drive a forklift to load and unload semitrailer trucks. It was interesting and sometimes challenging. One day my forks were too high, and I punctured some oil cans. The company had a rule that a picture had to be taken of every accident, so my foreman got out an Instamatic and took a picture of this tall kid with long, skinny legs that had big feet sticking out the bottom, standing next to a forklift that looked just like him.

I loved working the late shift. When my parents would allow it, Ricky, Lee or Jeffrey would come get me after work at about 3:00 A.M., and then we'd go to an all-night bowling alley and bowl the rest of the night. When daylight came, we spent hours next door in Mrs. Brannon's backyard. We bounced her crazy every day. If we wanted to go full court, we'd run to the park, then back to our house to take a swim, then over to Mrs. Brannon's again.

Life was good for me. I had a wonderful family. And on the outside I loved seeing my name in lights. On the inside, though, I couldn't handle the pressure. Even with all I had going for me, I had very low self-esteem and felt insecure about who I was. I was full of inner pressures, unsure of anything in myself, afraid to make decisions and always relying on other people or external circumstances to tell me if I was any good. I was pretty proud about my accomplishments but full of fear about my real self.

I'm certain most athletes, even in the pros, feel the same way unless they have experienced an inner transformation as I did. They feel great on the outside because of what they're able to do, but they're miserable on the inside because there's a shadow of doubt about whether they really measure up.

God was honoring me although I had never made a commitment to Him. I had attended church and Sunday school just because my parents asked me to. We all went together to our family church, Albina Pentecostal Church of God, with Pastor Samuel Irving. But inwardly I was untouched and didn't understand the need for church. I was a "cultural Christian," going through the motions without the emotion. Once my parents stopped insisting, I stopped attending.

By the time I graduated from high school, I thought God was OK, and I was OK with Him, and that was that. I didn't really need Him, and all He really wanted was for me to say nice things every now and then. I reasoned that if I were a good person and better than most of my friends, I had my fire insurance and was heaven bound.

In reality I was a rebel. I didn't go out and publicly hate God. I didn't vandalize churches or make fun of preachers. But inside I practiced hating Him by refusing to do anything He wanted me to do. I wanted control over my life. The only way I knew to exercise control was to do things my way.

Grace kept me once again. The Bible says that where there's sin, there's even more grace. I had a lot of sin in my life. I was determined to sin, but God's grace was bigger.

I wasn't even thinking about church that summer when nine good friends asked me to join them on a weekend visit to Hermiston, Oregon, to see one of our old Benson teachers, Rod Bragato, and his wife, Karen. I knew they were with the Fellowship of Christian Athletes, but that was OK because, after all, I was OK with God. A few seeds had been planted in my mind earlier in the year when different guys asked me to come to Bible studies. They even asked me to read the Bible. I didn't get offended, but I thought, Why are these guys asking me that? I had never heard anybody talk like that except a pastor. Their remarks were like a foreign language to me.

The weekend went fine. Rod and Karen asked us to attend church with them on Sunday morning, which was fine with me. It was business as usual at church until the preacher got up and gave a sermon titled "Do you want to go to heaven, or do you want to go to hell?" I found myself getting very uncomfortable as he spelled out the plan of salvation. The message was certainly not unique, but the timing was perfect. I realized I was totally separated from God, totally guilty of sin.

The god I thought I knew did not exist in reality, only in my mind. I had a god complex, not a relationship with the living God. I had thought that I was in sync, that my engine was fine-tuned, that I had picked out the right tie to go with the right suit, that I had a first-class plane ticket to heaven. But this pastor was reading a different story, telling me I wasn't even on the first page of being OK with God and that the one true God who created me had a right to my life.

I'm sure I had heard such a message before, but on that day my eyes were suddenly opened to my need of a personal relationship with Jesus Christ. Being better than the nine other guys in my pew wasn't going to get me into heaven. Because I was out of line with God, my destiny was hell. Not only that but I was also missing out on my true purpose in life. I thought my purpose was playing basketball. I thought life was about the friends with whom I was hanging around. I thought I was doing right for my parents. But, in an hour and a half, my standards got blown to pieces. I realized I was missing it, that I was guilty before a holy God and that I had better get in sync while I had the chance. In God's timing He made me understand that.

God might not always come when you want Him, but He is always right on time. He was right on time for me that day. His Holy Spirit was reaching out to me, and it was up to me now to catch the pass and dunk the ball.

Until that day I was the biggest people-pleaser around. I'd do anything to make people think I was cool. In that moment of crisis, of change, that very attitude worked against me. When the pastor asked for people to come to the altar to get straight with God, I wanted to sprint down the aisle, but something stopped me.

"Let someone else go first," a voice inside said. Again I felt the urge, but again I stopped.

"They're going to laugh at you if you go first," the inner voice said. I was shocked. I looked around, but obviously no one heard it but me.

Ricky Stewart was standing right next to me, between me and the aisle. I was waiting for him to go first, hoping he'd make a move, but he didn't budge. Finally, as the pastor asked for about the third time, in a forced act of courage, I thrust my way past Ricky and into the aisle. It was "my step into destiny." Ricky's and Lee's steps would come later.

I was the only guy down there. The pastor looked at me kindly. "Do you know what you are doing, son?" he asked.

"No, I don't," I answered honestly. All I knew was that in my heart, this was right, even though I didn't fully understand anything. The pastor came down and talked and prayed with me while I stood with my back to the audience.

"You may turn around now and face the congregation," he finally said. Once again, the voices started in.

"All your friends are going to be laughing at you."

"They're going to call you stupid."

"You've just made the dumbest move ever."

"They won't talk to you now."

"You're not one of the homeboys anymore."

I obeyed the pastor and turned around, and, to my amazement, everyone was smiling at me. They started clapping, high-fiving and saying, "Yeah, way to go."

In that instant I realized that I had heard a pack of lies, and later I learned that the voices were lying spirits if not the devil himself. I had a real enemy I hadn't even met yet who would do anything to keep me from believing the truth about God and myself. He wanted to run my life and treat me like a puppet on a string while fooling me into believing I was in control, making my own decisions.

For the first time in my life I felt free. The fear of others that had motivated me for so many years, the people-pleasing habits and peer pressure, were simply gone. I instantaneously realized that the outside of a person wasn't what mattered; it was the inside that counted. I could now face those doubts that had plagued me. It was miraculous. When you come to know the miraculous God, miracles follow.

Along with all that, my bad habit of cursing instantly left. The habit was stupid anyway. In high school we'd say a curse word just to practice saying it. "Look at this new one I got," we practically announced to the guys. Then we used it all the time. I felt it was an uncontrollable habit when I was with my friends, but I could always stop myself in front of my family. That's what made it such a joke, so hypocritical. It was just a way for me to be accepted at school, to fit in. It was part of my insecure, people-pleasing attitude, and *boom!* — it was gone.

That Sunday was August 2, 1981, just weeks before I left for Oregon State. Later on that summer I was playing a pick-up game and said the "d" word after I missed a layup. I instantly felt convicted by the Holy Spirit. I just stood, frozen to the spot, while all my teammates ran to the other end of the court. I was dumbfounded that I'd said it. I had a choice: Continue slipping back into my old habits or stay with the new me. In that moment of reflection the old ways didn't look like much of an option. I enjoyed being in control of my life, feeling I didn't "have" to do anything, especially not to be "cool," to be "in." That high school mentality was behind me, and in those few seconds I chose never to return.

That doesn't sound like much today, but for me it was a stepping stone, a hurdle I cleared to continue moving in a new direction.

A decision can change your whole life. Other guys I knew made decisions to follow Jesus Christ, but then they made other decisions down the road that took them in a different direction. Once we decide to be champions, we're faced with the same question: Will I keep going, or will I give up? We not only make the decision once, but we keep affirming and reaffirming that decision so we can go after our destiny and fulfill it.

My first decision in the right direction was to stop following my peers and instead follow a proven leader. I needed a hero to identify with. To do that I first had to admit I didn't know everything. In order to learn, you must be willing to be taught. If you go through life believing you know it all and don't need to learn anything, you'll end up looking as foolish as I did with those fireflies.

I often meet people who think they're fooling others by acting as if they've done it all and know it all. In the NBA, even though men have mastered a sport, command a huge salary, land endorsements and have people catering to them, they can still be fools in the eyes of others because they're not teachable. They think they're cool because no one tells them the truth. They simply look foolish. In every field, at every age, regardless of the amount of success and accomplishment, everyone has something to learn from others. We just need to seek out those who are a little further ahead in some particular area. A teachable spirit is the key.

PRINCIPLE #8
Admit you don't know everything. Open yourself up to learn from others. Develop a teachable spirit.

I had great parents and a great first coach, but other people are not so fortunate. You need a leader, someone you can respect, almost a "parent." It could be a teacher, boss, older brother or sister, neighbor, grandparent, godparent, Sunday school teacher or coach. It could even be a sports announcer or referee. Once you find that person, make sure of him or her. Get confirmation. Watch others who have followed that person. Examine the results of the person's life. How often does the individual set goals, and then how often does he or she reach them? Whomever you link up with, you will begin sharing that person's destiny. If your leader is running from the police, you'll soon be doing the same. If your leader is going to the top of some particular field, you'll soon be doing the same.

If it hadn't been for Dick Gray, I don't know if I would have pursued basketball. Coach Gray taught me, pushed me, challenged me and believed in me to become better. I'm not the type to waste time just doing things. I wanted to have a purpose to whatever I did. He was instrumental in that. Now all I needed to do was find someone who could do the same for me in college.

3

THE BIG PICTURE

A.C.! HEY, A.C.!" I heard someone calling me at the Portland airport recently. When I turned around, I saw Archie, Diane and Mike Jamison heading straight for me — my old Little League coach and his family! Archie's the one who taught me the fundamentals of baseball. We hadn't seen each other in ten years.

"Remember how much taller I was than you?" Mike asked,

laughing and tilting his head all the way back to look up at me.

"I remember you guys," I assured them.

"We've followed your career all these years," Archie said. "I still remember the day you asked me to make you a shortstop."

"Yeah, I remember that day, too, Coach," I said. "You put me between second and third bases and said, 'Stand here, and don't let a ball go past you.' Then you hit balls to me, and I used my body to make the stop!"

"I remember that," he said. Archie taught me the mechanics of blocking the ball with the side of my knee and calf. Then he drilled me on how to field the ball with my gloved hand and throw it to first.

"You learned the techniques flawlessly," he said. "You were one of the best shortstops that came to the league."

"Thanks," I said. "That's how I remember it, too."

Coaches like Archie who teach the form and technique of a game are priceless. Those fundamentals become the foundation for everything a player does. On the basketball court what some fans see as razzle-dazzle moves and spontaneous bursts of talent are really well-rehearsed plays and trained moves that we practice over and over until they become second nature.

Building a solid foundation is the most important thing you can do in sports or in life. Only the strongest, best foundation can support the gifts, talents and abilities of a champion. You can start building at any age, but the sooner the better. People who have talent and ability without a strong foundation eventually crash.

PRINCIPLE #9
Lay a foundation. Only the strongest, best foundation can support the gifts, talents and abilities of a champion.

A child's greatest years of physical and emotional development are generally between the ages of two and seven. Mine were between the ages of seventeen and twenty-two, because that's when my spiritual and basketball foundations were built.

During my freshman year in high school I played basketball for fun. In my second year I noticed older players — how they played and what happened to them. I saw a couple of guys get scholarships. I thought, Hmm, scholarships. Coach, what's a scholarship? My junior years of both high school and college were the pivotal years. Those were the years I blossomed as a player.

During my senior year of high school, after starting the year as an unknown, I started to attract the attention of coaches from big regional schools: Marv Harshman of the University of Washington, assistant coach Jim Marsh of Utah and Jimmy Anderson of Oregon State. Most recruiting was done over the phone or with Dick Gray, who screened everyone. But one day we had a home visit that turned into an important, lifelong relationship.

I was in the back room watching television, waiting for my visitor. The house was clean, and Mom had cleared out the grandkids for the afternoon. She had snacks and drinks ready. I heard the doorbell ring, then my dad's booming voice.

"Hello!"

"Hello. George Raveling from Washington State University," said a strange voice. I turned the corner just in time to see the two men grasp hands.

"My wife," Dad said, and Mom shook hands with Coach Raveling.

"And I guess you know this is Junior," Dad said. Coach Raveling's big hand clasped mine firmly, and he looked into my eyes with a fatherly expression. I liked him instantly.

"Please sit down," Mom said.

"Portland has changed quite a bit since I was here last," Coach Raveling said.

"Hasn't it?" Mom said.

"Did you have any trouble finding the house?" Dad asked.

"No, I've been in the area before," Coach said. "This neighborhood is real nice."

"The Northeast sector has really grown up," Dad said, and the three adults were off to the races. I didn't need to be in the room. This wasn't a meeting about basketball, about my future, about me at all. This was our long-lost Uncle George talking about the state of the community; young people these days; good, old homestyle cooking; and The Way Things Used to Be. They may as well have moved to the back porch and rocked for a while before they ever got on the subject of basketball.

Coach Raveling didn't promise I'd be a starter; didn't assure Mother that Pullman, Washington, was a good place to live; didn't tell Dad he could see me on national television five times a year; didn't try to get on their good side with "Hey, we're all black, so let's keep it in the family." He talked realistically and honestly, making sure they understood the process, and we melted into his big, gentle hands.

"A.C.," he said as he left an hour and a half later, "you have a wonderful family."

I beamed. I wanted to go to Washington for the sole purpose of playing for Coach Raveling.

Deciding which college to attend is one of the biggest decisions a person will make. Athletes have to sign a letter of intent by the day we are legally allowed to declare, usually sometime during our senior year of high school. When my day came, I was far from God, but again God's grace was there. My parents and other praying Christians brought me further into my destiny, though I didn't know it. The love of God is amazing. He is willing to lead even an unbeliever into a right decision. He cares for us long before we ever start to care about Him.

My choices were either to move five hours away to Pullman, Washington, where I couldn't see my family a lot, but I'd be with George Raveling; or to go an hour and a half away to Corvallis and Oregon State (OSU) with Coach Ralph Miller. My parents would have been happy either way, although we were all leaning toward Coach Raveling.

Oregon State was playing good basketball. The team won the Pac-10 championship in 1980, the year I started paying a little attention, and went on to become the number-two team in the nation in 1981. The distance to Washington State and the championship level of the basketball program at Oregon State ended up being the deciding factors. I chose OSU.

My friendship with George Raveling during that decision-making time was highly unusual for him. He saw thousands of kids and had his own family, but he took a genuine interest in me. We stayed in telephone contact after I chose OSU, and he was instrumental in my college development. Years later, when I was with the Lakers, he came to L.A. to coach USC. I attended USC's football games, so I started going to their basketball games as well to support him. Our friendship deepened even more when we moved across the street from each other in L.A. When I moved to Phoenix in 1993, Coach Raveling offered to let me house-sit a home he co-owns with some sweet friends of his, Jerry and Selma Roth. Because of their generosity, while I got used to a new city, I spent a year as the world's tallest house-sitter. George knows he's Mom's favorite. His first question when we get together is always, "How's Mom?"

Oregon State, with its broad range of programs, was a good school for someone like me who wasn't big on academics. I didn't know what to major in or what I wanted to become, so a school with a specialized academic program wasn't even on my list. I was just looking to play basketball, though I still didn't think I would become a professional. Once again I started a freshman year thinking I was playing just for fun.

Lee Johnson and I got to the campus early, before school started, to get oriented. His brother, Jay, had been at OSU for two years and became our self-appointed host.

"Let's go play some hoops," I said.

"OK, there's only one place to play," he said, "and that's Dixon where most of the team probably is anyway."

We put on our shorts and walked straight across campus to Dixon, a recreation center on campus where students go to play basketball, handball, badminton and volleyball, and to work out with weights. Jay opened the door to a new-looking, two-story, red brick building behind the baseball field. I was used to stuffy, sweaty gyms, so I noticed immediately that for an athletic facility Dixon smelled strangely clean. We walked into the bottom level and saw three full-length basketball courts. Two were in motion with the jumps, squeaks, thumps, thuds, yells and grunts of basketball players. On the third court someone was playing either badminton or volleyball, but I hardly saw them.

I leaned back against the wall, trying to hold my mouth shut, thinking, There's William Brew. There's Lester Conner. There's Charlie Sitton. There's Danny Evans.

"Here we are, fellas," Jay said, gleaming.

A.C., you have a choice, I thought. You can stand here oohing and ahing at the guys you used to watch on television, or you can get out on the court and get busy.

I had to force myself to move toward the game. Entering college and the pros is a rude awakening. Guys come from schools where they were the star players and find themselves up against guys who were the star players four years earlier and are now much, much better. I got no shortcuts at Oregon State. It was do or die.

"Yo," one of the younger players called to me. "Are you playing?"

The only way to stay on the court in pickup games is to win each time, so senior players always teamed up to keep playing. I was on a team with younger players, some of them freshmen like me.

Boom! A pass found the side of my head. Whack! An elbow found my ribs. Fear helped reality set in. This was a different game, the real deal. Adrenaline started pumping, telling me to try the moves that every freshman's adrenaline says to try. I used my little high school layup move that used to fake everyone out. I drove up to the right side of the basket, and when the defender jumped to try to block the shot, I brought the ball down, under my chest, and reversed the layup to the other side of the basket. That move works nine times out of ten in high school. Ka-boom! The ball was swatted from the other side by another defender.

"Get that garbage outta here," Charlie Sitton said, running back down the court.

I went up for a rebound and got knocked down.

"You better pump some iron," Lester Conner said.

I was nervous, thinking, No, this is not high school. This is college ball.

"Don't be coming in here with that weak junk," William Brew said after another ill-fated attempt to score.

My mind was answering, OK, sir, excuse me, sorry. This is definitely not the same.

"You're too weak, young boy," Danny Evans said as he muscled another rebound.

Mercifully the game came to an end.

"Who are the next losers to come on?" one of the seniors challenged boastfully. "Come on — don't keep us waiting. Who has the next game? We need some fresh meat."

Those guys were not just three-times better athletes. They were also ten-times better talkers, totally intimidating me with their "trash talk" as much as with their play. I wondered if I could compete. When I went to the pros, I felt the same way. You have a gut check. You ask yourself, Can I play at this level? Mentally you can be telling yourself that you can do it. You know you have to go out there. Your faith can be really high, but there comes a time when you're just there. The battle lines are drawn. You're face-to-face with your opponent. Then you confront the moment of truth. Can you do it?

Sometimes it takes a week to bring yourself to cross that threshold — maybe a month or a year. I'd rather get that road crossed as soon as I can. That's why it's important to build a foundation: When you get to the moment of testing, you can withstand the pressure and go on to achieve your next victory.

Jay's and Lee's eyes were like saucers when I came off that court. I knew what they were thinking: You want to finish touring the rest of the campus?

I doubted they knew what I was thinking: I wonder if Benson would let me do a fifth year.

I knew I had to stay, however. The older guys never let up, and I kept playing, but I struggled for every point. Lee and Jay joined the "rat" ball game eventually. The other freshmen were trying to dunk, to show them anything to make them think we belonged, but nothing worked. Sympathy was nonexistent on their team. For the next few weeks I thought I had missed the bus to the school where I was supposed to be. These guys were monsters. But pressing on was the only way to achieve my goals, as uncomfortable as it was.

Staying in your comfort zone is one of the surest ways never to excel in life. Taking even one small step prepares you for all the others down the road. In the Old Testament, David fought a lion and a bear for the sake of the sheep. Each time he had to strengthen himself and add courage to his faith, which prepared him for stronger and stronger opponents. As he continued to grow in faith and ability, he kept winning victories right up to defeating the giant Goliath for the sake of an entire nation.

There are no "gimme" victories in life. You must have courage to work for the victory. Remember that. The reason you enjoy winning is that you know there is a chance of losing. You've got to have respect to become a champion. Respect life; respect your opponent; respect yourself. Victories are not cheap.

PRINCIPLE #10
Add courage to your faith. There are no "gimme" victories in life. You must have courage to work for the victory. Have an attitude of respect.

PRINCIPLE #11
Respect life. Respect your opponent. Respect yourself. Victories are not cheap.

My college coach, Ralph Miller, was a disciplinarian. He's a college coaching legend, having retired in 1989 as the eighth-winningest coach in college basketball history with 657 victories, just behind John Wooden, who had 664. In 1981 he was the United Press International coach of the year, and his team was rolling. That's the team I joined, and the expectations were high.

I learned in one day of practice that if we didn't do things Coach Miller's way, we sat on the bench. The discipline I brought from my childhood served me well. Everyone had to learn the coach's rules.

"OK, no shooting until you pass the ball five times," he announced at practice. "Dish it out. Pass the ball."

Sometimes he carried that over into the game to teach us how to play unselfishly and to perfect our passing game.

"Stop right now," he said angrily when someone bounce-passed at practice. "What do you think you're doing?"

We couldn't move when he said to stop. We stood frozen in place while he grilled us. That was his way. He made sure we thought about what we did on the court, and we accepted it. He didn't allow a lot of slack in practice or in a game, so I got used to playing the game with a high sense of energy, to give everything I had on every possession.

A couple of weeks after I got to OSU, some friends came up to see me and Lee. We had an unofficial traditional football game that we played every year, and even though it was raining, we decided this year would be no different. The rain poured down. We played, slipping and sliding in the mud, until about 1:30 in the afternoon, when I suddenly remembered I had practice at 2:00. With no time to run back to my room and clean up, I ran straight to practice, drenched and caked with mud.

"What happened? You fall?" the team asked playfully.

"Yeah, I sorta kept falling," I answered. The coaches were not happy, especially that I was playing football. That was another wake-up call for me. They didn't pay my way to OSU to hang out with the guys. I had a job to do.

Coach Miller was a defensive specialist. He lived for defense. In high school Coach Gray was an offensive man, teaching us to run our opponents into the ground. Coach Miller rounded me out, helping me understand the game from a half-court standpoint. At first he didn't know where to play me because I was versatile, and so was the team. Besides that, the seniors from the championship season were still playing. Coach Miller started me as one of the two forwards for my freshman year and through the first half of my sophomore season. I tried my hand playing guard sometimes, too. Then he switched me to center, where I played the rest of my college career. I stayed in the paint most of the time in the half-court set.

I had always been a rebounder and runner, but OSU played a slower-paced game. We were a tempo team — a Ralph Miller team. He taught us to control the ball, but the born-to-be-wild side of me loved to get out of Miller mode and fight the teams that had the fast-paced tempo.

Rebounding is what the pros call "hard work." Some don't like it because staying in the paint beneath the bucket is one of the greatest danger zones for injuries. Rebounders are kind of like soccer goalies — you have to be a little crazy to want to do it. But for a kid who enjoyed cleaning the school cafeteria and wrestling with his brothers, it was just my speed.

In the neighborhood we often played to get our own rebounds, so we all had to learn how to get the ball. We played a game called Crunch, or Twenty-One. You could have any number of players from two to ten, and it was every man for himself. After you scored a bucket, you'd go to the line to shoot a free throw. To win you just had to out-rebound and out-pursue your opponents. The first person to twenty-one, wins. On those playgrounds I learned to see the angle at which the ball would come off the rim or backboard in order to beat Ricky, Jeffrey, Steve, Lee, Terrel and the rest of them.

I couldn't be taught the instinct for the ball, but my skills could be refined. Our whole high school team knew our job was to get every rebound. I took special pride in that. Rebounding was neat, fun, exciting. My talent was basketball, but my gift was rebounding. When I got to college I learned how to get different inside positions, and I honed my skills in the mechanics of the game. God always put someone there who was willing to teach me. All the coaches — Jimmy Anderson, Lanny van Eman, Steve Seidler — did their part to work with me. In time I developed a real "nose" for the ball.

My coaching didn't stop at basketball. In college I began a journey of growth — spiritually, physically and academically. Probably 80 percent of the time, school athletes can "jock" their way through the graduation line. It's easy to slide through school, to take Mickey Mouse courses. I had friends on campus who were skating through, but many times it caught up with them. Some of them came in our freshman year, but by their junior year I didn't see them anymore. In many colleges guys have girlfriends taking their tests and doing reports for them. Some teachers let it go. They don't want to give athletes special favors, but they just look the other way a lot of the time. Schools don't always mind because it keeps players eligible to play.

When I saw the system, the seeds Coach Gray planted in me began to grow. I didn't want to be "just another athlete." I didn't want to do it the jock way. If I was there to learn, I would learn. A woman from the OSU administration office named Tootie Systrup had worked with other athletes and saw them come and go, many of them doing their four-year degree on a six-year plan. I had other encouraging influences, but Tootie became my tutor, my counselor, my academic coach.

"So you want to graduate?" she said, looking down her nose at me my freshman year as if she were inspecting to see if I had brushed my teeth.

"Yes, ma'am, I do," I said.

"But you don't like school much?"

"No, ma'am, I don't," I said.

"OK, then take these courses," she said, and she started scribbling on my scheduling form.

She knew what she was doing, and I didn't. It was a no-brainer to follow her lead so I could graduate. Every semester I was in her office, figuring out my schedule, doing what she told me to do.

"If you want to graduate as you say you do," she said one spring, "and if you don't want to come back to school because you don't like school much, you'd better go to summer school."

Summer school! She was determined to see me graduate. She had the bigger picture for me academically. I went to summer school.

Discipline was my tool, my weapon, my ally. When the other guys watched football or a basketball game on ESPN, I packed my books up and walked over to the library. Discipline created character within me that would tell me "Get it done" when it was just as easy not to — especially when it came to academics. Discipline saved me from procrastination. What grows within your character shows up in every area of your life. The Bible says a double-minded man is unstable in all his ways (James 1:8). For me, the strength of the discipline I exercised academically started showing up in every way, in basketball and in personal matters.

"It's time to declare your major," Tootie told me one year. "Have you decided what you want to do with your life?"

"I know I like basketball," I said.

"Keep going," she said.

"Well, I think I could be a good broadcaster, like Ed Whelan," I said. "Plus I want to tell people about Jesus. I really need to learn how to speak publicly."

"OK, let's see here," she said, looking over my transcripts and the course catalog. "You could major in speech communications."

"Great!" I said, and it was settled.

Three months later I was in her office again.

"So, Junior, you failed sociology," she said. "What happened? Did you turn in your work?"

"I turned in all kinds of papers," I said, "but the professor was less interested in my papers than I was in his class."

"And you barely passed biology. You know what this means?" she asked.

"Summer school?"

"Take these classes," she said, shoving my second summer-school schedule across the desk to me.

It was tough because that summer I had the Pan Am trials, the Olympic trials, and I was elected to the USA Select Team. But I fit in summer school.

With Tootie's coaching I got my degree in four years. The process of becoming educated became as valuable as the education itself. I still don't know everything, but now I know where to find it. I haven't explored all areas of life, but I have a foundation from which to understand them.

In basketball we can foul out of a game by doing the wrong thing too often. Students can foul out of class the same way. And if you're really messing up, you can get an ejection. Being ejected from a game only makes players feel stupid. Dropping out of school makes students feel stupid, too — if not immediately, then somewhere down the road. There's no reason not to get an education when you have the opportunity to do so.

4

NEW PEER PRESSURE

ONCE I WAS lined up academically and physically, I still needed a spiritual coach. Pastor Irving encouraged me to find a church when I got to school as a freshman, so I visited a couple, but more often I went home on weekends and attended church with the family. I was proud to escort my mom with her beautiful clothes and matching hats.

Then one day in November, Ricky Stewart called from the University of Oregon, which he was attending. He sounded as if he had just finished running back-to-back marathons.

"There's this guy," he said, "and people are getting saved, and it's great, man." Stop, pant, breathe. "My life has changed. I'm a Christian. Everyone is going to hear him." Gasp, inhale. "I think he's coming your way sometime soon. His name is Greg Ball."

Who is this that could have led Ricky to the Lord? I thought. After all, Ricky was the guy next to me in Hermiston who wouldn't budge when I took my step into destiny.

"Greg Ball prayed with me at a revival here," he said. "You've gotta meet him."

A few weeks later I passed some guy on campus and sort of looked at him because he was looking at me. I was just a few steps past him when he spun around and caught up to me.

"Hi, I'm Greg Ball," he said. "Want to come to a meeting we're having here on campus?" Another step toward destiny.

The part Ricky has played in my life is amazing. We're not as close as we used to be, but we still have that bond. Ricky was the guy who got me to Benson Tech, so because of him I met Dick Gray. He was the guy who stood between me and destiny in Hermiston. Then, even though we went to different colleges, he met Greg Ball before I did, which is another major part of my life. It's interesting who and what God will use.

Greg Ball was a real example to me of true Christianity. He was preaching a week-long revival on the campus. I admired his courage, coming to a campus cold and just starting to witness. His goal, under the direction of Bob and Rose Weiner out of Florida, was to help start churches on college campuses. Dave and Joan Elian were already on campus to become the pastors. Greg was the evangelist, the spark plug of the church engine. His few words to me, a perfect stranger, challenged me in my Christian walk.

On Tuesday I went to his small meeting, which was more of a social gathering in one of the student halls, helping people get oriented and make other Christian friends. When it was over, about ten of us hung around talking, getting to know each other.

"So you play basketball," Greg said.

"Yeah. You like basketball?" I asked.

"I love it — love all sports. Used to play football in college, but now I'm into kick boxing."

"Kick boxing?"

"Yeah, I have a speed bag I work out on, but I'm not competing anymore. I love shooting hoops, too. Anything for a challenge."

Everything about Greg was so challenging. This guy was no wimp. During the conversation I made a decision to be serious about God as he was, instead of just another Christian student on campus. I didn't want to do the "shoulds, oughts and musts." I wanted to pursue spiritual things as seriously as I was pursuing basketball and academics. In his meetings Greg challenged people to be 100-percent committed to Christ. But even when he wasn't preaching, his life commanded the same respect.

"I'd like to know Jesus the way you do," I said as we continued talking. "I need to get my focus realigned."

"OK, let's pray," he said in a flash. People were milling around, but Greg thought nothing of putting his hand on my shoulder and praying out loud for the power of God to be active in my life.

When he prayed, as sudden as a bolt of lightning, I felt a power surge. I had never experienced anything like that before. It's one thing to know you're saved, but another to be saved and have the power of God living inside you. I was so excited! I had been baptized as a kid, but now I wanted to get baptized again, only this time with understanding. Greg had been baptizing people in bathtubs, but when he baptized Roger LaVasa, a football player, it emptied the tub and flooded the apartment below. On a chilly November morning two days later, Roger helped Greg, along with Dave Elian, baptize me in the school swimming pool.

"Man, where are you going?" Lee asked me when I headed outside with a towel at 6:00 A.M.

"I'm going to get baptized," I said.

"You're crazy, man," he said.

"I've got the power of God in me," I answered.

We all have the free choice to set our wills in any direction. When I set my will to follow Jesus seriously, God filled me with His power. Some people believe just in their own willpower — mind over matter and all that. Willpower is good and useful, but when you set your will to follow Christ, you get God's power as well. His power overwhelms the power you have within yourself. Willpower will get you only so far, but God's power will give you victory.

Two days later, on a Saturday, we played Pepperdine for the third game of the season. I had come off the bench in the first two games, so this was my first start. As it turned out, everything was different. I was no longer the lonely little freshman on the court. I had God inside me.

"Man, the power of God is happening!" I said excitedly as I raced down the court after scoring. I went for a rebound and dished it out to my teammate, who drove down and scored.

"It's happening!" I shouted.

I got eighteen points and ten rebounds. We won 82 to 76.

Lee didn't stand a chance now. I was going to Greg's revival every night, and I nailed Lee with it every day.

"Lee, guess what happened today!"

"Lee, you're missing out, man!"

"Lee, man, you've gotta come! You've gotta come!"

Finally he said, "Yeah, OK, I'll come in about a week."

Two nights later Lee and two friends, Mike and Clark, went with me. About twenty or thirty people were there that night, many of them visitors. Lee surrendered. Mike and Clark never did. The small group of us who got saved became a Bible study group, which then turned into a church. We started with about ten, and more came as we grew and evangelized others.

Until that time I was totally involved with sports. But as I attended church and followed my spiritual coaches, God purified my mind and ego in a process called sanctification. In 1 John 1:9-10, the Bible says that if we confess our sins, God will forgive us and cleanse us from unrighteousness — the habits of sin. Many Christians are forgiven, but they don't get cleansed, so they stay in old physical and mental habit patterns. My mind had to be renewed by daily Bible reading and attending church. My ego had to be humbled. I couldn't be out on the court using God's power like at Pepperdine, then take the credit for myself.

I began to see victory not as a stroke to my own ego but as a witness for God, something that proved how great He was within me. A new, purer desire for winning branched out in other areas as well. I wanted to win academically not just for myself, but also to show people what the power of God could do inside a person. After all He was doing for me, I wanted to do all I could for Him. I had the feeling players have when playing for a great coach. I didn't want to disappoint God. I wanted to achieve all that He had created me to achieve.

PRINCIPLE #12
Purify your motives and your heart. Get a pure desire for victory that wants victory for the Lord's sake, not just for your own.

Pastor Dave Elian taught me a lot about the Word and building character. First I learned about serving others. We were a small group, so everyone had to pitch in. Even though I was the star athlete, I cleaned toilets, both at church and in my apartment. Once again I felt ownership. As my "star" rose, work like that helped keep my feet on the ground and my head out of the clouds. I realized I was always going to be a person as well as an athlete. I also learned that unless you're willing to serve, you cannot earn the right to lead.

Pastor Dave taught us about the importance of daily Bible reading and prayer. Sometimes he challenged everyone in the church to pray for thirty minutes every day that week. Lee and I followed that to the letter of the law. We sat in our bunks, trying to fill our thirty minutes with one eye closed and one eye on the clock.

"Lee, how much time have we got left?"

"Ten more minutes."

"OK.... Lee, how much time have we got?"

"Five minutes."

"I don't know what else to pray about."

"Pray about that test coming up."

"Oh yeah, good idea.... Lee, how much time have we got?"

"Just a few more minutes."

"I don't have anything to pray about."

"Just close your eyes. It'll count."

God honored our obedience to our pastor, even though our approach was all wrong. It was a stepping stone for us.

Pastor Dave also emphasized keeping our word. He lived integrity and challenged us to a high level of integrity ourselves.

"The honesty of a man's heart, the depth of his manly character, is shown by how he keeps his word," he taught us. "God spoke, and there was. That's how important words are. God doesn't speak careless words, so neither should you." He taught us to honor whatever we said we would do, to control our tongues and not make careless promises. Lee and Roger called him "Mr. Integrity." If we didn't make it to a 6:00 A.M. prayer meeting after saying we'd go, we were rudely awakened with a telephone call.

Dave could have said, "Brother, are you coming? Are you late?" But he didn't. "Brother," he always said, "*where are you?*"

For years after that, whenever a phone call woke me from my sleep, even during an afternoon nap, I'd jump up thinking, Oh no, I'm late.

Pastor Dave drilled integrity into our lives not out of legalism but out of respect for ourselves, others and God. He was the same with tardiness. There was nothing glamorous about being fashionably late to his church. He stood at the church door to give a special greeting to stragglers — hint, hint. He taught us to be at meetings at least fifteen minutes early. We learned to plan on being there thirty minutes early just in case, then wait fifteen minutes in our cars. He expected the same attitude, promptness and integrity in our classes and everything else we did.

One day I was at a prayer meeting with Lee and Roger when I realized I was going to be late for class. We had driven my car, a 1972 Continental Mark IV just like the one Frank Cannon used to drive on television. It was the biggest, widest, longest car on campus. Just about the whole team could sit across the front seat. My parents had bought it for me as an early graduation present the year before. When I got to college, I wanted a new car, so my dad and brothers painted it for me. It was turf green, so they painted it white right down the middle — trunk, roof and hood. Now I had a skunk-white and turf-green Mark IV. Everyone on campus knew it was mine. Roger and Lee dropped me off, then hit the main drag. It was the morning rush hour, and students were scurrying to classes, but Roger and Lee drove five miles per hour the whole way. People were honking and yelling while they sat there laughing like crazy about their big chance to ruin my reputation. People must have thought my stardom had gone to my head.

The church grew rapidly, and everyone who came was determined to learn from Dave and Joan. One of the major battles with young people today is the rebellious attitude of the 1960s that's cropping up again. They act as if they know how to do things when they don't.

"I've been doing that since I was five years old" is their attitude, even though they know it's not true. That attitude keeps people from listening to a coach and from learning properly. It's tough enough growing up today without making it hard on yourself. Moms and dads are trying to raise kids on their own. Spiritual atomic bombs have been thrown at our family structures. Maybe parents aren't taking the time to train their children, or maybe parents think kids should grow up the way they want. But everyone has his or her own power of choice. The key is to develop a teachable spirit whether you're the parent or the child.

Having a teachable spirit was crucial to getting my foundation built. I never miss basketball practice, and I go to every Bible study and church service I can. A lot of Christians think they're not hurting anyone if they miss church. They go once or twice a month but intend to go the rest of the time. They don't realize what message they send others. If a Christian isn't interested in church, how can he or she interest a non-Christian in the difference between life and death?

Many athletes and other "stars" use their identity as an excuse not to go to church. They believe they can't go to church or Bible study because people will bother them or they'll take the attention away from the speaker. Their attitude is: It's harder for me than it is for you. I just went. Getting reinforcement from other Christians was extremely important, so it didn't matter who or what I was. I needed it. I went. I still go.

The Bible became my manual for living. Pastor Dave influenced me, but I had to take the initiative to develop good habits myself. Even though I had 7:30 A.M. lectures and labs some mornings, I made it a practice to get up by 6:00 to spend time with God. Each day I wanted to be led by the Spirit of God in making decisions, whatever they may be. I read my Bible in the morning and prayed. I did a Bible workbook in the evenings before I went to sleep.

Pastor Dave emphasized that we needed to memorize Scripture, too. I can't take the Bible with me on the basketball court, and you can't depend on looking up a verse in an hour of need. You have to have it inside you already. Greg Ball and Pastor Irving were big on that, too. I memorized little verses at first, then whole chapters later.

Jesus' disciples, after He left the scene, wanted the power to be witnesses, to be bold, to move further in their faith. I identified with those guys. I loved reading the power book, Acts. I could see those guys in my mind. All of a sudden, the hair stood up on the back of the disciples' necks. Power welled up inside. They felt righteous indignation in certain circumstances. They said, "Wait a minute! This isn't the way things should be." Their zeal for righteousness, their love for the Man who changed their lives — I can feel it, see it. I want to be just like that. Those guys weren't wimps. They were just learning, being groomed when Jesus was around. When their time came, they had power.

Pastor Dave and Greg both encouraged us to go out and witness, to open-air preach on campus just as the New Testament church did. When our church went out open-air preaching, I went with them. There was no reason to exclude myself from what the others did. My first time out was with Roger, Dave and Lee. Pastor Dave took his Bible and walked out into the quad, the open area where students milled, ate lunch, read and talked.

"Man, my knees are knocking," I told Roger as we stood off to the side.

"Don't worry," he said. "Just watch what I do."

Dave finished his sermonette and introduced Roger. Roger gave his testimony, read some Scripture verses, then introduced me. I walked forward and stood there.

What am I doing here? I thought. I looked like a fish in a fish bowl, with big, bulging eyes staring at the people milling around and the twenty or so who were actually listening, waiting for me to say something.

"I'm A.C. Green," I started. Duh. "And I'm a Christian." I gave my testimony, and one of the other guys wrapped it up. That was the first time people on campus knew I was a Christian, and I couldn't believe what a difference it made. While other students lost their virginity that year, I lost my reputation; but in God's eyes I was just starting it. I was no longer A.C. the basketball player; I was A.C. the Christian. People on campus were on the lookout for me now. I was definitely not "just another athlete."

My first "convert" was Darryl Flowers. We played basketball together, and he was a little nervous around me because of my stand for Christ.

"Come to our meetings," I said.

"Well, maybe later," he said.

Others from the church invited him, too, until he finally came and got saved.

"Wow!" he said. "This is great."

Our conversations got more serious as the weeks went by. "I can't do enough for God," he told me one day. "I just want to do everything I possibly can."

"Darryl," I said, "there's one thing you can do that you probably haven't done yet."

I took him out to the quad and told him to give his testimony. Darryl was so funny. Unlike me, he really got into it. I should have known right then that he'd become a preacher. In the middle of his story he blurted out, "So put that in your pipe and smoke it!" What Darryl didn't see was that right then one of his professors walked past with a pipe in his mouth. I had to control myself until we left. Then I burst out laughing.

Darryl eventually graduated with a degree in engineering, went to L.A. and stayed with me for a while. Then God called him into full-time ministry — at Oregon State! I'm a proud supporter of him, his wife, Yvette, daughter Gabriella and the campus church that helped build my foundation.

As was evident in my first attempt at open-air preaching, my self-confidence didn't appear instantly. I needed spiritual reprogramming and restructuring. My spiritual man had to be built bigger, stronger and faster, just as my body had been. Pastor Dave and Greg helped me understand who I was, why I was living, where I was going and how I was going to get there. They helped me understand power, authority, what the war is, where my battles would be, how to get victory in battles and how to rebound after defeats. I'll teach you all that.

Confidence is the start. It only comes through tasting victory. To get confident, you have to set some kind of goal. My goal at OSU the day I got to campus was just to have the courage to play with those guys. When I reached that goal, my confidence grew. Then I could set another goal: to play them and actually score one time.

Maybe a goal for a young basketball player is to make ten free throws in a row. When you try and you make eight, that gives you a sense that you can eventually accomplish what you set out to do. Maybe a goal for a new Christian isn't to win ten people to Christ in one day, but to admit to just one person that you've become a Christian. With each admission of Christ, your confidence grows. Each victory builds confidence.

If you don't set goals, you can't possibly reach them, because even if you get there, you won't know it. So set goals. Take practical steps to reach them, little steps of faith, courage and boldness. Face the challenge head-on. If you want to memorize a Scripture verse or a series of verses, go at it. It's a step, and that builds confidence. When I was in that church in Hermiston, I took a step out from my insecurities and peer pressure and into more confidence.

PRINCIPLE #13
**Set goals. Take practical steps to reach each goal —
little steps of faith, courage and boldness.**

Another step of confidence came somewhere around my junior year when Lee and I got fed up with pornographers. I'm not a big mouth, but when it comes to speaking what I believe, I can tell it. We went into convenience stores near our home to see if they had pornography. If they did, we got vocal about it.

"Why are you selling that stuff here?" we'd ask the clerk. "That is so degrading, so filthy. How can you stand to have that in your store and in our neighborhood?"

If a child walked in, we turned up the heat.

"Look, you've got little kids coming in here, and you're feeding that kind of stuff to them. What if he looks at it? What if he thinks it's OK because he saw it in the store where he buys his candy? Ted Bundy admitted this is the stuff that twisted his mind to kill all those people. Why do you keep selling it?"

We went on and on, voicing our protest in all the convenience stores around campus. If someone came into the store to buy it, he wouldn't while we were there. But one time we caught a guy buying it, and we lit into him.

"Why do you want to buy that stuff? It violates women."

"Come on, man," he said. "This isn't a violation. I'm not going to rape someone just because I read this. I just want the magazine. It's art."

"Right — art," we said, laughing. Then we challenged him. "It degrades women. It gives you no sense of virtue. Why do you want to look at something like that?"

We turned to the clerk, who was a young woman.

"Does that stuff make you feel wholesome or violated? Would

you want to date a guy who was buying trash like that?"

She was embarrassed at first and turned red. As we kept badgering the guy, she sided with us. "I guess they're right," she said to him. "I wouldn't want my boyfriend looking at that stuff."

He bought it anyway. His pride was at stake. But I'm sure he had a gut check every time he bought another one, if he ever did.

Ours was a little two-man crusade until we realized that right on campus, in the campus bookstore, OSU was selling pornography. Now we were fired up. Lee and I and a friend named Scott Smith took a stand first with the bookstore manager, then with the administration. The campus newspapers wrote about us. Soon local newspapers and television picked up the coverage. We felt as though we had just stepped off the pages of Acts.

"This is wrong," we pronounced like Bible characters standing up in the middle of a sinful society. We didn't just step on toes; we stomped them and mashed them into the ground. Lee brought legislation before the student council to ban pornography from the campus. The administration was upset. Here I was, one of their star athletes, taking a stand against their policy.

"They're being used by the right wing," people said of us as if we didn't have brains of our own. Rumors and accusations about us spread. News raced through the Pac-10. When I played at other schools, hecklers lowered their own dignity by waving centerfold pictures at me. The more opposition I met, the more insistent I became. I didn't want to be associated with the selling of pornography in the school I represented. The administration finally backed down and required that the store put the junk in covered boxes out of direct eyesight.

Standing your ground is often a victory in itself. You must learn to follow the leader, but when the leader — in this case, an institution — violates your faith, you can no longer submit to that leadership. When we stood our ground and refused to bow to their rules, our stand in itself was a huge personal victory. We set a goal and did not back down regardless of the adversity. That propelled us into a higher level of boldness, tenacity, grace, confidence and faith all at the same time.

We had other victories as well because of the exposure we received. Hundreds of high schoolers and aspiring athletes saw that we weren't afraid to air our beliefs, that we could be Christians without being wimps and that we could even excel at sports. One local teenager had just moved to Corvallis when my reputation was growing. He was Dave Johnson, who committed his life to Christ and then competed for Olympic gold in the decathlon. Now he inspires young people around the world with his life and testimony. When we finally met recently, he told me I had been one of his inspirations.

The episode gave me strength that showed up in all areas of my life. To play basketball well or to focus on any goal in life, you have to be mentally tough. I've been compared in basketball to both a longshoreman and a collection agent for the mob. The choice I made to follow Jesus meant I had to be a solid, focused person. I don't focus on others who might distract me or pull me down. Just because others are doing it doesn't make it right or mean I need to get involved. Likewise, on the court I keep my eye and my mind on the ball.

At OSU, basketball is so popular that athletes from other sports played with us and other friends at Dixon when practice was over. Lee and I often played together. When the season ended, we were there just about every day with everyone else. Basketball was king.

Students at OSU got free general admission tickets to games. Since it was first-come, first-served, they often had to camp out in line to wait for the ticket booth to open. Then they camped out in front of the gym to get good seats when the doors opened on game day. During my first year the whole student body was enthused when USC came to town. But the Trojans were ready for us, and we were down 26-21 at the half. Southern Cal had both the lead and the tempo.

At halftime Coach Miller reminded us of what Miller ball was all about. We pulled ourselves together and during the entire second half limited them to just ten points. Our defense was that strong.

Our whole team was competitive. My high school nemesis, Dean Derrah, played with us for a couple of years, but injuries kept him from pursuing the pros. I was often matched during practices against Greg Wiltjer, a 6'11", 245-pound center. I was 6'8" and 205 at the time, skinny by most standards. Hours in the weight room helped me to even the odds. Lester Conner, one of the seniors, became sort of a mentor to me, and we have stayed close in the NBA. I always enjoy going up against him or anyone from

OSU. Charlie Sitton had been the All-American player of the year in high school and played center for OSU when I played forward. We also developed a good relationship. He was drafted by the Dallas Mavericks and played overseas, and now he's back in Oregon.

Our team went on to win the Pac-10 conference title that first year, which was becoming typical of a Ralph Miller team. When the regular season ended, we went into the National Collegiate Athletic Association tournament as the number-four team in the nation. Coach Miller said we were the best defensive team he had ever coached, which for him was saying a lot. In the tournament we tromped Pepperdine 70-51, rolled past Idaho 60-42, then were served our heads on a platter by Georgetown, losing 45-69.

In 1983 we had an adjustment year, changing our game because of the loss of the previous year's seniors. We were still competitive but didn't win the Pac-10 crown. So in 1984, my third year, we were on a Miller mission. Besides being known for our defense, our team was a scoring threat because of our quickness. Even though we were still a defensive, tempo team, we were effective in a spread offense because we were so fast.

In the race for the Pac-10 championship we pulled even with the University of Washington Huskies by defeating them 64-52 in front of a sellout crowd at our own Gill Coliseum. I went head-to-head against Detlef Schrempf, a 6'9-1/2" German import who was the talk of the league. He was very versatile, able to dribble, drive, shoot outside or score in the paint. It was hard to predict what he was going to do. He went on to be a high-scoring forward for the Seattle SuperSonics and made it to the All-Star game one year. I led the team that night with nineteen points, and Darryl Flowers got a career-high of fifteen.

We played Coach Raveling and the Washington State Cougars in one of our last games of the season and won 66-55. He hated losing, but he couldn't hide the pride he had in me. Then we went to Arizona State to keep alive the drive for our Pac-10 title.

I was rested and ready for that game. All day I bugged my teammates. "Let's get this thing going!" I said.

We went out and ripped the Sun Devils 69-58, our sixth victory in a row. A couple of days later I was named Pac-10 player of the year. I was fourth in the nation in field-goal percentage at .667, and I topped OSU with a 17.5 scoring average and 8.5 rebounds.

On the night of the player-of-the-year announcement we played

California, where Kevin Johnson was a freshman. Kevin went on to become a major scoring force for the Phoenix Suns. The first time we saw each other after I signed with Phoenix years later, he came up and hugged me. "I can't believe this. We're going to play together," he said.

"Kevin," I said laughing, "I used to own you in college!"

I enjoyed playing Kevin because at 6'1" he was a feisty little competitor. He was hard to contain because he could penetrate the ball, and he also had a decent jump shot. But it was his quickness that caused me problems when they got to the open-court game. California was not an up-tempo team, and neither were we, so we usually had low-scoring, tough battles together.

That night, however, their 6'9" sophomore center, Dave Butler, was on. He scored twenty-six points. Coach Miller tried three different defenders on him, the final choice being me. I did my best, and Coach left me with him, but I still couldn't shut him down completely. With Kevin zipping around out there, too, we got in trouble.

They had us beat until our Alan Tait sank a fifteen-foot jumper and tied the game with just seconds left. They still had time, however. Kevin Johnson got the ball. As the clock ran out, he shot a forced jumper from the top of the key. Everyone held his breath for a split second, then watched it bounce from the rim and put us into overtime. We ended up winning 64-60.

The win was important because it kept us in the running for the Pac-10 title. Washington State had already won its final game, so if we beat UCLA in our final contest, we'd share the crown. Movies couldn't be scripted better, because UCLA was a huge rival of Oregon State. We played on their court. The fans were delirious, but we shut them down as we claimed our title by winning 70-65.

At the NCAA tournament that year, West Virginia squeezed us out 64-62. I went home and got myself ready for my last year, which turned out to be my best. I was selected third team All-American by the AP and UPI, and I won a place on the All-Pac-10 team for the third year in a row. I was also the region 8 player of the year. That's the year I was chosen to go to the Pan Am trials and the Olympic trials. At OSU, I won the OSU Most Valuable Player award for the second straight year. I led the team in scoring and steals for two straight years and in rebounds for three years.

In my senior year I had a game that became the highlight of my whole college career. We went to Stanford to play them on national television in February, just three months before I graduated. I love the floor at Stanford's gym. It's springy. You can notice the lift even during the pregame warm-up. It has so much bounce that it seems as if everyone can jump a half foot higher on it.

Darryl Flowers and Eric Knox decided they were going to make me score twenty points that night. Darryl was the kind of player that I found Magic Johnson to be later, where giving an assist was as exciting to him as scoring. Eric had been the next in line to commit himself to Jesus Christ after Darryl, so we were "three amigos" on the team. As players, Eric and Darryl wanted me to be highlighted, and as friends they wanted to see me win big that day.

Between the springy floor and Darryl and Eric, I had the game of my life. I had my hands on everything that went up. When I got to twenty points, Darryl and Eric couldn't stop smiling. It seemed as though I got passes a second before defenders could react. It was another power night of basketball. When I got to thirty points, we started laughing out loud. We couldn't believe it. I was playing defense the way I was supposed to, and I couldn't stop scoring. I ended up with a career-high thirty-nine points.

Darryl tells the best story of that year. It was the grudge match against arch-rival UCLA at our own Gill Coliseum. They were out to avenge their loss from the last game of the year before. The game was televised nationally, which always heightened the anticipation. Students who were lucky enough to get tickets camped out starting on Thursday to be ready when the doors opened on Saturday. When the players got to the gym on game day, we saw human huddles parked all over the grounds. They screamed just seeing us. The excitement was intoxicating.

Darryl remembers a play that was like the breakaway slam dunk over Grant in high school. We had a skirmish for a loose ball under the UCLA bucket. All the players were scrambling to find the ball inside the paint. Somehow the ball shot out toward the sideline, and someone from OSU got it. He threw it to Darryl, who took it up the sidelines with one defender behind him.

Darryl was looking out the corner of his eye, seeing what angle he needed to beat the guard. I saw Darryl get the one-on-one breakaway, so I started following him, coming up the left side. Darryl made his move to the free-throw line, which drew the defender to him so he couldn't score. Somehow he flipped a

"Magic Johnson" no-look pass under the defender's arm back to me.

I was about five feet behind him. I got his pass and took one dribble, but the defender turned on me to block my shot. I jumped, he jumped, and we went in the air together. As I came down, I dunked the ball. The way Darryl tells it, I dunked the ball *and* the defender through the hole.

Darryl started jumping up and down. He might as well have done cartwheels. Eric ran down and high-fived Darryl, not me. The play set the crowd in an uproar. The alumni, sitting closest to the court, erupted. I'm sure we set off pacemakers and saw toupees flying. Until then it had been a close, defensive game that needed a spark. That play proved to be the momentum swing we needed to win 59-49.

We went on to the NCAA tournament and played Notre Dame. That was exciting, because when we boarded the plane, I was going somewhere I'd actually heard of before. That's education for you. They beat us 79-70, but the interesting trivia of that game is that it was the last NCAA tournament game ever played on a home court. Ever since, they've been played in neutral facilities.

Our team also played that year in Japan for the Suntori Bowl. We stayed for about ten days. It was a great trip, but it was the physical challenge of a lifetime, like being trapped in a junior high school. Nothing fit. Beds weren't long enough. Our legs didn't fit under dining tables. Transportation was cramped. Still we had a great time, and my parents have the souvenirs to prove I was there.

College was most important spiritually because it was there that I decided not to be a closet Christian but a success in everything I attempted, everything I valued. The Bible says that when you do something, you're to do it with all your might for God's glory. That kind of winning attitude is important to cultivate. You don't just throw down a crossword puzzle and give up. You get the dictionary and fight for that win. Don't be a quitter. You don't give up when the science project is due tomorrow. You go out and get it done to the best of your ability. Think championship. Think victory.

If you can't do something on your own, which no one usually can, find someone who has been there and is willing to help you. If that person says to go to summer school, don't fight it. Go. The teachable spirit is key. On the other hand, when someone in leadership tells you to violate your faith, your character or your person, then stop, resist and stand your ground.

Like me, you may need to find different coaches physically, academically and spiritually. They will help draw out the potential within you, to develop qualities into true character, to give you direction and guidance, and to show you the big picture. The spiritual coach does the same types of things. There's never a reason to reinvent the wheel. I figured other people had this Christian business down pat, and I wanted to learn from them, so I found good coaches. People who start from scratch may end up with a wagon. People who accept the wheel that is already invented can end up on the Indy speedway.

With college behind me, everyone felt certain I'd be drafted into the pros within weeks. My family, as always, made sure my head was out of the clouds. They keep me humble. Faye and my brothers, Lee and Steve, came to help me pack up my apartment after graduation.

"Junior," Faye said while we were moving, "do you remember the time you got jumped from the bushes and beat up real bad?"

I knew immediately what she was talking about. I was walking home from the neighborhood store one summer day when I was real young, wearing a brown corduroy jacket even in the heat. All of a sudden, a band of hoodlums jumped out from the bushes, pulled my jacket over my head so I couldn't see and started hitting me. I got away and ran for my life, never looking back.

"Never start a fight, but never run from one, either," Dad always taught us. When he saw me, he asked how many kids were involved.

"I don't know, Daddy," I answered, trying to think of something good to explain why I ran. "Probably about five or ten."

Faye looked at me mischievously over the box she was packing, her eyes twinkling above her deep dimples.

"Do you know who did it?" she asked.

"No."

"You had told on us again, and we were tired of getting in trouble, so Lee, Steve and I waited for you. It was us three."

"No!" I said, but I instantly knew it was true.

"Hey, Junior," members of my family still jokingly ask, "were there five or ten people that jumped you that day?"

My family loves to tease me, but by the time I graduated, they looked up to me, and it was me, the baby, who was getting the midnight calls asking for advice. During my four years at OSU, I had won the greatest accolade of all, the respect of my family. Now I just had to prove that their faith in me was well placed.

5

DRAFTED INTO YOUR MISSION

I N MY JUNIOR year of college, everything started coming together for me. I heard constant praise for my playing ability,
thanks to my coaches — Ralph Miller, Jimmy Anderson, Lanny
van Eman and Dave Elian, my spiritual coach. I was twenty years
old and seemed to have the world at my fingertips. This time when
I blossomed, I was a Christian. It made such a difference.

The harder I worked, the better I became. I was a regular in the weight room, turning myself into a lean, mean Green machine. When I wasn't in the weight room or playing basketball, I was in class, at church, with my church friends, at Denny's or at the library fighting that "just another athlete" syndrome. I was determined to succeed, to win, to graduate. Lee and Darryl were serious basketball junkies, so they kept me up on what was happening.

"OK, man, it's that time," Lee said from his perch on the couch one day as I was packing up for the library. "Where are you going?"

"The library," I answered.

"How about the Lakers?"

"How about them?" I said, shoving my books in a backpack.

"They're only the best team in basketball," Darryl said, walking in from the kitchen with a soda.

I knew something about them. Pat Riley took over in 1981, the year after the 1980 finals when Magic Johnson helped win the championship against the '76ers. In 1982, two years later, Coach Riley took them all the way to another championship over Dr. J. and those same '76ers.

"Man, they're running over everyone and everything," Lee said. "That's who you ought to play for."

"Yeah, right," I said, then headed off for the library, leaving them to watch another ESPN triple-header.

The guys knew their basketball. That season the Lakers toppled the Celtic dynasty in the NBA finals. Not only did they crush them, but they did it in Boston, on the Celtics' own parquet court. This was in-your-face basketball at its finest. Their fast-paced style, "Showtime," was my kind of basketball, and I found myself getting as enthused as the junkies during the play-offs. I finally took time to watch some basketball, instead of just playing it.

As the Lakers heated up, so did my mind. I started seeing the bigger picture myself, watching older teammates drafted to play professionally, catching on that you could get paid for it — a lot! But was it right for me? I prayed seriously for what God wanted me to do. I had learned what the Word says, that if we ask anything in Christ's name, our Father will give it to us. I didn't want to make a mistake. I wanted to ask correctly and take the right step.

Lee had made a big decision to go to law school in Texas, where Greg Ball lived. Now he was concerned about my decision. Roger LaVasa shared his concern.

"What about AIA?" he asked one day. Athletes in Action is a Christian basketball team that tours the country, and the players give high school kids and adults their testimonies.

"I'm thinking about that," I said.

"Or the NBA?" Roger asked.

"Yeah, or quitting," I said.

"I can't see God bringing you this far just so you'll quit," Roger said.

"I can't either, but I have to be willing if that's what He wants."

"That's not what He wants," Lee insisted.

"But I'm willing," I said.

The whole church prayed for me. I finally gave God my request: I wanted to serve Him. That's all. When I prayed, however, nothing happened. No bells, whistles or lights. Phil Bonasso, a pastor friend, later taught me that if you can't see a clear green light from God, giving you the go-ahead signal, then at least train yourself to see the red light so you'll know when to stop. That worked for me even before I knew about it. Like Lee, I eventually felt that quitting wasn't an option. In time I felt that AIA wasn't either.

"Lee," I said one morning after my devotions, "I'm going with the NBA."

"Man, that's great!" he said with genuine excitement. "But you could get drafted anywhere."

"I know," I said.

Taking a step toward the NBA took as much courage as taking a step away from it. It's a fearsome thing to know you have a God-given destiny, that you're responsible for something bigger than yourself. You have the gut check again. Am I going to be able to handle it? What am I going to do? Do I have enough character, patience, wisdom, discernment and spiritual fortitude to do it? Have I learned well enough to play with the big guys on a new level?

God says that we have not chosen Him, but He has chosen us. When the time is right, He brings us into what He has for us. In the draft the teams choose you, too. You don't choose them. Once I made the decision, I was helpless. It was in God's hands now. He'd have to work within me, as well as in the circumstances, to take me where He wanted me.

Besides the fear, I faced the temptation to jump the gun. Once you know where you're going, you want to be there now. I got restless my senior year, itching with senior-itis.

"I can't wait to be king!" Simba sang in the movie *The Lion King* when his father told him he would one day be king. His father took Simba out to a meadow to teach him about timing. As they walked, Simba looked down and saw his tiny paw inside his father's humongous paw print. It's a great object lesson. Simba thought he was ready to be king, but the paw print proved his time had not yet come.

Jesus taught us timing when He went to the mountain to fast and pray, and the devil came to tempt Him. Satan showed Him all the kingdoms of the world and said he'd give them to Jesus right then if only Jesus would bow down to him. Jesus refused, then left the mountain to do the difficult missionary work His Father asked Him to do. By doing it God's way, Jesus became the King of kings. He had to wait for the proper time. There are no shortcuts to victory.

I had to keep my eye on my game, on what I was doing, and not let the NBA distract me or intimidate me. My friends helped me out there — Buster and Lois Fenner, Heidi Croissant, Kristi Peschka, Bob Schroeder and Shavon Dennis. Their prayers helped me through the decision time and the waiting period.

Friends are like teammates, fitting into complementary positions that help you reach your victories. I don't know how I could make it through life without good, solid friendships. God knit our hearts together at church, cementing us into tight friendships that strengthened each of us and kept us from drifting away from Him during those turbulent college years. The Bible says that if you want to have friends, "show yourself friendly" (Proverbs 18:24). We showed up, making ourselves available for friendships, and God did the rest.

Pastor Dave taught us to hold each other accountable, responsible for our actions and decisions. We didn't skip out on each other. We didn't ditch church or church activities. We were part of everyone's lives. We prayed for each other, socialized together and became accountable to each other spiritually, physically and socially — even financially when we would go out for frozen yogurt and split the bill.

People were not created to live alone. You need true friends, quality people who are working toward finding and fulfilling their destiny, who see your potential and help you to achieve your calling and purpose. True friends won't let you stay in a comfort zone. They challenge you to a higher level. They see you on the beach and challenge you to get out in the water and fight some waves. They encourage you to stand for yourself, to believe in what the Word of God says.

As I contemplated the draft, I asked my friends to pray with me for just two things: that I could go to a team in a city that had a good church like ours and that, if possible, I could stay on the West Coast.

PRINCIPLE #14
Make true friends. Show yourself friendly to quality people who are working toward finding and fulfilling their destiny. Pray for God to cement your friendship together.

My college season ended, and then I just waited.

I was referred to a local sports representative who helped introduce me to the NBA. He arranged interviews with teams that flew me all over the country. The men I met were courteous and genuinely interested for the most part, but almost every one of them seemed nervous about the fact that I was a Christian.

One interview was back east with some gentlemen I was to meet for the first time. A team assistant picked me up and put his best foot forward. "How was your flight?" he asked.

"Fine."

"Have you been here before?"

"No, sir."

"You never played here in college?"

"No, sir."

He took me to a posh hotel and up to the suite the team had rented. When we walked in, I had to adjust my eyes because it was so dark. The curtains were drawn shut. I was introduced and shook the general manager's hand.

"How are you, sir?"

"How are you, young man?"

He motioned toward a table in the shadows, which I assumed was arranged with the usual spread of food. But as my eyes adjusted, I saw it wasn't food at all. The entire table was full of every kind of liquor imaginable. Fat bottles, tall bottles, round bottles — every kind of bottle filled that table from edge to edge.

It must have cost a small fortune. Then I realized they were trying to test me, to see if I could handle it! I almost laughed out loud.

"Could we get you something to drink?" the general manager asked, lifting his glass toward me as if in a toast.

"No, thanks, I'm not thirsty," I said with a smile. I rearranged a chair to sit down, hoping that after springing this, the rest would be routine.

"How do you like our city?" he asked.

"So far, so good," I said. "The ride from the airport looked nice. But the weather's a little brisk."

"And our team?"

"They're great, competitive."

"Well, I'm sure you would fit in here," he said. "Can you imagine yourself playing here?"

"I guess I could," I answered.

I didn't know how any general manager or coach could estimate how I would fit into their team. They had expertise in that field, but I was just a big-eyed kid in a new city talking to people I'd never met before.

"Your college team structure kept you inside the key most of the time," he said.

OK, I know what's coming, I thought.

"It leaves some questions about your shooting from the outside."

"I'm very confident that I can stick it from the outside," I responded. "As you said, Coach Miller's system was designed for me to post up all the time, but I believe that, with a different system and some practice, my shooting game will be fine."

"You would have a good position with us," he said. "We'd use you as a small forward or big forward, wanting you to get out on the fast break and fill the lanes. You would be quite an acquisition for us."

"Thank you, sir," I said. I knew there was a perennial All-Star in that position, and I could have trouble finding playing time.

"You've had quite a colorful career."

"Yes, sir."

"You've been involved in some extracurricular activities, too, I see. Preaching on campus and fighting pornography."

"Yes, sir," I said, and then I thought, Oh, great! What next?

"Now you know that in the NBA you might hear players talk about their girlfriends. Can you handle locker-room talk?"

"Yes, sir," I said, thinking, What does he think I've been doing for eight years? Locker-room talk started on the playground!

"People in the NBA might not have the same values as you. Will that be a problem?"

"No, sir," I said. I'm a Christian, I thought, not a space alien.

"We'd really like to have you," he said.

"Thank you, sir," I said. I was glad when I felt the wheels of the plane fold up under me as I flew out of that city.

His team ended up not getting me. And *Sports Illustrated* reported them as saying, like a case of sour grapes, that they didn't want me because they feared I'd hold Bible studies in the back of the team bus! It didn't matter, though. My Father had it all under control.

While I didn't appreciate his sterotype of a Christian, I understood that the man's concerns about my playing ability were genuine. General managers are all concerned about getting rookies who can make it at the professional level. The intensity of the pro game is incredible. Only about 320 players play in the NBA at any given time, and dozens of energetic young legs wash out every year.

I had my own concerns right up to the day of the draft. I didn't know if any of the teams who said they would take me really would. Boston, Denver, Philadelphia, Los Angeles, Portland and a couple of others had expressed interest, including that East Coast team. I was excited, nervous and amazed that this could be happening to me.

On draft day most of the guys who expected to be first-round picks flew to New York to be at the Felt Forum, where the draft was conducted. I agreed to go until I thought better of it. If I was going to have one of the greatest moments of my life, would I really want to go back to a lonely hotel room while my family celebrated without me at home? No way. My representative arranged for my family and the media to watch the draft in the presidential suite of the Jantzen Beach Red Lion Hotel just north of Portland.

My immediate family took time off from work. Along with Pastor and Mrs. Irving and Dave and Joan Elian, we drove up to the hotel that morning to await the announcement of my destiny. We were at least an hour early, beating the media by thirty minutes. We entered the gorgeous suite and had fun making ourselves at home. It was full of beautiful, overstuffed furniture, what looked like original paintings, and a bathroom with a Jacuzzi. The hotel made sure we were well stocked with catered foods and drinks. We sat down nervously.

"Are you comfortable?" Mom asked me.

"Yes, I'm fine," I said.

"Are you excited?" Sister Irving asked.

"Yes, a little," I said.

"Can I get you something?" Joan asked.

"No, thank you," I said. I had eaten breakfast before going and didn't feel like eating again until later that afternoon.

Long lapses in conversation added to the tension. My brothers found relief by playing in the hotel, alternating between awe and acting as if they were raised in fancy hotels. They tried to entertain themselves and everyone else, cracking jokes with photographers and helping them set up.

At 10:00 A.M. all heads turned to face the television as the draft began. Faye sat next to me, eight months pregnant and trying not to be too tense or excited. Mom sat next to her, totally tense and excited. Sister Irving and Joan sat beyond them. They kept checking each other.

"Are you excited?"

"Yes, are you?"

"Yes, and how do you feel?"

"I'm really excited."

They were in their own world. Dad walked around for a while, revelling in the big moment, enjoying every passing minute, which turned into almost two solid hours. Eventually he set up shop as the sheriff in a corner chair, making sure everything was running smoothly and talking knowledgeably with the two pastors.

"Who do you think will choose you?" reporters asked me.

"Oh, I don't know," I answered evasively.

"What team do you want to play for?" they asked.

"Oh, I don't know," I answered.

I may have secretly hoped for the Lakers, but I couldn't admit it even to myself. Jerry West, their general manager, impressed me on our first meeting. I felt he was someone I could learn from as well as look up to. From his playing years Jerry still holds probably dozens of NBA records. He is an honest, classy gentleman who knows the game from the courts to the contracts, from playtime to showtime. If they drafted me, he said they wanted me playing small forward and big forward, filling the lanes and rebounding. I couldn't have asked for a better job description. It was right down my alley and with a fast-paced team, too.

The Lakers had the twenty-third pick. Portland had the twenty-fourth. I found out later that as late as the morning of the draft,

Portland still tried to trade and barter for an earlier pick than the Lakers so they could keep me at home. I appreciated their confidence in me and would have been happy and proud to play for them, my home team. My family especially appreciated their efforts, because they didn't want to see me go.

Phone calls kept our pulses racing. People jumped each time the phone rang, as if it were the red phone in the Oval Office. No matter who was near it, they all looked at me and called, "Junior!"

I answered it with my heart in my throat. The front desk called. Catering called. Housekeeping called. Whew!

The hot summer morning wore on, and the room became stuffy. Many of the reporters smoked, weighing the air down even more. Weary photographers sat around trying to hold their position to get the perfect shot at the moment of the announcement.

As each draft choice was announced, my heart pounded. The first pick, ninth pick, fifteenth pick and twentieth pick went by. Each set my pulse racing and then I'd relax again. But what if I didn't go in the first round after all? Sports analysts felt certain, but I wasn't so sure.

At 11:52 A.M. the twenty-third pick was made. The Lakers announced, "Out of Oregon State, A.C. Green."

I was drafted in the first round. I was drafted by the number-one team. I was joining the champions. Incredible!

A shriek went up in the room. My family jumped, clapped, hugged and kept screaming. I covered my face with my hand, feeling almost embarrassed at being so incredibly happy, so incredibly fortunate, so incredibly blessed. That's the photo the local newspaper ran — A.C. with his hand over his face.

"How do you feel?" reporters asked.

"I just thank God. I just thank God," I said.

Finally I was able to answer a little more clearly. "I want to play the Laker style," I said, "to run the ball, get banged up and rebound to my heart's content."

My heart was pretty contented right then. Actually it was almost bursting. Television reporters interviewed me, live on national television, my first time as a Laker. I said what everyone says, that I was happy to be chosen. But my answer wasn't hollow. God had given me all I'd dreamed of and even more.

The party started breaking up, and Mom left to prepare the bigger celebration at home for the extended family and friends.

Faye, her son Terrance, and my brother Lee's son, Jerray, went together to Lloyd Center in downtown Portland to kill some time while the family assembled. We walked around and ate frozen yogurt. It was so strange to be in such familiar surroundings with such a totally different feeling inside, a feeling that I was coming into my own, into God's plan for my life. I celebrated late into the night, surrounded by the people who meant the most to me, those who had seen me through and helped make my dreams a reality.

Years would go by before I realized that basketball wasn't the only draft God had for me. He chose me for a vocation of basketball and, in time, for an avocation of influencing the next generation.

I went into the NBA knowing that the men there were my mission field. They are hurting men, men who are crying out for truth. Some desire the God of their youth but don't know how to find Him or draw close to Him. I've had a great time with my teammates and other athletes, counseling them, praying with and for them, challenging them and sometimes just loving them.

But God had even bigger plans. One day in Los Angeles, as I was reading my Bible, I read the proverb that the "good servant" will be given the children of the wicked son and will receive his inheritance. We have an inheritance from God because we're His children. But if we're wicked, we lose the right to that inheritance. Another verse says that children are God's inheritance to parents.

As I studied those verses, I started thinking about where I lived. In Los Angeles, drugs, gangs and sex routinely destroyed young people all around me, many of whom came out of broken homes or had no caring parents at all. I realized what God was saying to me. God would use my basketball career as a platform from which I could influence young people. Where parents were wicked — hooked on drugs, abandoning their children or just not taking the time to train children properly — I was to be the good servant. So many parents today want the pleasure of sex but not the responsibility of its results. When the sex is over and the children are growing up, they don't have time, patience or inclination to raise them properly. God was telling me to step into the gap.

My own nieces and nephews, like so many kids today, are not being raised the way I was, in a traditional, two-parent household. Nothing is ideal. You work with your circumstances and make adjustments, but not compromises. I had a choice. Either I could watch kids grow up and make mistakes they didn't need to make, or I could help them understand what it takes to become a champion. It's a fragile position sometimes, especially because I'm not even a natural parent myself. I can offend parents, step on toes and be seen as an outsider who gives advice but doesn't live under the same roof. Yet I have a sense of responsibility, purpose and obedience.

We don't ask for certain things to happen. God puts us in positions that surprise us. Looking through His Word, it's amazing how often He chooses the least likely person. Parenting, mentoring and helping kids is an odd hobby for a single basketball player to take up. But it's a great mission, a great goal, and I love it.

Everyone has a God-given destiny to fulfill. It's usually in two parts: a vocation (career) and an avocation (mission). For some people, like Greg Ball and other full-time ministers, the two are the same. When I teach young people how to find a career, I teach them to discover their God-given strengths and talents, then find a way to express them in the marketplace. If you're not a career person, that's what you need to do. As I've heard it said, "Find something you love to do, then find someone who will pay you to do it."

In finding your mission, remember that God will give you the desires of your heart. Some people believe God will tell them to do exactly the opposite of what they desire. That's not right. But it is true that we have to learn to desire Him more than anything else. That's why we build our foundation. We need courage to take our steps into destiny.

One of the most exciting things about being a Christian is that you get to know for certain that you're doing exactly what you were created to do. And you get the power to do it. You personally have a purpose to fulfill. Your life has meaning because you're the only one who can do what God wants you to do. Nothing makes a greater impact on the world around you.

PRINCIPLE #15

You have a destiny to fulfill. You're the only one who can do it. Nothing is more fulfilling personally. And nothing makes a greater impact on the world around you.

One important part of your foundation is to accept yourself the way you are. Your strengths, talents, characteristics and desires will enable you to fulfill your destiny. You will never fulfill that purpose if you constantly deny those characteristics that are meant to get you to the goal. You have to understand and accept that you're different from everyone else on this earth.

On every team I've played with since becoming a Christian, about ten guys have been roughly alike, while one or two have been different. I'm always one of the more unique guys on the team. I'm convinced that the others are alike not because they were born that way but because, at a young age, they started following the crowd, giving in to peer pressure, and became just like everyone else. They weren't willing to let their uniqueness come out.

Christians are naturally going to be different from everyone else. Once we give God our lives, the uniqueness that has cried for recognition suddenly becomes unchained. We are set free from following the crowd, from peer pressure and from self-imposed limitations. We are free to be exactly who God created us to be. A kindred spirit, a common bond, unites Christians, but that's the only characteristic we all share.

PRINCIPLE #16
Accept that you're different from everyone else. Your qualities, talents and gifts enable you to fill perfectly the position God has for you on His team. Don't hide or be ashamed of them. You're unique. Take joy in that.

At one time when I was younger, for example, people wanted to tease me about my name. My name is unusual. Very few people share it. I have just one little cat named after me, the kitten a friend gave his daughter. At another time in my life, my skin color was unique. When my family moved to Gresham for a year and a half, Faye, Lee and Steve went to other schools, making me the only black kid at a white school. In fact, the Little League team Archie Jamison coached was all white except for me. There was nothing I could do about my skin color except to accept who I was. So I did.

Differences aren't an issue unless people make them one. To say that I'm better because I'm black or worse because of it makes no sense at all. Race was never an issue with God's people in the Bible, so it's not an issue for me.

I heard far more about my height than I ever did about anything else. Again there was nothing I could do about that. I had to adjust to being bigger, taller and heavier than everyone else and then just accept it. At my basketball camps sometimes I see young people trying to hide their size, to pretend they're not quite as tall as they are or don't have quite the arm span they have. But adolescence is the age to learn that people are different and those differences are good.

Other people will recognize your differences. You have to accept them, too. They see something unique in you, and it comes right out of their mouths. "Wow, you have big feet!" they may say.

It's easy to be offended unless you realize where they're coming from. You don't need to get upset, to deny the obvious or to be embarrassed.

"You should see Ralph's if you think these are big" is not something you need to say.

"It's just these shoes."

"Shut up."

Those are unnecessary responses.

"Yes, they're big" is all you need to say. It's the truth. So what? None of your uniqueness is an issue unless you make it one.

If people say something to hurt you, that's different. It's their immaturity and insecurity talking. But you don't need to get down and fight on that level, either. Recognize it, cope with it, pass on and let it fall to the background. People will get used to your differences if you don't make them an issue. Take joy in your uniqueness.

After the draft, I had to go to Los Angeles to meet with the Laker management and negotiate the terms of my contract to play for them. While I was there, I checked out a church that Greg Ball had helped start, and I loved it from the first minute. Both my prayer requests were answered: to be on the West Coast and to have a good church to attend.

The Lakers agreed to pay me a certain amount in return for my promise to play for them for four years. I agreed to the terms and shook hands, and the deal was done. Then they wanted me to sign a contract! It was so strange for me after four years of indoctrination in making my word mean more than anything else. I couldn't understand why we couldn't just shake on it, but I signed the contract.

Regardless of what the contract said, what I promised them was to play at the highest I could, to be the best sportsman I could be and to represent the Laker ball club in the most positive way possible. My name was going to be out there across the back of my jersey, and I wasn't going to let it get dirty. The Bible says a good name is to be chosen above riches, so I valued my name more than any money they could have offered me.

The Lakers and I ended up going through two four-year contracts together without any disputes, haggling or broken promises. They were fair to me, and I kept my word to them. Integrity is essential in championship-level living. People need to know they can count on your word — that you'll follow through with what you say you'll do. Value your name. Value your word. Value your reputation.

PRINCIPLE #17
Develop integrity. Integrity is essential in championship-level living. People need to know they can count on your word. Value your name. Value your reputation.

I flew home after signing with the Lakers and tied up all the loose ends left from my childhood and developing years. I said my good-byes and got myself ready for my next big step into destiny.

While I was at the house a few days before the move, Dad came to me and asked how I was getting to Los Angeles. "You gonna take that car?" he asked, meaning the Mark IV.

"Sure."

"Can I borrow the keys?"

"Of course."

I gave Dad the keys and went on about my business. In a little while he came back to the house, pulled an envelope out of his pocket and shoved some money into my hand.

"Here, Junior," he said. "Use this money to get to L.A. I sold your car."

I was shocked. My dad sold my car? But soon I was on a plane, on my way to Los Angeles, without even my old, trusty, skunky-looking car for a friend.

6

ROOKIE

BRIGHT LIGHTS, BIG city. Los Angeles was a world away — a planet away — from Portland and Corvallis. I found myself in a foreign atmosphere of fast cars, fast talkers, big money and even bigger egos. I stopped in L.A., then went straight out to Palm Springs where the Lakers' training camp was held that year. We played at the College of the Desert and stayed at the

Ocotillo Lodge, a rambling, ranch-style hotel east of the city and far from the main strip. That's where the rich and famous hang out during the winter to escape the sixty-degree chill of Los Angeles.

Our hotel had good food with fast room service. I later learned those are two of the most important concerns when housing a team of basketball players.

On our first night there, we had a team dinner to kick off training camp, a Laker tradition. I walked into the dimly lit ballroom and saw a single podium and video screen standing in the middle of one wall. A buffet table stretched along the other wall with waiters scurrying around it, bringing on the mountains of food necessary to feed a squad of professional athletes. Delicious aromas filled the room and made me instantly hungry. A dozen round tables, each set for six, were spread far enough apart to allow big bodies to move easily among them. I threaded my way to a table where Dexter Shouse and other rookies had already found seats, careful not to bump any of the million-dollar arms or legs belonging to the living legends who were filtering into the room.

Every time you go up a level in life, you start at the bottom all over again. This was overwhelming, like the first day of kindergarten. The stars gathered in that one room could have taught the least-educated basketball enthusiast a history lesson of the sport. Kareem Abdul-Jabbar is a walking historical monument on his own. By that night, with sixteen years in the league, he had played with, for or against most of basketball's greats. I heard people at his table call him by his team name, Cap, short for Captain.

I got into the pros just in time to play with Kareem and against another basketball legend, Dr. J., Julius Erving. Kareem presided at Dr. J.'s farewell the next year, and two years after that Doc presided over Kareem's retirement ceremony in Philadelphia. The two were strong competitors. After Kareem and the Lakers beat Dr. J.'s Philly team for the title in 1982, Doc returned the favor, beating the Lakers the next year to earn the only world championship of his career. By the time I came along, their competition had turned into friendship, which was interesting because Dr. J. became a fiery Christian, while Kareem turned to Islam. Kareem was serious about his religion, too.

"You should watch these," he told me once on a road trip, shoving four ninety-minute videos by a Muslim teacher into my hands. "They'll give you a better understanding."

I was willing to view them and discuss them with him, but two days later he approached me. "You have my tapes?" he asked.

"I barely watched part of one," I started to explain.

"I want them back," he said.

He probably would have viewed, digested and written a forty-page thesis by that time. That's Kareem.

He played center on the court, but off court he was a guard. He monitored everything he owned, from his old jeans to his jazz collection. He always played practical jokes and stole jewelry and stuff from guys for fun, then kept them for a long time. But if anyone got anything of Kareem's, he demanded it back soon. He always got it back, too.

That night everyone was dressed casually. I learned later that Kareem is *always* dressed casually. He was especially fond of one pair of jeans that he wore to home games without fail. On the rare times when he dressed up, he still didn't look like a man at the top of his profession.

Two years later when he retired from a twenty-year career, each NBA city honored him in a pregame ceremony while the teams waited to play. We never saw him until he came to the locker room after the ceremony. The players could hardly wait to see him. He walked in — wearing a tie that was barely long enough to cover his chest. We kidded him until we got sideaches from laughing.

"Cap, take off Amir's tie next time you go out there," we told him. Amir was his nine-year-old son.

Jeff Lamp was the Kareem imitator of the team starting in 1988. He did a merciless Kareem routine in the locker room at almost every game. We would howl with laughter when he imitated the way Kareem slightly nodded his head forward to acknowledge the crowd, looking more like the pope blessing the people than a sports figure.

Kareem had room to laugh. He was, and is, an all-time great. In college he had played for the legendary John Wooden, who left Indiana to take UCLA to eleven NCAA titles, three with Kareem. Kareem won the MVP award all three years. Kareem redefined the center position. At 7'2" he wasn't the immobile big man typical of that era. John Wooden changed his game plan to cut Kareem loose, and Kareem, with his incredible coordination and power, dominated the game.

His ability to dunk the ball — which scored, fired up the crowd and intimidated the opposition — caused the NCAA to outlaw the dunk before his junior year. (That ruling lasted ten years.) Kareem responded by perfecting his trademark skyhook, an almost indefensible move that lobbed the ball over defenders' heads — which once again scored, fired up the crowd and intimidated the opposition. Coach Wooden helped him perfect his game with ruthless practices in which Kareem might shoot a hundred skyhooks in a day. In the pros he continued to dominate the game, and he's the only player ever to win six MVP awards in the NBA.

Kareem was well known for being an introspective, proud man with a hungry intellect and a fierce appetite for privacy. But because he elevated the game, he drew crowds from the beginning. In his junior year of college Kareem commanded a standing-room-only crowd at the new, enormous Houston Astrodome for a game against Elvin Hayes and the University of Houston. They packed in over fifty-two thousand fans, with four thousand standing-room tickets, at a time when the pros thought they were doing great to get ten thousand out to a game. Playing under the expanse of the Astrodome was an experience Kareem likened to "playing on a prairie." He always sees things from a slightly different angle. He continued to pack in the crowds throughout his career, and he always shunned fans and reporters. When our friendship bloomed, I came to know him as an intelligent man who enjoys reading, thinking deeply, analyzing everything — and playing those practical jokes. I got my fill of those, but I got him back, too.

Jerry West was Kareem's senior by nine years. He left West Virginia to become a Laker in L.A., where he stayed throughout a brilliant career. He was "Mr. NBA" at one time, the only player in history to win the MVP of the finals even though his team lost. He represented the previous generation, the ones who didn't always get the pay or attention but brought basketball into its own, on a par with baseball and football.

Jerry and Oscar Robertson were drafted in the same year, 1960, and both ended up in the Hall of Fame. He played against Bill Russell, who led the Celtics to eleven championships in the fifties and sixties, six of them over the Lakers. He played K.C. Jones, Connie Hawkins, Bob Lanier and John Havlicek. He was a teammate of Elgin Baylor and Wilt Chamberlain.

My relationship with Jerry grew throughout the years into a

strong friendship based on trust and respect for one another. Although he manages a team located in the shadow of Hollywood and whose playing style was nicknamed "showtime," he never became flashy or superficial himself. He's an intensely loyal person who always keeps his cool and is always confident. He affectionately called me "son," and I affectionately called him "Mr. West." By the time I left the Lakers, I was one of the players who best understood his contributions to the sport, and even then I was still learning.

Earvin Johnson was another history maker, known to the fans as Magic, but to the team as Buck. Once we became friends, he and I fell into our family names and just called each other Junior. The 1979 NCAA final between Larry Bird's Indiana State and Earvin's Michigan State is still a classic, and it became a pivotal event for basketball as the two big men fought for the title, which Earvin narrowly won. The rivalry between them became legendary, both on and off the court.

Earvin left college after just two years and was drafted by the Lakers for $500,000 per season in 1979, a record-breaking salary during the days when $150,000 was considered high. Two weeks later Bird was drafted by Boston for $600,000. I think it still irritates Earvin that he came in second.

The year before I joined the team, Earvin and Larry met in the off-season and started a friendship that grew stronger every year. The two of them changed the game of basketball, bringing the sport even further into the national spotlight and the kind of game we play today. At 6'9", the same height I am, Earvin was considered too big to be a guard, to maneuver the way he did, to orchestrate the game from his position on the floor. Yet he executed all that, and even more, flawlessly. He studied the great players like Marques Haynes, the "shifty dribbler" who was famous for dribbling lower and lower to the floor until he was lying down, dribbling just six inches off the ground. Marques was from the Jerry West era, but Earvin copied his moves in practice and developed skill in ball control unequaled by any of his contemporaries.

Earvin seemed to have eyes all around his head, always knowing exactly where everyone was on the court and able to toss his trademark no-look passes when and where he wanted. Earvin passed the ball unselfishly — "passing out the sugar" as the first great assist man, Bob Cousy, called it. Earvin eventually broke

Oscar Robertson's all-time NBA assist record in 1991, the year he retired. It was a bittersweet accomplishment because of the conditions of his retirement, but he left the game a champion.

Earvin had already won three championships with the Lakers before I got there (in his rookie year, 1980, then in 1982 and 1985). Yet he kept his attitude of being one of the guys. To this day I've never seen him in flashy jewelry or clothes that proclaim his success. With all he has earned and accomplished, he has always understood relationships and valued them above all else.

Earvin didn't wear any of the rings he had earned, but others did. You couldn't help but notice the rings in the room that night in training camp — big rings, with big diamonds and intricate engravings that made the rookies' class rings look like Cracker Jack toys. When sports figures earn a championship ring, I guess they want people to see it from across an arena. The rings bore the year, the score, the player's number, the Laker emblem and the words "World Champions." I knew I was in line for the next one.

Head coach Pat Riley wore his latest championship ring from 1985, when the Lakers beat the Celtics in Boston. That's the ring Jerry West prized even above the one from his 1972 win against the Knicks as a player. The Lakers and Celtics have enjoyed one of the longest, strongest rivalries in basketball. I found out later how sweet taking the cake from Boston could be.

Coach Riley had been a great player himself and a teammate of Jerry West's for a while. He even played against Kareem, starting back in high school. He had coached the Lakers for four years when I got there, taking them to the finals every year and winning the whole show twice. Critics said he was good only because Earvin was on his team, but after Earvin retired, Riley went on to New York and proved that he was the man. He's a great coach and masterful storyteller. He prides himself on his locker-room talks. With the results he gets, he has every reason to.

We had an ongoing controversy in the Laker organization and in the media about who really called the shots for the Lakers: Was it Jerry West, Coach Riley or Magic Johnson? All three were amply qualified. Sometimes even the players asked each other, "Who's the coach around here?" Jerry never seemed to want to interfere, yet he was very opinionated and had a deep understanding of the game that couldn't be ignored. The controversy seemed to affect management more than the players. Fortunately, our quality of play was never sacrificed. It probably most affected sports writers who got a lot of great stories out of it.

Coach Riley's right-hand man, Bill Bertka, was another ring-wearer who would come to remember me as the "one who affects the many." He coached the big men like me, James Worthy, Kareem and, later, Mychal Thompson. Randy Pfund was a new assistant coach that year, a rookie like me, who came from a basketball family and had impressive high school and college stats of his own. Years later, when the coaching staff was juggled, leaving him on top as head coach, his faithfulness made a deep impression on me. I admired a coach with convictions and principles. During eight years together we developed more than a coach-player relationship. We really became friends.

I took a seat at the table with the rookies and free agents that night in Palm Springs. I was glad when I caught Byron Scott's eye and nodded to him. He came right over to talk a little. We had played each other in college, so there was a connection there that relieved me. Byron was the team jester on road trips, but on the court he was all business. He had perfected the off-guard position. He was a deadly shooter from the three-point range and closer. With the Lakers' chemistry we had during those years, Coach Riley counted on him for twenty points every night, and he generally delivered. He became my first friend on the team, a friendship that continues.

Byron left, and I continued to gaze around the room. I felt as if my eyes were bulging out of my head. There was James Worthy, the same height as Earvin and I and one of the best small forwards ever to play the game. When he gets fired up, he's unstoppable. He is lightning quick and able to shoot the ball outside or inside, creating a deadly situation for defenders. I had heard the critics say he only looked good because of Earvin, but I found out differently. Earvin said that the Lakers could not have beaten Boston in 1985 if it hadn't been for James. I was proud when, in 1988, James won the finals MVP, an award he richly deserved.

James became one of my mentors. His style of play is both courageous and brilliant. He is highly intelligent. He reads about 25 percent of what Kareem reads, which puts him two notches above the average person. His quick, intelligent wit had earned him the team nickname, Clever. He always chose a training camp rookie to pick on, and I must have been the one that year, but it lasted for the next eight years. I had no idea as I gawked at all these men that we'd blend into a huge family, but we did.

"You should see A.C. eat," James said to Byron Scott one day during my first two years. "I invited him over to watch my alma mater's football game, and he ate all the chicken wings in the whole house!"

"I believe it, man," Byron said.

"Angela said, 'Don't invite that A.C. again unless you give me a week's notice,' " James said with a squeaky voice.

"Same thing happened to me," Byron said. "I told Anita, 'Baby, I want to invite A.C. over for enchiladas.' "

By this time, the whole team was listening in and laughing.

"We ate and got up after dinner, but A.C. was still sitting there. I said, 'Man, what are you doing?'"

"He said, 'I'm still hungry.'"

"I said, 'Then help yourself.'"

"So he got into the refrigerator and finished off twelve more!"

They got the whole team roaring.

They loved to tease me about anything, especially my name. One of their favorite taunts was, "A.C., your dad had to be drunk to give you that name!"

I spotted the veteran Michael Cooper at the next table, laughing and swapping off-season stories with some others. But I soon learned that beneath his calm exterior, he was Mr. Nerves. Before a big game, you could just look at him and he'd start sweating. I avoided high-fives with Coop unless I had a towel handy, because he had the wettest palms in basketball.

Coop was a strong competitor. Even from across the room, anyone could see what good shape he was in. He was slender but thick and solid, not skinny. During the off-season he would hone his body into a machine at his home in Albuquerque. Every year when we checked in for training camp, we'd get our preconditioning reports, and his would always come in showing a tiny percentage of body fat, the best on the team.

His determination for training off the court was matched by his determination for winning on it. When the rest of the team couldn't stop someone from scoring, Coach Riley called in the defensive specialist, Coop. He was known as the Lakers' "hit man," and he was true to his reputation. Any handshake or hug with an opponent, such as before the game when you saw an old college friend on the court, would bring Coop's wrath down on your head. He didn't want any of his teammates fraternizing with the enemy. In the five years we played together, I never saw him back down or become intimidated by anyone. He could stop the best.

I recognized Kurt Rambis when he walked in because of his trademark glasses. He wasn't a dirty player, but he did the dirty work on the team. He got the ball out of bounds after an opposing player's basket or after a missed shot and started the fast break going the other way before the ball ever hit the ground. He was quick and agile and a necessary component to a world champion-ship team. He was known as Superman because of the dark-rimmed glasses he wore. A cheering section of his fans dressed like him in the stands — glasses and all. He was also a power forward and rabid rebounder, so I spent most of my practice time with him to learn his skills.

In that first year the media tried to make a controversy about my being groomed to take Kurt's position. When I took his starting job in my second year, I was still too young and inexperienced in dealing with high-stakes careers and egos to realize fully what was happening. But I did know that I took someone else's job.

"Do you deserve this position?" reporters asked me. "Are you better than Kurt Rambis?"

"I just do what the coaches say," I said. I felt so honored by God to become a starter in the NBA. I didn't want it ruined by hurt feelings.

Kurt turned out to be a much bigger man than all that. "A.C. works hard," he told the press, "and he does what the coaching staff wants. There's nothing personal between me and A.C."

It was true. Joining the pros was to me a do-or-die environment. That kind of pressure situation makes you learn things quickly to survive. Just about everything I picked up those first years, I learned from Kurt. He guided, trained and helped nurture me as a player. He was funny, too. He went back and forth with Coach Bertka about proper techniques at practices. He always had Bertka repeat himself two or three times. When he played, he pulled my shorts, gouged me and elbowed me, all in good, sporting fun. We became very good friends on and off the court.

Kurt's fans weren't quite as friendly to me. Every time he came off the bench to play, they roared their enthusiasm. I lived with that for four years, but I appreciated that he was a champion and had earned their respect and admiration.

Jerry Buss, our owner, made a point of coming by the rookie table to say hello to the newcomers. He had a lot of hopes pinned on us. He was not a player but was a serious enough fan to buy his own team. He earned a doctorate degree in chemistry at USC, then made his millions through real estate investing, working out deals as far-flung as the Chrysler Building in New York in order to acquire the team from Jack Kent Cooke in 1979. I respected him during the draft process because he never played the games with me that some other owners did. Although he had a notoriously "Hollywood" lifestyle, he never tempted or taunted me with it. We had a mutual respect from the beginning that lasted until the day I left eight years later.

Once we were settled for dinner, the players went through the buffet lines, ate, talked, heard introductions and watched some special Laker videos prepared to pep us up for the season. By this time, everyone at my table was at ease. The evening was warm outside as well as inside, and I was beginning to feel comfortable in my surroundings. Then management left, the players were alone, and Earvin took the podium to host what he called the "Buck-A-Roam Show."

"OK, now it's time to introduce the rookies and free agents," Earvin said. We realized immediately that this was not exactly to honor us or make us feel welcome but to set us up for the "dissing" we were going to take all year. The tension at our table resurrected itself.

"When I introduce you one at a time, you come up here," he said, looking at our table with a gleam in his eye. "Then you can sing your school fight song, a Top 10 song or a rap."

I don't remember who the first guy was, but of the five or six new guys that year I was the last. Earvin introduced the first rookie, and all the players applauded as he approached the podium. "Come on up and give us your song," he said.

The rookie sang or rapped while the veterans kept time, beating tables or singing backup. None of the rookies had any musical skills whatsoever. The only singer in those families was the sewing machine. As they performed, for a while everyone laughed and helped out. Then sooner or later the veterans started yelling. They booed and hissed, and some even threw food.

"Go sit down!" they yelled. "Get off the stage!"

I think Earvin enjoyed himself more doing that than all the rest of training camp. Kareem and the others laughed their heads off.

My eyes got wider with each performance. My anxiety level rose with each new burst of laughter. I wanted to laugh, but inside I knew I was in trouble. Sooner or later I was going to get called, and I didn't know what to do. At OSU we won a lot of basketball games, and they sang the fight song each time. But with my adrenaline still pumping from the game, it was always just noise to me. They sang it at football games when we won, too, but we didn't win enough of those for me to memorize lyrics. I never learned the song.

My other option was the popular tunes, but I had listened only to Christian music for the last four years. I sat there sweating it out and racking my brain for a popular tune I could sing to get it over with, but my mind went blank. These were the days before Christian rap artists, so that choice was out, too.

I already felt like a kindergartner. Now this was like the teacher calling for your crayons. You take out your twelve-crayon box and look around to see that all the other kids have ninety-six-crayon boxes complete with sharpeners. It was a feeling of total inadequacy.

"And now, fresh from Oregon State University," Earvin finally announced, "it's Mr. A.C. Green."

I started walking stiffly, my legs trying to take me the other way.

"Come on up, A.C., and give us your school fight song," he said with his famous smile spread ear to ear.

I stood looking blankly, trying to forget whom those faces belonged to in front of me. But, like anyone else, I wanted to find a way to do whatever Magic Johnson asked.

"I don't know my fight song," I said.

"Come on — you have to know your fight song!" he said.

The other veterans started laughing. I just stood there and shrugged my shoulders.

"Come on, man — hum it or something," he said.

I fumbled around, looking for a way out.

"I know we were the Beavers," I said.

They loved that. Everyone rolled with laughter at my expense. I laughed, too, but I also hoped I could go sit down soon.

"OK, give us a Top 10 R&B selection then," he finally said.

"I don't know one."

"You've got to know one," Earvin insisted.

"How about a song by Little Richard?"

"Little Richard? That's not in the Top 10!"

"Al Green?"

"No, man. What are you, a golden oldie?"

"Otis Redding?"

"Quit jiving. You're gonna sing something. Let's hear a rap."

"I don't know one." At this point I wasn't gutsy enough to break into "Victory in Jesus," but I considered it. I was facing a decision about whether or not to give in to peer pressure. Don't let them unnerve you, I thought. Don't allow them to make you ashamed of your Christian music. Roll with it, but stand your ground.

"I only know gospel songs," I said with a grin. "Do you have any requests?"

"Swing Low, Sweet Chariot," James Worthy called out in his deep, James-Earl-Jones voice.

"Clevvverrrr, Clevvverrrrr," the veterans called out.

"Swing low...," I started as soulfully as I could. The veterans joined in, "...sweet chariot, comin' for to carry me hooommmmme...."

Buck let me go with everyone laughing harder than ever. I knew right then that they were wondering about me.

Veterans are assigned rookies at that dinner to be their waiter, valet and attendant for the rest of the season. Earvin had been Kareem's rookie years earlier. The rookies get water, deliver juice, coffee and a newspaper in the mornings, make wake-up calls, carry the veteran's gym bag, and do whatever menial chores the veteran wants done. When they made the rookie assignments later that night, I noticed that no one was saying, "I want A.C. to bring me my paper." They later confirmed what I suspected, that they were thinking, I want A.C. to stay away from me for right now. All the others got assigned, but I never did that year. I was a little too strange for that crowd.

They had the wrong impression of me at first, but I also had the wrong impression of them.

7

THE STUFF
OF HEROES

I REMEMBER SITTING on a bench in the locker room the day after the training camp banquet, actually looking forward to practice so I could start to redeem myself. Maybe that's why they did Buck-A-Roam, so we'd want to play basketball against them the next day.

I leaned over to tie my shoes. Out of the corner of my eye, I saw a pair of huge shoes walk right past me. My eyes followed. I wondered who owned those feet.

I pulled back, raised my eyes and slowly panned up until finally I saw Kareem Abdul-Jabbar's shaved head. I felt like thousands of other people: There's Kareem Abdul-Jabbar! I shouldn't have been surprised. After all, this was his team. I just couldn't get used to it. I did the same with James Worthy and Kurt Rambis.

Most of the time a veteran player doesn't speak to a rookie, but on that first day Kareem spoke to me. During practice he said, "Rookie, get me some water." Wow. This was real. Months later, or maybe it was the next year, he actually used my name, and in time he started calling me Junior, too.

Practices were tough, intense, and so was I. We had daily doubles where I made mistakes — got hit and faked out time and again. Every day I called Lee Johnson and told him what I had done.

"Let me tell you what happened today," I said on the third or fourth afternoon. "Coop came in from the baseline and tried to dunk the ball on me."

"Are you serious," Lee said, still awed that his homeboy was talking about Coop as in "Michael Cooper," not chickens.

"I was at the free-throw line," I said, "so I took a couple of steps to jump and block his shot."

"Did you get it?" he asked.

"Almost!"

"Dog."

"Lee," I said, still trying to believe it myself, "I almost blocked Michael Cooper's shot!"

Coop probably didn't even notice it. But I was a different person when I got to practice for the intersquad game that night. I really believed I might be able to make it in this league. They put me on the red team along with the rookies and reserves from the previous year. We played the gold team, which was made up of Kareem, Byron, James, Magic, Kurt, Mitch, Maurice and Coop. Refusing to be intimidated, I jawed with them and played harder than anyone out there.

"We're going to beat you," I told Kareem.

"You don't even know the plays," Byron said.

"We'll still beat you," I said. Kareem just looked at me calmly. He reminded me of the time I went to an outdoor park in Oregon and watched an ostrich. I yelled at it and took pictures, but it just stood there, unbothered, blinking at me.

I got about twenty points and twenty rebounds that night. As we took a breather, I overheard them talking.

"That boy's going to be something," Coop told Magic.

His statement became my confirmation that I was at the right place, that I hadn't missed the bus regardless of how tough it might be.

The first weeks and months in Los Angeles were like living behind the lens of a slow-motion camera in a Hollywood movie. I hung out with one famous crowd, the Lakers, and the Lakers attracted another famous crowd, the movie stars. People came to our games to see the stars as much as to watch the game. It was like finding yourself sitting in your living room watching TV, when suddenly everything you see comes right out of the television and envelops you. Jack Nicholson is talking to you, directing you. Denzel Washington is cracking jokes on the sidelines. Dyan Cannon is flashing that familiar smile. Kareem Abdul-Jabbar is hitting skyhooks right over your head, and Earvin Johnson is shooting no-look passes to you. It's amazing.

I would find myself playing against someone I used to watch on television, and I'd think, Man, I remember watching you while I was in college. You did that same move, went for the rebound that same way! I could hardly believe they did in person just what I had watched them do on television. I was shocked and awed once more.

For a while I fell into the trap that anyone can fall into. I generalized a person's outward success to his inner character. I looked at what he did on the court and figured he played at the ultimate level off the court, in his everyday life, too. I figured these must be cool guys through and through. If they were married, they must be good family men with great marriages. If they had a business on the side, they must be good businessmen. I was swayed, utterly in awe of them. I didn't want to believe anything else. I didn't want to see anything else.

Reality set in within weeks. I know the Bible says a man's heart is evil apart from Christ, yet I was surprised at how wide the gap was between a man's public and private life. Throughout my career I've found that many players, and some of my teammates, are very insecure and misinformed in their identities. Some don't know who they are. And most of them, because they have such great talent, think they should be viewed as better-than-average people and should get respect. But many have no foundation. They're shaky, uncertain, and they try to cover up for it with bravado, talent and talk.

I held them in such high regard that I could have allowed them to influence me. When I realized that, I had to separate in my mind their talent from their character. I could admire the talent, but I couldn't copy the character.

For anyone, when you determine to do something new, such as live a Christian life or graduate from college, the people you look up to have to change. You have to find new heroes, people whose lives match up with how you want to live your own. You have to find new friends, even, people who will influence you to do the right thing, to press on into championship living in every area of life, not just one.

PRINCIPLE #18
**Admire the talent, but don't copy the character.
Don't substitute performance for substance.**

It wasn't just the players I looked at. I met a lot of people at whom I had to take a second look. Some famous Hollywood personalities came to every game, and we'd chitchat a little afterward. I liked them, but it didn't take long to find out that they also had no real foundation. One of them thought he was cool with God, as I had thought years earlier, because his dad was a preacher. He called himself a "P.K.," preacher's kid. But being a P.K. isn't going to save anyone from anything. God doesn't have grandchildren, only children. You have to be born again and walk the walk yourself. I could appreciate his talent, but I didn't want to be influenced by him. Even though I genuinely liked him and the opportunity for friendship was there, our relationship stayed at the surface level, which suited me fine.

Mike Tyson was a different story. Like me, other players were big boxing fans. So when he came to our games, it was a big treat for all of us. I saw one day on television that he was supposedly baptized. He was wearing some ceremonial gown, and they said he was taking a new direction in life. When I watched that, I prayed, "Lord, bring him my way. I want to have the opportunity to talk to him."

A week or two later he came to the game with his promoter, Don King. I talked to Mike casually before the game.

"What's happening, Mike. How ya' doin'?"

"I'm fine. Just came to check out the game tonight."

"Are you coming to the locker room after the game?"

"Yeah."

When he came back there, we made our way into the training room for as serious a conversation as we could manage. It was like trying to talk on the freeway in L.A. during evening rush hour.

"I know that you've taken a stand for Jesus Christ," I said.

"Mr. Tyson," some people interrupted, trying to cling to him.

"Later," he said, waving them off impatiently.

I chose my words quickly and basically just challenged him. "Don't be religious," I told him. "Don't make a public appearance to get man's approval."

"Mike," his manager said.

"What!" he answered abruptly.

"We need to — "

"I'll be out when I get out," he said, waving him off.

"You need a real relationship with Jesus," I said, "not just a head knowledge but a heart knowledge."

My teammates and some stars who wanted to meet him came up and stood there for a minute. He didn't acknowledge them, so neither did I. When they heard what we were talking about, they slinked backward until they were out of the room.

"This is all new to me," he said.

"Mike," said his bodyguard.

"Chill out!" he insisted.

"But — "

"Just wait one more minute," he said.

"Get trained, discipled and committed," I told him.

God must have arranged for us to talk. He asked a lot of questions, although every fifth word was a curse word. Yeah, I thought, this could be a little bit new to him. We had at least twenty minutes together, and he was definitely challenged to follow Jesus with his whole heart.

Within weeks after that, Tyson was in serious legal difficulties. I tried to contact him several times but was never able to see him again. I still admire his talent and the character I saw in him, and I pray for him to find the real Jesus Christ.

From my childhood I had more boxing heroes than basketball heroes. But Lee Johnson had a big basketball hero — Bernard King. King was a great player with the New York Knicks and was known for a quick-release jump shot. He could get his shot off before a defender could get a hand up there to block it. Besides gunning from the outside, he also shot a turn-around jumper in the low post and a baseline jump shot. Lee was totally enamored of King's talent.

In college Lee and I were always going one-on-one. We still do it in any sport or game you can name, but in college it was mainly basketball. Lee wanted to prove he was as good as I was, even though he wasn't on the team. He always talked a bunch of junk to me.

"OK," I would finally say, "we're going to take care of this right now."

Then we'd get out on the court, and Lee would become Bernard King.

"I'm Bernard Kiinnngggg!" he yelled as he drove to the baseline, pulled up and shot.

Whether he made one out of ten or nine out of ten, it didn't matter, because every time he shot he acted as if he made it.

"Bernard King — two!" he yelled after shooting the turn-around jumper, and he'd run down court.

We all have our heroes. They might be sports figures, a political figure, our parents or someone in our school. But heroes can be dangerous. We usually measure them according to some outward performance, but we need to get below that to their character. We cannot substitute performance for substance.

PRINCIPLE #19
Find new heroes. Heroes can be dangerous. Find people whose lives match up with how you want to live your own.

The men I've known, more than the women, have especially seemed to need role models. It's as if men have a mechanism that triggers us to place someone in the position of a hero. Some people put me on that kind of hero level now. They look up to me and try to be like me. It's nice, a compliment, but the truth is that there are no superpeople, no super-Christians, no superheroes.

And there are certainly no superathletes.

We need to look instead at the Hero who will never disappoint us — Jesus. He understands that men need heroes. He had His own hero and role model — His Father. Jesus always talked to the disciples about what His Father gave Him, showed Him or told Him. Jesus saw His Father's habits and patterns, and He followed them exactly. He set the standard for us to copy. He intends for us to look up to Him and copy His works.

PRINCIPLE #20
Make Jesus your biggest hero. He intends for us to look up to Him and copy His works.

Our desire for heroes is also a desire to be part of something greater than ourselves. We want to be known as Laker fans or Suns fans because we want to be identified with a champion, a hero or heroes. But just because some man or woman can achieve some great thing doesn't mean he or she deserves to be a hero. We can appreciate people without putting them on a pedestal.

In Christ you can become identified with something far greater than yourself — the Lord God. Lew Alcindor lost his identity to Islam and became Kareem Abdul-Jabbar. For the same reason Cassius Clay became Muhammad Ali. We don't change our given names in the Christian faith, but we change our team name. We are not Lakers, Bulls, Celtics or Suns. We are Christians.

Being part of God's family means becoming part of something bigger not only than ourselves, but also bigger than anything else on earth.

PRINCIPLE #21
Identify with something bigger and greater than yourself.

While Jesus is my ultimate hero, I recognize that other people affect me, too. And sometimes they prove to be true.

"Look at this, Ace!" Dave Soto, my roommate, said a few years after I joined the Lakers. He rushed into the room with an *L.A.*

Times article about Evander Holyfield.

"Look!" he said excitedly. "This guy gets up at 6:00 A.M. and prays before he trains. He trains in the spirit first, then in the flesh. Look at those T-shirts he wears, too — 'His Pain, Our Gain' and 'Lord's Gym.'

"We've got to keep up on him," he said firmly. "We've got to believe in this brother."

When I read the article, I found in Evander an athlete to whom I could relate. He definitely went up on the wall of people I admired. I was cautious, but I admired his principles and courage. Years later I got to meet him in person. He came to a game at the Forum and sat courtside, right next to our bench. Normally I want to play the whole game, but that night I was happy to come out.

"Sub!" the coach called. "A.C., you're out."

I thought, Great — thank you. I've been waiting for this.

"Move, rookie," I said to a rookie sitting on the last seat of our bench, right next to Holyfield. That's the privilege of surviving your rookie year — you get to dish it out from then on.

"Mr. Holyfield," I said, "I appreciate your stand, your walk with the Lord."

He sort of smiled.

"I've been praying for you," I said. "Me and my roommate."

He's a reserved man. That night he was so quiet that I didn't know if I was talking to myself or to him.

"I just wanted to encourage you and let you know there are other brothers out here with you," I said.

That was our first encounter. I've talked to him about four or five times since then, but he's always quiet. People say *I'm* quiet, but he's quieter. I still admire him and follow his career.

I have my spiritual heroes, too. Bob and Rose Weiner were early ones. They orchestrated the start of dozens of campus churches in the U.S., then went on to Russia and did the same there in whole cities, not just campuses. They are never-say-never people, and that kind of faith transferred into me. David and Joan Elian are other heroes. By the time I left OSU, they probably had seventy-five to a hundred strong, committed students in church. The church now runs about two hundred with Darryl Flowers as an associate pastor.

Friends are the same as heroes in that they can influence you for good or bad. They can lead you toward or away from your destiny.

You will eventually walk a path similar to that of whomever you attach yourself to, either as a hero or as a friend. Whatever route he goes down, you'll go with him if you attach yourself to him.

A teammate I spent a lot of time ministering to was torn away from God by listening to someone close to him, a member of his own family. He was really getting with the Christian walk, reading his Bible on his own and spending time in prayer. But this one family member kept planting seeds of doubt in his mind.

"How do you know you can trust this religion?"

"What makes you think this is right or even real?"

"Is this some kind of cult you've got yourself mixed up in? This isn't the way you were raised."

It was like the temptations of the devil coming right out of this person's mouth. My friend became full of doubt and finally left the faith altogether. By attaching himself to that person, believing that person over others, he became like that person instead of achieving his God-given purpose.

To get to where God wants me to be, I've had to break away from lots of relationships and cultivate others. Greg Ball is both a hero and a friend. He limited his campus ministry so he could start Champions for Christ with Rice Brooks to help college and professional athletes in their walks with the Lord. I am proud now to serve on their board of directors. Greg has been a great role model for me. I can pattern my life after that part of Jesus I see reflected in him. His spirit is so zealous for the things of God! He's a man of character, holiness and integrity, and a family man, too.

I've been with Greg when he was really down, when he had made bad decisions. We have talked right then, and I've discovered that no matter how disappointed he is, in himself or others, his faith in God remains strong. I'm not crushed by his mistakes because I understand that he's just flesh like me.

When we do admire someone, it doesn't mean we have to copy the person. Men like Greg, Rice, Lee, Dave and Phil are my covenant brothers. I trust them because their characters have proved true. Still that doesn't mean I'm going to become just like them. So often people start to copy the way other people talk, sing, preach, laugh, play or pray. We don't need to. No one needs to copy my personality. I want to learn to lead others, but I don't want a bunch of A.C. clones running around. We can appreciate the character but not copy the personality.

PRINCIPLE #22
Admire the character; don't copy the personality.

I've already taught you to make good, solid friends. Now I'm saying to let go of old heroes and old friends that are bad influences. Sometimes you even have to put your own family behind you — not by dishonoring them but by not allowing yourself to be swayed — in order to go forward with God. Some people you cannot cut off completely, but you can lessen their influence on you by not hanging around with them or by staying out of certain situations with them.

Now that I was known by the team as a Christian, the oddball in the bunch, I had to prove myself on the court. The guys didn't know how to handle me, didn't expect me to play with the style and intensity that I had. I guess they expected me to have marshmallow elbow pads — and not to play rough enough to put anyone on the floor.

My dad taught me never to start a fight, but never to back down from one, either. I play basketball the way I think Jesus would play the game. I'm not angry or mean to other players, but I definitely stand my ground and get the better of opponents any time I can. That's the name of the game.

First I had to prove my game, and then I had to show I could shoot from the outside. People were saying I shot so bad that I couldn't hit the rim even if the ball had a metal detector in it. I had to prove that I couldn't shoot better if I had a *magnet* in the ball. The Laker coaches drilled me on my outside shooting, and I drilled myself. My outside shooting naturally improved, and time, plus a few three-pointers, soon silenced the critics.

In one early game, however, I just about earned the reputation they had been ready to hang on me. On my first trip to Portland I was so nervous and excited that I could hardly remember my name. We played Denver in L.A. on Thursday, and our next game was Saturday in Portland, so I flew up early to spend some time with my family and friends. When I joined the team up there, Byron and Earvin tried to calm me down.

"Just get your first bucket," Earvin said. "Once you get that out of the way, you'll be fine."

"But score in our basket," Byron said, laughing. "And don't let the ball hit you in the head while you're looking for your family in the stands."

Ed Whelan did a special "Boy made good and returned home" show with me and my family before the game. Then the team went to Memorial Coliseum, site of my high school state championship and many college tournament championships. I was so nervous when I ran out on the court, but at least I didn't fall the way Earvin did at his first pro game!

Just get a bucket, I kept telling myself. My teammates dished the ball to me, but I couldn't score. I caught a pass and went up for my first attempt, a basic jumper. I teach my kids at summer camps to tuck in their elbows and not make chicken wings; to follow through as if you're waving "bye" to the ball; to go up about twenty-four inches and come back down on the same spot, with your legs shoulder-width apart. This is as easy as breathing once you've played for a while. But that night I had no form or rhythm, and my muscles, instead of being loose and fluid, were tight as drums. I jumped about two inches; my elbows shot out; I had no follow-through and didn't know where my legs were going; and I just about fired the ball right through the backboard.

"Uncle Junior shot a brick!" my nephews chanted after the game. It seemed like nine years before I made my first basket that night. But, as Earvin said, once I did, the butterflies quieted down, and I was myself again.

I ended up being the first Laker rookie in over twenty years to appear in every game. Michael Cooper was the only other Laker that year who did the same. In my second pro game we played Dallas. I scored seventeen points and got sixteen rebounds — not too shabby for a marshmallow. The team started to take notice. I became a starter after the first few games of the season and led the team in rebounds, averaging 7.8 per game. I did what they hired me to do. In 1989 I was named by NBA coaches to the All-NBA All-Defense second team, and in 1990 the fans voted me into the All-Star game. Accomplishments like that helped my teammates put the team dinner and their initial impressions behind. I wish I could say they've forgotten that night, but they haven't. They still "dis" me whenever they have the chance.

Even though I proved my game, in many respects I remained the odd man out throughout my career with the Lakers. Byron and Earvin were the first two teammates who noticeably cleaned up the way they talked around me. Byron respected me because he talked to me more than anyone else, and we knew each other longer, so he knew I was serious. Earvin just has a great deal of respect for the Christian faith. He often asked me to pray for the team. At my second training camp he asked that I pray over the team on the first day before we did anything. I prayed with everyone there and asked God for His grace to be with the team and for the team to glorify Him through our play. That's the first year we went all the way.

The respect was there, but so was the desire to do what they wanted to do. I remember seeing guys talking privately after one game, getting dressed in sportscoats and splashing on cologne. There was enough aroma from Cool Water and Eternity to asphixiate everyone in the locker room.

"Why are you all dressed up so nice?" I asked someone.

"Oh, well, a couple of us are just going to so-and-so's house," he said.

That subterfuge became the rule of thumb for the next eight years. I was never notified of unofficial team parties or nights out on the town. I knew what was going on only by seeing my teammates dress up for their postgame activities. I'm sure they thought I'd ruin their party or that they would feel too intimidated with me there to have their brand of fun. Not telling A.C. about parties became a Laker tradition.

I loved my teammates, but I didn't require their acceptance to play the game or to live happily. I didn't have to try to live on their level to prove anything to them. And I didn't miss out on anything by not going with them. The Laker press book listed me my first year as a twenty-one-year-old who enjoyed tennis, bowling, baseball, football and eating frozen yogurt. Yes, frozen yogurt was a major activity for me. If you added church and church activities to the list, that about summed me up.

Training camp was in Palm Springs for a few more years, and then we started holding it in Hawaii. Once camp was over, we played our games at the Forum in Inglewood and practiced at

Loyola Marymount University in Westchester, right next to Inglewood. Loyola has a beautiful campus. The first time I went, I was struck by how clean and new the facilities were. The gym was the kind of place that made you feel good just being inside it. It had huge, high ceilings that kept it light and airy, even during the grueling practices Coach Riley was known for.

One day during my rookie year I got ready for practice and walked into the gym before it started. Earvin was always the first guy in the gym. He and Byron Scott, James Worthy and a few others were sitting around when I walked in — right into a rookie trap.

Buck said, "Hey, A.C., you've got a phone call in the training room."

To get to the training room, you had to walk down a very long hall, hook a left, then another left and you were there. I guess they thought they could make me late for practice, which is one of the things you can get fined for. I hurried down to the training room.

"Do I have a call?" I asked Gary Vitti, our trainer.

"The phone hasn't rung all morning," he said.

I felt like a little boy wearing red, polka-dot underwear with his white shorts. As I quickly walked back, I knew I had to do something. It took about a minute to walk down that hall, so I had time to think it over. I walked through the door and saw them laughing at me, pointing at me, eyes sparkling and teeth flashing like a pack of wild animals who had just made a kill.

"Rookie, we got you!" one of them shouted.

"That country boy from Oregon doesn't know anything."

"Hey, who was on the phone, A.C.?"

Very solemnly and seriously I looked at them, then gazed up toward that lofty ceiling. "It was my Father," I said softly. There were a few seconds of hushed silence.

I brought my head back down slowly, looked them each in the eyes and said, "And now He's waiting to talk to you."

They erupted in laughter.

"Hooo, he got us!"

"The rookie got us!"

8

NO
COMPROMISE

I STARTED LIFE in the pros during the 1985-86 season with a good training camp behind me and high hopes in front of me. But I certainly didn't understand what a grueling life it would be.

The basketball season is eighty-two games long, roughly fifty games longer than a college season, plus the preseason and play-offs. We play nine months out of the year instead of four or five, traveling from city to city for one-night stands in each place, then coming home for short stretches.

We play right through Thanksgiving, Christmas and Easter without stopping, not to mention Mother's Day, Memorial Day, Martin Luther King Jr. Day and a dozen other days that most people remember for something more than the flight schedule in their hands. I was happy to be where I was, but I had to adjust to the new style of life. The veterans tried to help.

"You've gotta get an hour or two nap on game day," they warned me.

"Make sure you get some food," they said after the morning shoot-around on game day.

I still had my college habits, thinking I could get by without sleeping or eating a square meal. It took only one bad experience to figure out the veterans knew their business.

I went to the shoot-around one morning, then stayed busy all day before the game that night, because the next day we were leaving on a ten-day road trip. As a single I don't have someone at home taking care of business for me. I had to do laundry, pick up dry cleaning, go by the post office and take care of all those other good responsibilities. I always handle my own business, so I had bills to pay and needed to go to the bank, too.

I showed up at the game hungry but mentally ready to play. I grabbed dinner out of the vending machines at the Forum — some candy bars and fruit drinks. That was a big mistake. By the end of the first quarter I had the worst sideache I'd ever had, got dehydrated and fought cramps throughout the game. I was able to play, but only at about 50 percent of my normal energy level. That cured me forever from looking for shortcuts.

Coach Riley's practices were worse than games, and we had a lot more than eighty-two of them during the season. Even though most of my teammates were seasoned veterans, he drilled us on techniques and fundamentals every day. We usually spent thirty minutes drilling on double-teaming a post man. Then we spent thirty minutes on the pick-and-roll game. Then we put in thirty minutes on something else, and by the time we were done, we had been at it for about three hours total. The practices were hard, fast and heavy, but they were like a religion to us.

From Kareem down to the newest rookie, we drilled thirty

minutes on each aspect of the game until we were totally ex-hausted. Then Riley would drill us some more so we'd be ready to keep playing even after we got tired in the real game. Finally we practiced free throws for a while before going to the locker room.

That year the Lakers were in transition, changing from using the dominant center position to a more balanced offensive game that utilized everyone's talents. You could say we were changing from being Kareem's team to becoming Earvin's team. It was the right time. Opponents were figuring out the traditional Laker plays that keyed on Kareem. One or two could even beat us at our own game. Coach Riley led the transition, and both Kareem and Earvin helped. It wasn't until the next year that it really paid off.

From the start I went for the ball on defense like a hound after the fox, but I was pretty tentative offensively. In addition, the short, quick passes of the pros require soft, swift hands, which I was still developing. After I dropped a few key passes, James started calling me Hands of Stone, after Roberto Duran, the boxer. It had been a compliment to Duran. The name reappeared throughout my career any time I dropped a pass. I laughed at the time with everyone else, but later I learned its significance. If the veterans give a rookie a nickname, it means they like him. I may have been the odd man out, but I was "in."

Byron and James dogged me all the time. They gave it to me for my hair, because I wore it in the greasy style that was popular at the time. They called me Billy Dee for Billy Dee Williams or Valdez for the infamous Exxon oil spill. When I made a mistake during the game, Byron showed no mercy. He's a natural impersonator. He memorized whole stand-up comedy routines to entertain the guys in the bus on road trips. If I missed an assignment, he came after me. If I was supposed to trap a player like Hakeem Olajuwon, but I got brain lock and forgot, I heard about it for twenty minutes in the locker room. Byron would invent an entire routine about my brain.

"I said, 'Double-team,' but my legs said, 'No, we're too tired,' so all of a sudden my mind said...." On and on he went while everyone laughed, including me. The team always kept each other in check, but we did it in a brotherly way and with a lot of humor.

All that year I believed we were going to go all the way. The whole team thought we would. Some guys may say, "We should have won," or, "We were the best team," because of pride or ego. But, objectively, we really were a cut above. The league had parity at the time, making every team almost as good as the next, but we were at the top in league statistics. We won sixty-two games, making our won-lost percentage .756, way ahead of Houston, which was at .622, and just behind Boston at .817 with sixty-seven wins.

In the play-offs we shot the ball well, rebounded well, got the loose balls and generally did the things that are supposed to win championships. *Sports Illustrated* said we might prove to be the best team in the history of the game.

My play had improved by the play-offs, and my confidence level was soaring, right up there with my faith that God would make me a champion again. I found I still had a lot to learn about faith.

We blew threw the first series of the play-offs, eliminating San Antonio three games to none, then beat Dallas in six. When we started the Western conference finals, we were ready to win in four straight.

The Houston Rockets met us in that conference final, pitting the "Twin Towers" of Hakeem Olajuwon, 6'11", and Ralph Sampson, 7'4", against our single tower, Kareem. Kareem had to work. He had other players to help him, but Kareem expected to defeat those guys himself. He had already scored forty-two points against them earlier that season.

Going into the series, sports writers and critics were calling Houston "the team that could beat L.A." We won the first game in the Forum comfortably by a score of 119-107. But then they squeaked by us to win the next three games by a total of twenty-eight points. We were soon on our way back to the Forum knowing we needed to win or we'd be out of the play-offs. We were confident, however, that we would still prevail in the series.

I can't remember if I was on the floor or the bench during those last fateful seconds of game 5. Because I was a rookie, I sat out part of that series. We were ahead at the half, and we held the lead until late in the fourth quarter. One thing we knew we could not do through that whole series was let Ralph Sampson or Hakeem Olajuwon have the ball. The way Houston was playing, if their team got ninety points, those two guys would account for eighty of them. If either of them could get the ball, we knew they could score.

TOP: My brother Steve is "Mr. Popularity," even with the hundreds of thousands who crammed the streets for the Lakers' 1988 championship parade. *From left:* Me, Steve and Kareem Abdul-Jabbar.

PHOTO: © 1988 ANDREW D. BERNSTEIN, NBA PHOTOS

AT LEFT: My basketball coach, Dick Gray, from Benson Polytechnic High School in Portland, Oregon. I was thrilled to see him again in February 1994 when they retired my high school jersey number (#45).

PHOTO: HOA GIANGI, BENSON POLYTECHNIC HIGH SCHOOL

TOP: I played for the Lakers from 1985 to 1993, went to the Finals for four years and won two NBA Championships —in 1987 and 1988.

PHOTO: CRESTINE VILLANUEVA

AT RIGHT: Earvin "Magic" Johnson became a good friend as we played together for the Lakers.

PHOTO: ©1993 ANDREW D. BERNSTEIN, NBA PHOTOS

TOP: Darrell Green, David Robinson and I work together on a video. They have both contributed their time and resources to my programs for youth.
PHOTO: CRESTINE VILLANUEVA

AT LEFT: It was hit or be hit by Adrian Dantley against the Detroit Pistons in the 1988 NBA Finals.
PHOTO: ©1988 ANDREW D. BERNSTEIN, NBA PHOTOS

TOP: Dave Soto (my roommate from the L.A. days) and I presented a basketball signed by all the Lakers to our pastor, Phil Bonnasso, to thank him for screaming with the rest of "Green's Gorillas" at every home game.

AT RIGHT: My friend Greg Ball and I appeared on "Lunch Date," a show equivalent to "American Bandstand," during a mission trip to the Phillipines. At high schools and colleges there I preached and played pickup basketball games.

TOP: James Worthy, a good friend on and off the court, hosted the first gala event for the A.C. Green Programs for Youth in Los Angeles.
PHOTO: CRESTINE VILLANUEVA

AT LEFT: Here I am with my lifelong best friend, "The Judge," Lee Johnson.
PHOTO: WILL LANGMORE

TOP: The first time I played golf was at a tournament sponsored by David Robinson. My friend Lee Johnson (far right) told me to go out and "shoot a birdie," which I'm holding.

AT RIGHT: "A.C. who?" That's what people were saying when I was chosen to play on the All-Star team in 1990.

PHOTO: ©1990, NATHANIEL S. BUTLER, NBA PHOTOS

I started playing for
the Phoenix Suns in
the 1993-94 season.

TOP PHOTO: © 1994 BILL BAPTIST,
NBA PHOTOS

BOTTOM PHOTO: COURTESY OF THE
PHOENIX SUNS

THIS PAGE AND OPPOSITE:
Each summer my
foundation for youth
and other sponsors
send hundreds of kids
to day camps where I
teach basketball. At the
camp in Los Angeles,
I take them on
educational field trips.
PHOTOS: CRESTINE VILLANUEVA

Darryl Flowers
and I played
basketball
together at
Oregon State
University.
I was able to
become a big brother
to him and influence
his life. Today he's the
associate pastor at our
old church in Corvallis,
Oregon.
PHOTO: MIKE SHIELDS

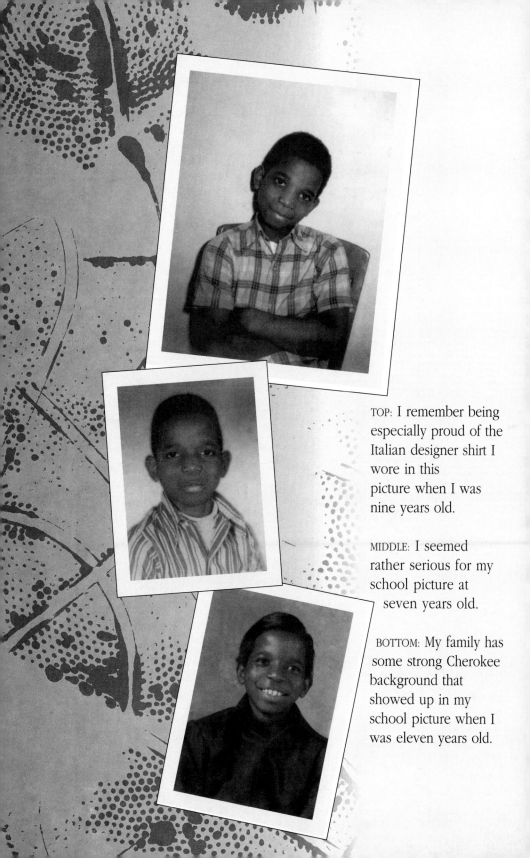

TOP: I remember being especially proud of the Italian designer shirt I wore in this picture when I was nine years old.

MIDDLE: I seemed rather serious for my school picture at seven years old.

BOTTOM: My family has some strong Cherokee background that showed up in my school picture when I was eleven years old.

TOP: This was most of the family in 1987. *Top row:* My brothers, Steve and Lee; me holding my niece Paris; my sister, Faye. *Middle row:* My nephew Terrance; my parents, Leola and A.C. Green. *Bottom row:* My nephews Jerray and Kevin and my niece Ashley. We're missing baby Nicholas and all the kids since then—Austin, Sierra, Christina and Lee.

AT RIGHT: Leola and A.C. Green, the world's greatest parents and my heroes.

With five minutes left Mitch Kupchak and Hakeem Olajuwon got into a tussle and were both ejected. Down to Sampson against Kareem. We knew the game was ours. With thirty-seven seconds left we were still up by three. Then Houston's Robert Reid hit a three-pointer and tied it. We attempted another shot, missed, and they called a time out with the score tied and two seconds to play.

All of us were worried, both on the floor and on the bench. The guys on the bench weren't sitting in their chairs. They were flat out on the floor throughout the fourth quarter, lying face down, grasping the ends of towels that they held stretched across the tops of their heads. They were yelling out defensive moves to their teammates and possibly even saying a prayer or two.

Time out ended, and Houston's Rodney McCray took the ball out of bounds right in front of our bench. He lobbed it in to Ralph Sampson. Sampson caught it about five feet from the basket, with his back to the net and Kareem on him, trying not to foul. A second ticked off by the time he caught it, so he didn't have a chance to dribble, to reset himself or even to land. We all caught our breath to see what he would do. He sort of twisted in the air and threw it back behind his head with a limp, weak toss that seemed to say he would settle for a tie and overtime.

Was it over? We all watched as the ball hit the front of the rim and rolled slowly to the back. The world was frozen in slow motion for everyone in the Forum. The players were all eyes, watching that slow ball take its time to decide what it would do. The roll to the back brought it to a stop, and it seemed to hang on the back of the rim just for fun, to prolong our pain. After a moment it dropped down, right through the hoop.

The Forum was dead silent. We heard the dull thud of the ball bouncing on the floor beneath the basket.

"Incredible!" we heard the announcers say in the background. "Ralph Sampson hits a behind-the-head shot to win the game and the series. Unbelievable! Ralph Sampson has done it. The Twin Towers have won the game for Houston."

Laker players were on the ground already, so their heads just dropped to the floor, towels covering them. Michael Cooper had been playing under the basket and fell down there like he was dead. He didn't move. People started wondering if he was OK because he laid there so long. We were all stunned. That marked the end of my first professional season.

I hate to lose. I especially hated losing that day. If I'm going to get beaten, then beat me. Don't make me lose because of some lucky shot. I was frustrated, disappointed, and had a lot of work to do on my knees to figure out what God was doing in all of this. My faith had been so high. God had to show me His ways.

The last thing I expected when I came back the next season was an injury. That's something the average car salesman or home builder probably doesn't think about, but it's something professional athletes think about every day. We have to stay healthy and in top condition to compete and win.

Health concerns everyone, but most people usually don't notice it until they lose it. Developing good health is essential to championship living, however. You have to get healthy, then maintain a healthy lifestyle to keep it.

Conditioning starts with staying alive, like avoiding drunk drivers and gang shootings and wearing your seat belt. Then comes not putting drugs into your body like tobacco, alcohol or anything stronger. After that comes diet.

I've had to continue to refine my diet, but there are still things I treat myself to when I'm hungry. By the time I hit L.A., I had developed a habit of hamburgers served from a fast-food drive-through window. When the team was on the road in a strange city and the other guys went out to clubs, relatives' homes or the movies, Kurt Rambis and I headed for the closest fast-food restaurant. After games Denny's is my all-time favorite place to eat because they serve me breakfast twenty-four hours a day, anytime I want. When the other guys go off to Chasen's, Studio 54, The Mansion or clubs, I go off to Denny's and a Grand Slam breakfast.

But eating right becomes a way of life once you get started. When Lee and I roomed together, we had the usual squabbles about who ate whose food. I found out he hated raisins, so I always bought Raisin Bran cereal. That way I knew he'd never touch my breakfast. Usually I eat a muffin or cereal for breakfast or maybe waffles or pancakes. During the day I eat lots of vegetables, fruit juices and just plain fruit — pineapples, apples, oranges, bananas and melons. To avoid fat, I eat a lot of chicken — baked, broiled or grilled. And I can level a mountain of pasta.

Normally I try not to eat after 8:30 at night except on game nights. During the off-season I'll eat desserts, but I seldom have them when I'm playing. Of course, frozen yogurt isn't a dessert; it's a staple food. I usually start the season at 225 pounds, and I easily fluctuate 10 to 15 pounds during the regular season, so splurging on frozen yogurt never worries me.

Then there's Mom's poundcake that's irresistible and Mama Johnson's banana pudding. Lee won't allow me to touch a bowl of that anymore until it's time to eat it. He says it has something to do with how I ate the whole bowl once while he was driving the ninety-minute trip back to college. He's probably exaggerating. But I do love her banana pudding whenever I can get it.

When my mom cooked for the team, Lee's mom always made her famous banana pudding, which Byron Scott also got addicted to. He would heap his plate full of that precious stuff and take it to his table to eat right in front of me, knowing that since I was the host, I would wait until everyone was served before I got mine.

To maintain good health, exercise comes next on the list. During the off-season I generally get up before dawn, read my Bible and pray, then stretch and ride my bike the half mile to my neighborhood park. I run three or four miles around the park, then jog to a nearby track, where I run sprints. That keeps my wind ready for the following season. I'll run six or eight hundred-yard dashes, then six or eight fifty-yard dashes. Then I'll go to the gym to lift weights.

I use free weights to work the basic muscle groups. Then, because of the demands of my sport, I tone my legs for endurance using lighter weights and more repetitions. I also work on upper-body bulk and strength, using heavier weights and doing fewer reps. After weights I shoot hoops for a while.

During the season I go to practice for my workout, then to the weight room afterward. I try to have all my conditioning done by the time I reach training camp so that throughout the season I can just work to maintain what I've already acquired.

Besides diet and exercise it's important to get enough rest, take vitamins and antioxidants, and get regular checkups. Then there's the spiritual aspect of praying daily for supernatural health.

The Bible says that physical exercise profits only a little compared to spiritual exercise and godliness. But that "little" can often mean the difference between winning and losing. No matter what field we choose for our careers or what our mission is in life, we need to have physical conditioning to see it through. We need to have consistent blood sugar to be creative, and we need to release tension through exercise to be even-tempered and maintain self-control. Of course we can only maintain coordination through activity as well.

PRINCIPLE #23
Good health is essential to championship living.
- Modify your diet.
- Learn to exercise; find out what your body can handle.
- Get enough rest.
- Take vitamins and antioxidants.
- Get regular checkups.
- Pray daily for supernatural health.

I recommend to my campers each summer that they start exercising while they're still young. But whatever your age, find out what your body can handle. Weight lifting is great, but don't do it to keep up with the Joneses or Jamaals. Get to know your own body, respond to its needs and work at your own level. Even if you're older, studies prove that your rate of improvement is the same as for youngsters. You just have to rise out of a deeper deficit.

All the time, in season and out, I stay active with a variety of sports. Lee and I haven't lived in the same state for nine years, but when we get together, we often stay up all night competing. My bowling ball is always in my carry-on bag on trips to see Lee. We'll go out and bowl the best two out of three games; then we'll shoot pool for the best three of five; next we'll shoot hoops; then we'll have our Mark Spitz swimming contest; and finally we'll end up indoors playing board games. He just got married, so we'll see how well his wife adjusts to my visits.

The point is to have fun while you're staying in shape. Then it won't seem like work.

Your mind has to get in shape, too. Pat Riley had hard practices, but they prepared us well. I call it "toughness with gladness." We forced our minds to control our bodies, like in Byron's skit: "Legs, get out there and double-team, and don't tell me you're too tired!"

It's the same principle in the kingdom of God. You tell your body to get up and go do something right, and all of a sudden your body starts talking junk to you.

"Oh, no, I want to stay in bed."

"I don't want to go to Bible study."

"No, I don't want to confront my sins."

You have to control your mind and body to make yourself do what you know to be right, what you know to be the habits of a champion. I'll show you later how one guy who took the shortcuts fared under Coach Riley. Those who accept compromise or want to find the easy way can never perform at the highest level. Coach Riley didn't have time for such players.

PRINCIPLE #24
Control your mind and body. Make yourself do what you know to be right, what you know to be the habits of a champion.

People get into that syndrome where they say, "I'd do this if I were in the finals" or "If I were the pastor...." That type of person never gets to the top. He's talking and comparing more than working and preparing. Failure to prepare is preparation for failure.

You have to will to win. If you don't. you won't win. Coach Riley knew he could work and mold, but if he didn't have players who wanted to win, all his efforts would be wasted.

In the same way, if it's not your desire to fulfill your destiny, your destiny won't be thrown on you. God won't make you do it. You have to will it.

PRINCIPLE #25
Will to win. If it's not your desire to fulfill your destiny, your destiny won't be thrown on you.

We always practiced with more intensity than we had in an actual game. Coach Riley wanted us to react instinctively to game situations. The only way to do that is by practice.

"If you stop and think during the game, it's too late," Coach Bertka often said.

Practices prepared us mentally as much as physically to endure to the end, to keep our concentration, to react quickly and instinctively, and to win the game.

This runs a close parallel to spiritual training. If you haven't been in spiritual training every day, when the real situations come, you won't be ready.

When I left the Lakers, I went to the Suns where training camps were easier in terms of physical conditioning. The guys there would get mad and start snarling at me when I requested more practice. But I was used to such a high standard of performance that I was self-governing. Some guys only work hard when the coaches are watching. My ultimate Coach is always watching, however, and He knows if I'm really doing it or if I'm shucking and jiving. You'll see why this is important a little later.

Like any athlete I get little injuries. I call them game souvenirs or fender benders. I twist a finger, suffer a knee in the thigh or get the smile to the back of the head that I seem to attract. But I had a serious injury at the beginning of my second year with the Lakers.

We were playing our last preseason game against the Suns at a New Mexico college. In the second quarter I bent my thumb back. I thought, Ouch, that smarts. It was like one of my nephews pulling on my thumb, but I kept playing. I scored twenty-four points and got thirteen rebounds, and we won.

Before we left, I asked Gary Vitti to tape my thumb, but it kept hurting, even then. We flew back to L.A. and I had it checked out thoroughly. I had hyperextended it up and over the back of my knuckles. No wonder it hurt. I had a torn radial collateral ligament that required surgery. Coach Riley knew what was happening because he'd had the same injury as a Laker player. He had needed to have steel pins inserted and to wear a splint for six weeks. Earvin had suffered an injury his second year that kept him out for four months. Besides all that, basketball players and coaches are notoriously superstitious. So the coaches were pessimistic about me. I was wondering myself where those angels were that I thought were stationed around me.

I drove myself to the hospital in L.A. for my second appointment. The next thing I knew, the nurse started preparing my hand for surgery and said I was going to be hospitalized overnight.

"We're going to give you something before the general anesthesia," she said, then pulled out a needle and poked me. "This should make you feel a little drowsy."

The same nurse was on duty when I came to the next morning.

"I don't know what happened to you," she said laughing, "but we never did give you the general anesthesia. You were out for the whole operation just from that relaxer."

I'm no doctor, but I believe I went under as soon as a foreign substance went into my body because I had taken care of myself. A clean body responds.

After surgery my hand was put in a huge splint the size of a Ping Pong paddle. Gary Vitti fitted me with a smaller one that I ended up wearing all season. I missed just three games total, the last one on November 18, 1986, which turned out to be the last game I have ever missed as a professional. I now have the record for the longest consecutive string of games played by a current player. My record stands as the sixth longest of anyone in basketball history at the time of this writing.

Keeping my body pure from immorality is another part of my overall conditioning. It affects every part of life, not just the physical. When I became a Christian, I made a vow like Samson's, but my strength wasn't in anything external; it was in my word. I resolved not to be with a woman until I married. My convictions were obvious when I joined the Lakers but not proven, so a few players taunted, teased, tempted and tried me to see if I'd hold up my standards.

"Hey, wait 'til you see what's waiting for you," they said at an airport as we waited to go somewhere they were familiar with.

"How much will you want to bet A.C. can't stay away from so and so?" one said.

"I'll bet twenty dollars he can't," said another.

Still another piped up with, "Count me in for a hundred dollars."

"You won't last two months in the NBA," one of the guys told me. Some even threatened to set me up with women they knew.

"Let's see how strong you really are," they said.

When they didn't win, they tried new tactics. They learned that if they could get me to say I'd do something, I would be committed to do it. It's that integrity Pastor Elian drilled into me. So they tried to get me to commit to something that would put me in a compromising situation. Eventually they got tired of the game and started believing in me.

Professional athletes attract women the way lottery winners attract friends. For whatever reason, NBA players especially are known for their sexual conquests — like Wilt Chamberlain, who boasted that he had sex with twenty thousand women, and Earvin, the ladies' man on our team. I had to hold my standard against tremendous pressure.

I launched into the professional world of sports with a healthy self-respect, self-control and two words to govern me: *responsibility* and *timing*.

At first it was shocking to see women throw themselves at players. Once after a game against Philly, as the bus backed up the ramp, someone in the back of the bus said, "Hey, look at that freak," talking about a woman outside. "Freak" is what the players call the groupies who throw themselves at them. She caught his eye and pulled up her top to expose herself. The applause by the team seemed louder than that of the spectators in the arena earlier that night. Such women wait in hotel lobbies, flirt in restaurants and watch for our buses and planes. Believe me — such attention is not glamorous. It's not what some guys would think is, "every guy's dream." It's ego-inflating and flattering, but it's just as often pathetic and disgusting.

It isn't just women who are after us, either. One guy called me in my hotel room in Milwaukee just as I was finishing my pregame meal. When the phone rang, I thought maybe it was someone from Darryl Flowers's family, because they live there.

"Hello."

"Hello. Is A.C. there?"

"I'm A.C."

"You guys going to win tonight?"

He started into some small talk while I was still trying to figure out who this guy was. Then he got to the point.

"What are you doing, resting?" he asked.

"No, I'm eating."

"Well, I'm a friend of —— " (they always insert one of your teammate's names here), "and I normally see him when he's in town."

"Cool," I answered, as I got more suspicious.

"I'm in the neighborhood right now. Would you like some company?"

"No, I wouldn't," I answered. "Actually, do you ever read the Bible?"

"Not really. Not normally."

"Well, God talks about immorality such as homosexuality, and that's something He certainly doesn't condone. Matter of fact, I think you should probably seek out some help and let Jesus Christ have first place in your life."

"OK, well, it was nice talking to you." Click.

I always have a choice to make. If I'm tempted by some woman or even a TV commercial, I don't have to look. I don't have to treat women like a piece of meat in a shop even if that's how some of them treat themselves. They can call my room, but the same hand that picks up the phone can hang it up, too. It's my choice. I exercise my power of choice to keep control of my own body, my own life. I choose what hairstyle I wear, what clothes I wear, how much I'm going to work out and whether or not I'll throw my body around like a dirty rag.

We all have the power of choice. But once used, our choice then has power over us. We have to live with the consequences.

PRINCIPLE #26
We all have the power of choice, but once used, our choice has power over us. Weigh the consequences of your choices.

In high school I had relationships that never resulted in sex. But that's not what I told people. Most of the guys I hung around with pressured me to have sex to be included with the homeboys. Like a lot of kids I talked a lot even though nothing happened. It was all part of wanting to be in the in-crowd, not playing in left field alone. I had the guys fooled that I was "doing it," and they had me fooled that they were, too.

My parents never emphasized abstaining from sex, but under their leadership I developed respect for myself and others. When curiosity was trying to kill the cat and my friends were telling me how much fun I was missing out on, the grace of God kept me. It wasn't that I didn't want to have sex or didn't think about it, but my self-respect never broke down before I got saved, and it strengthened afterward.

Birth control and disease control wouldn't be issues if people exercised self-control. I face temptations that may be greater than most people's, but everyone is bombarded with sex today. The media, athletes and entertainers scream in word, action and life-style, "The normal, natural way of sex is to have it whenever you want to, but try to do it safe, and don't worry about the conse-quences." People believe the lies.

When my nieces and nephews and others I care about start believing that junk, that raises my flag. I look at the babies in my family now, Sierra, Christina and Lee, and I wonder about the world in which they're growing up.

Condoms are hailed today as the answer to sexually transmitted diseases (STDs) and unwanted pregnancies. The facts are, how-ever, that they fail to prevent pregnancies 15 to 36 percent of the time; they leak the HIV virus, which is said to be 450 times smaller than sperm; and unwed pregnancies have increased among teens 87 percent since the start of the government's birth-control cru-sade. We'll never stop the AIDS epidemic unless we stop sexual promiscuity, which is the most common way of transmission.

I heard about a young woman who went to Florida on a six-week vacation, met a charming man, ended up staying with him and was given a small jewelry box to open on her trip home. Instead of the engagement ring she expected to find inside, she found a tiny coffin with the words "Welcome to the world of AIDS." Three months later she tested positive for HIV.

Even more widespread than disease are the emotional scarring and deep wounds that come out of broken relationships. No mat-ter how strong a condom is, it won't protect you from a broken heart.

I am sick of people being sold a false bill of goods. It's great to let people know their options, but the options given today are faulty. We need a higher standard by which to govern our sexuality. Young people are told when they're old enough to smoke, drink, drive, vote, go to school and fight in the military, but we don't tell them when they can have sex.

Out of deep concern, during my sixth year in the NBA, I formed Athletes for Abstinence to teach that the only 100-percent sure way to avoid STDs, unwanted pregnancies and a lot of the consequences of ending a sexual relationship is sexual abstinence. We teach that sex in itself is not wrong and was actually created by God, but that sex *outside of marriage* is not worth the risks. Just because everyone else is doing it doesn't mean that it's right. And besides, everyone else *isn't* doing it. They're just saying they are, the way I did as a kid.

Even if you've been sexually active, it's never too late to say no. You can't go back, but you can go forward. You might feel guilty or unworthy, but God will forgive you. Abstaining from extramarital sex is one of the most unpopular things a person can do, much less talk about. But it's the best alternative if you want to live a happy, healthy life.

If you can control yourself sexually, you can control yourself. Period.

Earvin was diagnosed with HIV in 1991, and most of my teammates went in for testing when they heard. Not me. It was one of the most traumatic experiences of my life, but I knew I was disease free. The way I've chosen is the best way. I've been criticized and ridiculed, but I'm not afraid to stand alone on this issue if I have to. I've seen all the options, and I'm not going to back down. Sometimes people stand around doing nothing until someone else takes the lead; then they step to the line. In the world of professional athletes I'm not the only one who resists sexual temptations, but I'm definitely the one who is willing to stand up and admit it.

I don't test my control by putting myself in compromising situations — all alone, tired, vulnerable. That's stupid. I don't hang out at my girlfriend's apartment, and she doesn't hang out at my house. I don't spend long hours alone or stay out late at night with her. Greater men than I am have fallen and made mistakes. I'd rather learn from someone else's mistakes than think I'm above that and make them myself.

In football, to keep the other team from scoring late in the game, the team that's leading uses what is known as a "prevent defense." Well, I have some "Prevent Defense Rules" of my own:

1. I don't feed my eyes or mind lustful images. I don't watch television and movies that show people having sex. I don't listen to music that tells me to have sex. The lower your exposure, the higher your tolerance grows.

2. I don't put myself in tempting situations. I don't invite a woman to my house at midnight to watch a movie or "have a Bible study." No one wants to be the party pooper, but you have to draw that line. If someone wants to keep talking when it's getting late, I suggest a time the next day when we can get together.

3. I use the buddy system. I often have a third party with me instead of being alone with a woman. I'm not likely to make a pass if someone is right there watching me, holding me accountable for my actions.

4. I have studied Proverbs 6. The adulterous woman is out to spoil me with flattering lips and seductive looks. It's a perfect picture painted by my enemy to get me to fall into his scene. You don't have to be a rocket scientist to figure it out.

5. I keep myself accountable to my friends. I've gone to Lee, Greg, Dave and others with egg all over my face more than once. They are the pit crew to my race car, and they always get me back on track. Even though they love me unconditionally, I don't like telling them when I've failed.

By my third year in the league, news reporters were calling me a "third-year pro" instead of a "third-year rookie." I felt that part of the test I had passed, in terms of achieving respect, was a moral test.

That year, after a regular-season game against the Mavericks, Greg Ball was waiting for me as I exited Reunion Arena in Dallas. Usually Earvin was the first one in and the last one out, but on this night he came out right after me. Three ravishingly beautiful young women were waiting for us. They came up to me, smiling and saying cute things to try to strike up a conversation.

"Hey, A.C." the first one said.

"How are you girls doing?" I asked.

The one in the middle answered, "Fine, now that you're here."

I wanted to be polite and get out of there as quickly as I could, but they boxed me in. Earvin got stuck right behind me and became part of the conversation. They chattered seductively, and then one got bold and made a comment about my virginity. I bent down so I could talk to them eye-to-eye.

"You know what you girls need to do?" I said. "You need to repent and get real jobs."

Earvin jumped right in. "Yeah, that's right!" he said.

I said a few more things to soften the blow and let them know I wasn't trying to put them down. I just needed to make it clear where I stood. Earvin and the rest of my teammates followed me as I walked away, leaving them behind. That became one of Greg's favorite stories — that and the fight, which I'll describe later.

One by one I earned the respect of my teammates. "We've heard rumors," a reporter said to James Worthy one day, "that A.C. preaches too much."

"People respect A.C.," James said. "A lot of guys who joke about him and give him a hard time probably want to be like him but don't think they can."

They asked Randy Pfund the same thing. Coach Pfund said, "A.C.'s religious convictions translate into basketball in terms of working hard and being competitive."

Though he was older and had his own religious convictions, Kareem respected me enough even to take up for me. Once during a shoot-around, one of my teammates was jiving, talking junk. "I'm a Christian," he said. "I'm just like A.C."

Kareem shut him down fast. "No, you're not even close," he said. "No one else on this team is like A.C."

Once you make your identification with Christ, people who can't stand it tend to run the other way. Like children, some of my family and friends do things wrong but don't want to get caught, so they avoid me for a while. Others boast about their wrongdoing. Even when others around me practice immorality, I take my stand

and lay down the law with friends and family. Usually they'll accept my stand, but they'll never accept condemnation. I don't preach to anyone unless I'm invited to. I don't tell anyone he's going to hell. On the other hand, I don't let someone's house burn without warning him. And I don't sit there listening to a person's stories of wrongdoing. I tell him the truth, I love him, and I pray for him. In other words, even though I don't compromise person-ally, I've had to learn tolerance toward others who don't share my convictions.

PRINCIPLE #27
**Practice self-control. Keep your body pure
morally. Tolerate others, but don't compromise.**

After a couple of years in L.A., I bought a house and equipped it with the best stereo system I could find. The speakers are enormous, feeding into each bedroom with incredible sound and resonance. I liked to play an assortment of music, from classical to rap. My brother Steve, our friends Terrel, Vincent and Tracy, and some of the other guys stayed with me sometimes for vacation. Not many of them have followed in my spiritual footsteps yet, so they didn't come to spend quality time with Junior. Their idea of fun was to go out club-hopping and partying. They came in from clubs in the early morning, long after I had gone to bed.

I always got up early for prayer, then left for practice at about 9:00 A.M. They stayed in bed, so I would leave a wake-up call. I programmed my stereo like an alarm clock to turn on at 9:00, with Little Richard queued up and ready to play almost at full blast. Then I would get in my car, pull in front of the house and wait for the fireworks. Suddenly the entire house would reverberate with Little Richard's voice. "GOOD GOLLY, MISS MOLLY!" I knew the guys were jumping out of bed, heads splitting, trying to remember where they were, fumbling for the controls.

Then I roared off and smiled all the way to practice. Those mornings ended up making their fondest vacation memories, or at least the ones we've laughed about the most. No compromise. Just tolerance.

9

APARTMENT
OF FAITH

FOUNTAINS DAMPENED THE air, and dense foliage dark-
ened the narrow, wooden walkway leading to my apartment
in L.A. It was like entering an enchanted fern grotto — until
you got inside. Then there was nothing enchanting about it.

The front door opened to a short corridor with doors to the left
that led to two bedrooms and a bathroom. Five steps later you

entered a large room. The first thing you saw there was one half of a well-worn, yellow corner sofa set with an orange lamp rising beyond it from its perch on a crate. In front of the half-sofa stood a blue coffee table, and beyond that were two chairs. Assorted boxes and crates were available for guests who didn't care what they sat on. The choice seat in the house was a rough, brown-tweed recliner that probably saw its best days about the time I was born. A fairly decent television and some degree of cleanliness provided the only clues that the residents might not be bums.

The far wall had glass doors opening to a balcony overlooking tennis courts. To the right a kitchen was hidden from view — which was the right thing for our kitchen to do. That end of the room, which some would call a dining area, was graced with a brown table that tipped when you leaned on it and shook when you tried to cut food. The assortment of chairs around it would have made for a very interesting game of musical chairs. They served their purpose until one of our many guests, Lawrence, got to them. Lawrence was a church brother who I was sure had the gift of clumsiness. One by one, our variety of chairs broke under his gift. We threw a bachelor party once for another brother, James Johnson, and invited Lawrence. That was basically the last night we had something to sit on for a while.

Apart from the television, the only other decent piece in the apartment collection was the bed in my room. Dave, my room-mate, put the other half of the yellow sofa set in his room to use as a bed. During the night his knees would hit the wall and startle me out of my sleep. Eventually I got used to it.

It wasn't exactly the kind of place you'd expect for a profes-sional athlete. I could have lived well with what I earned, even though my first contract wasn't great. But money was not the object. Deeper things motivated me.

With the crazy atmosphere of professional sports out my front door and Hollywood out the back, I faced temptations every time I moved a muscle in L.A. Besides women there was money, more than I ever thought I'd be dealing with. Then there was prestige or fame, and with it the desire not to trust anyone who could exploit those things — which meant everyone.

When I first moved to L.A., I wondered when I met someone, Does this person really like me for me? Or does this person want something from me? The veil of cynicism and mistrust that seems to hang over the L.A. area was trying to envelop me. God and I would talk it through in the morning, and then in the afternoon it would come at me again. I just wanted to withdraw, to stay away from people. I've seen the results when other players give in to that temptation. They become so isolated that they can hardly open themselves up again.

My superbrothers came to the rescue — Greg Ball; Phil Bonasso, who was my new pastor; old friend Lee and new friends Dave Soto and Tom Sirotnak. Greg came out from Texas and spent a lot of time with me. Lee Johnson was in Austin at law school, but I knew he was praying for me. Greg and I encouraged each other to become all that Jesus wanted us to be. We learned to be tough when we needed it and gentle when we needed that. Greg calls it "sweating in God's gym." We're like family, although it isn't human blood that joins us but Christ's blood.

Rick Hardville, the Lakers' team chaplain, and Keith Erickson, the former chaplain, made themselves available to me, too. They became men I could pray with about anything, whether or not it related to the team. Rick became a close friend as well.

My first four years of Christianity consisted of building a foundation and developing character and integrity. Under Phil Bonasso's leadership, the next four years emphasized believing God and learning to trust Him. I saw immediately how my teammates struggled when the big issues arose — contract negotiations, injuries or family difficulties. It's hard to trust and believe God during a crisis when you haven't exercised your faith regularly. Faith is what I needed. Phil was willing to teach it; I was ready to learn it.

PRINCIPLE #28
**No matter who you are, you have to live by faith.
It's hard to trust and believe God in a crisis when
you haven't exercised your faith regularly.**

My new friends from church, Tom Sirotnak and Dave Soto, prayed specifically with me that I'd be strong and wouldn't become like most athletes and break away into total independence. I was still living in a hotel during my first year when they befriended me, so I asked Dave, who was single, to room with me in an apartment. People thought it odd that a professional athlete would want to have a roommate, but since I was fighting a desire for isolation, I didn't need to be alone. I also wanted someone around to hold me accountable. I love myself, but I don't always trust myself. Dave stood with me and believed with me the way Lee had. Independence wasn't a problem after that. I just needed someone to help me walk it through.

Dave was saving money to go into full-time ministry as a campus pastor at Long Beach State. I had started financial planning with some experts under Jerry West's careful, brotherly eye. Pastor Phil was teaching us to believe in God, not to look even to our own salary as a means of provision. We were trying to look beyond the provision to the Provider.

So Dave and I agreed that to learn to live by faith, we would ask God to provide for our needs. Except for our food, gas and rent, we asked God for the rest — to furnish our apartment and provide us with the things we ordinarily would have bought ourselves.

I still spent money but only to put it to work. I was always taught that you cannot outgive God. In college, when my scholarship check came in, I tithed 10 percent of it off the top. Someone will probably read this and say that was an NCAA rules infraction. NCAA rules are very nitpicky. One time in college some friends took me out to dinner, and later I gave them tickets to a game. I got benched for a few games for violating the NCAA rules.

When I left for L.A., I asked God to enable me to give more than 10 percent and to allow me to increase it every year, which He has. I gave offerings on top of that to missions and ministries and to help my friends from college and in L.A. who were starting out in ministry or just trying to get through school. My attitude was to be a river, not a reservoir. I wanted money and blessings to flow through me to others. When endorsements started coming in, little television sets, stereos and radios slipped right through my hands to members of the congregation who couldn't otherwise afford them. When Dave asked, "Got any new endorsements lately?" it meant he could use something.

Some people thought we went overboard on the faith idea. It definitely was a little crazy, but that was part of a crazy personality we soon discovered we shared. We called ourselves "bachelors 'til the rapture" and agreed that the only way we'd move was to get married, which was exactly what Dave did.

PRINCIPLE #29
Look beyond God's provision to the Provider Himself. Remember that the resources ultimately come from Him.

Once the roommate issue was settled, I asked my teammates for suggestions on where to move. They were honest with me. They recommended I stay away from the area around the Forum, where many of them lived.

"There's a bunch of singles there — not your kind of atmosphere," one said.

"You'll get hit on a lot," said another.

Byron Scott suggested the area we finally settled on. It was in Hancock Park, on the dividing line between the mansions of famous people and a ghetto-type district, a regular riot area. When we brought our families to visit, we drove past White House-looking homes lined up behind manicured lawns. We pointed out the mayor's and Muhammad Ali's houses. We didn't tell them that six blocks in the other direction, gang members and drug addicts hung out on the streets all day, and gunfire kept us awake some nights.

When my brother Steve came to visit, I brought him in the bad way. The whole time we lived there, Dave and I would send him down to the 7-11 store at night and then sit home laughing about it. Knowing he could probably talk his way out of any situation, Steve went along with the gag. He and Dave ended up being the greatest of friends. Both of them even named their sons the same name — Austin.

Dave and I moved in with everything we owned — our clothes, some linens and the television. We wondered, Now what do we do? My cousin Harry was in the moving business and occasionally had used furniture available, so I called him. "I need whatever you have," I told cousin Harry.

"It's pretty worn out, Junior," he warned me.

"That's OK."

"I don't know if I can find anything to match," he warned me.

"No need to match anything up," I said, and I got exactly what I asked for.

Our apartment was a running joke at the church. People asked if we were decorating or desecrating. But we won the sympathy of some of the sisters. They brought us needed items or offered to come over and clean. I noticed, however, the same ones never came back to clean a second time.

We moved into the apartment halfway through my first NBA season. When I returned to the Lakers my second year and got injured, my outlook could have been a little dismal. Instead God had a better idea. The team heated up, and so did my play. In one of the first games with my splint on, I scored twenty-eight points and got 14 rebounds against Atlanta. I ended up that year with seventy steals and a 10.8 scoring average. My eighty blocks were the third highest on the team. I had a total of 615 rebounds, a 7.8 per-game average, which was the best on the Laker team and almost doubled what I had done the previous year.

I wasn't the only one having a good season. In a game against Phoenix in February, Kareem did something I would have thought nearly impossible. It happened like this: Coop missed a jump shot during the last minute of the second quarter. Kareem got the offensive rebound near our bench and spun, looking to pass or drive it inside. Since he was outside the three-point line, his defender headed for the basket, expecting Kareem to follow. As Kareem considered his options, Earvin got this mischievous look on his face. "Shoot it, Cap!" he shouted, stopping Kareem cold.

"Do it!" the guys on the bench chimed in. "Go for it!"

Kareem hesitated like a first-time bungee jumper deciding if he should take the last step. Then he pulled around to face the basket, did a soft jump and tried for the first and only three-pointer of his entire career. His shot dropped straight through the hoop. We exploded with excitement, thumping Kareem, laughing.

"Who told you to do that?" Coach Riley yelled. He looked at all of us. "Who told him to shoot it?"

Earvin just grinned.

Winning on the court directly paralleled winning off the court. That year we practically had a revival going on. Earvin, Byron, James, Coop, Billy Thompson, Adrian Branch, Mychal Thompson and Kurt Rambis all attended either chapels, Bible studies or one-on-one meetings where they asked me to tell them about Jesus. Three of my teammates made decisions for Christ during the season.

At the church, on the team and at home, we were all growing spiritually like we'd been doused with Miracle Gro.

Greg Ball flew in when he could and came over to the apartment to teach Bible studies. We invited everyone "BYOL" style. That meant bring your own lamp, because we were short on lights.

"Come on — can't we have the Bible study somewhere else?" people complained. Even Greg chimed in, and he's the one who always got the recliner. (We believed in honoring guests.) But we kept the studies at the most convenient place — the apartment of faith.

The first night that Byron and Anita Scott joined us, Anita's fine sense of style was evidently offended by our rich color scheme. Before she could catch herself, she let out a groan. "Junior! Oh, A.C...."

Later in the evening Anita tried to switch on the orange lamp near her, but there was no bulb in it. I quickly brought the lamp from my room, took out its bulb and put it in the orange one. She groaned again. Before she left that night, she offered to help decorate my house if I ever bought one. I tested her friendship months later when I took her up on the offer. She turned out to be a great friend as well as a great decorator.

Even though I was on a spiritual high, challenges came in many ways. One was the severe time constraints I had. The better part of most days was split between practice, games and travel, or all three. I desired more than anything to grow into the fullness God had for me, so I determined to keep that as a priority. Of all I was doing, I felt that my time with God was the best date I could possibly have.

Not much happens in the NBA at 5:00 A.M. I couldn't control flights and games, but I could control 5:00 A.M., so that became my standing appointment with God. Even if I was out late for a game the night before, I got up for my 5:00 hour of power. In those days the team didn't have chartered flights, so airports were my bed. Sleep could wait. Devotions couldn't.

At home or on the road I sit on the bed with my Bible in my lap and start talking to God, asking Him to direct me for that hour with Him. I generally ask what He wants me to study if I'm not on a regular course at the time. I read a chapter or maybe just a few verses, then meditate on that passage. After I think it over, I repeat it out loud several times until the passage sinks into my spirit.

Then, after maybe twenty minutes have passed, I carry what the Holy Spirit has ministered to me into prayer. I pray for my family, teammates, mission, church, friends and myself. It's very important to cover yourself with prayer. That's not a lack of humility. There's nothing wrong with praying for yourself just like everyone else.

I don't cut myself short. If I'm traveling and don't get enough time for devotions, I take my Bible and continue reading on the bus or plane. I don't feel guilty about it. It doesn't matter when I get my extra boost, just so I get it. I still depend on God's grace every minute of the day whether I spend one hour or nine thousand in prayer. It's important not to get legalistic about it. It's quality, not quantity, that counts. Let the Holy Spirit guide you.

PRINCIPLE #30
Cover yourself in daily prayer. It doesn't matter when you have devotions. Don't be legalistic about it. It's quality, not quantity, that counts. Let the Holy Spirit guide you.

In March 1987 God started ministering to me through specific verses on which I was meditating. He impressed upon me that He would give me an extraordinary season of favor if I would walk in covenant relationship with Him. He said He would move men's hearts toward righteousness as I ministered to them. That was certainly happening. I was winning on the courts and off. I felt we were going to go all the way.

I was still a youngster in Christ, however. For example, Pastor Phil was big on fasting. It wasn't totally new to me, but I struggled with it, especially if I had a day off. And Dave and I got legalistic about it before we ever got understanding.

Pastor Phil would tell us all to fast on Tuesday until dinner, about 6:00 P.M.. So Dave and I would wake up Tuesday morning and realize what day it was.

"A.C., we can't eat this morning."

"I know. Don't remind me."

We'd do whatever we had scheduled, then think of things to do to keep our minds off food.

I'd say, "How much time we got?"

"Four hours."

"Let's go play some miniature golf."

"OK, good."

So we'd go play some miniature golf. Then, "How much time we got?"

"Two hours."

"OK, ummm...." We would drive around trying to think of anything to do except eat.

"OK, now how much time we got?"

"One hour left."

"OK, let's go to the all-you-can-eat buffet."

So we'd drive around and park in the parking lot.

"Now how much time?"

"Thirty minutes."

"OK, turn the radio on." Then we'd listen to a few songs.

"Now how much time?"

"Fifteen minutes."

"OK, let's turn to a sports station and listen to some scores."

After a few minutes: "How much time?"

"Ten minutes."

"OK, get in line!"

We'd go in and let people move ahead of us in line until it was time. At five minutes we'd go through the cafeteria-style line. Then we'd sit at our table with forks in hand.

"How much time?"

"It's six o'clock!"

"All right, dig in!"

"No, hold it! We're supposed to fast until 6:00, so let's wait until 6:01."

Obviously, this was no real, spiritual fast for us. We were just starving ourselves because the pastor said it was a good idea. The only issue on fast days was how fast we could get to a meal line. At first we broke our fasts by eating whatever we wanted — steaks or hamburgers. Then we became dignified fast-breakers. "OK, we're going to break our fast, so let's eat light at first." We'd eat salad, then a little soup — then we went for it and chowed down.

In His grace God honored our obedience to our pastor. After doing it the hard way, in our flesh, we gained wisdom and understanding about the reason we fast. Now I fast to pray for breakthroughs on specific problems, to deliver people, to bring solutions. I spend the time in prayer when I would normally eat. I try to hear from God for His direction for family members, crises in friends' lives, decisions I have to make — for everyone from a coach to the president of the United States. When I was drafted I fasted, along with Greg Ball, Dave Elian and Pastor Irving. That's before I knew what I was doing. Just about anyone can fast. It's a tool in a champion's arsenal.

PRINCIPLE #31
**Fast for deliverance, direction and decisions.
Spend time in prayer when you would
normally eat.**

I soon lived up to the looks of my apartment, relatively speaking, because I became the lowest-paid starter in the NBA. I could have easily asked for and received more from the Lakers. Instead I asked God to increase my faith in Him before He increased my financial situation. The Lakers even offered more, and I listened. But when others pressured me to renegotiate, Greg agreed with me that I shouldn't.

"The Bible says you swear to your own hurt," he said. "It's not a good witness of Christ to whine about something you signed your name to."

It wouldn't have been a sin to ask for more, but because of where I was spiritually and how it would appear to others, I decided to leave the contract alone. I declined their offers.

I also wouldn't have sinned if I used what I made to improve my quality of life. Living by faith was not necessary, nor did it make Dave and me better than anyone else. But for personal growth, as well as for giving me time to adjust, it was a great boost. By the time we moved out a year and a half later, I had learned that everyone ultimately lives by faith. Even though others give us resources, those resources ultimately come from Him.

By not using the money I earned on myself, I also learned more about handling money. "If you don't work, you don't eat" is the simple principle. And if you work, you work hard, as unto the Lord. Then, when you get paid, you first give God His tithe. When I was making six dollars an hour, I learned to tithe, which was difficult because there was so *little* money. Now I had to learn to tithe off a thousand times that amount, which *could* have been difficult because it was so much money.

I gave God His 10 percent and even more off the top, and I learned to give it willingly. The government takes almost half my pay right off the top. Basketball agents can get up to 4 percent. An endorsement agent will get 10 to 20 percent. So why should I take my check, subtract taxes and expenses and give God a tithe off what's left? Everyone else gets his cut out of me based on the gross, so why shouldn't God?

"Who should I give my tithe to?" one player asked me when he made his commitment to God.

"Give to the ones who feed you," I answered.

"What about my church back home?"

"That's fine. Just be sure to give it to God, not charity."

Christians get confused on that. Offerings given to things such as charities come *after* tithes. Take care of God's business first, and He'll take care of yours.

PRINCIPLE #32
If you don't work, you don't eat; if you work, you work hard and give God His tithes.

Like most Christians, I believed God would act on someone else's behalf, but believing He'd come through for *me* was a different story. After months without one, I finally broke down and admitted to Dave that I needed a VCR to watch game tapes at home.

Dave said, "Let's pray about it."

"But, Dave, I *really* need it," I answered.

"Come on, man — we've got to believe God for *everything,*" he said.

I didn't want to let him down even though I was hesitant to put God to the test. As I drove to practice the next morning, I gave it to God.

"God, I need a VCR," I said. "I'm going to believe You to provide me with one."

Once said, I felt better about it. The next morning I prayed about it again during my devotions. Then I drove to the Forum, checked my box as usual and almost started laughing. There in my box was a note from a season-ticket holder named Doug Kanner. It said he wanted to give me a VCR. My faith soared. It was uncanny. I became friends with him and his family after that and always watched for them at games.

That VCR is one of the few things I kept for myself. It's a memento of God's faithfulness to me, even when my faith was weak. It reminds me of His willingness to answer prayer.

Dave and I eventually had to ditch the broken chairs, leaving us with just the yellow sofa and recliner, so we started praying for God to give us real living room furniture. My faith was high, but that answer didn't come as swiftly. That's when I learned to wait on God.

Living by faith helped me overcome the strong temptation to do things just for prestige, to feed my ego. Some guys who get drafted immediately go out and buy new cars, costing probably more than their parents earn in a year. I doubt that much consultation goes into those decisions. They're based on "I want." Most rookies don't even know if they'll be in the NBA the next year.

I couldn't see doing that. Besides, the opportunity came up to do commercials for a Toyota dealer in Corvallis. In exchange he gave me a Supra to drive for a year. Driving a Toyota was just fine with me. In the apartment neighborhood, nothing was safe. Midway through the year, the Supra was stolen from the apartment complex, stripped and gutted. The dealer gave me a new one. The first one had a lot of miles on it anyway. I got lost everywhere I went in L.A.

Every year God manages to get me from point A to point B. I have bought cars for others, but I have still never bought a car for myself.

God taught me His pattern: "Freely give; freely receive." I love to give and serve others. I love ushering, taking the offering and helping with the setup and tear-down at church. But having someone do something for me was a problem. It was hard to allow people to bless me, to do for me, to show concern for me. I struggled with that wall of mistrust. Could I receive from brothers and sisters in the church without their wanting something in return?

I'm proud of my accomplishments with what I think is a good, godly pride. But in another sense I have nothing to be proud of except what God has made of me. I'm humble enough to admit that. What I had to add was the humility to put my hands behind my back and allow others to bless me. I was like the guy who can't change the flat tire, yet he refuses to allow the mechanic standing right there to help him. "I'll fix my own flat," I was saying, thinking I was being humble. Then I'd fumble for the manual.

It is false humility that can't accept blessing. Ask for help. Receive help that's offered. This is God's blessing on your life.

"Freely give; freely receive" is the biblical pattern. When we refuse either part, we get in God's way. Humility is a weapon in itself. I'll show you later how to use it.

PRINCIPLE #33
Freely give; freely receive. When we don't do either part, we get in God's way. Ask for help. Receive help that's offered.

Living the faith-walking lifestyle wasn't all hardship, humility and struggle. We had fun, too: staying out all night, going to professional wrestling matches, taking short trips for sightseeing and fun. People from the church had fun together. A lot of them came to my games. I called them the "Faith Brigade." They called themselves "Green's Gorillas." My code word was "Champ," because we were trying to be champions for Christ. Even with 17,505 fans attending, I could hear them when they cheered, "Champ, champ, champ." I'd be on the floor hearing them, thinking, Those are my fans! It was great.

Ministry was fun, too, and more rewarding than just goofing around. Dave and I hosted an outreach at Long Beach State that year. Since then we've been hosting a summer rally in Torrance that has become an annual event. Students always get saved there. One of my teammates' wives made a public statement about her faith one year. A young woman named Ramona got saved one year and ended up as a leader at her church. She still calls me her spiritual daddy.

147

The 1986-87 season turned out to be everything God promised. My faith had been tempered and strengthened since the previous season. I was prepared to believe the best to the very end. Whatever that end might be, I could deal with it, but I wasn't going to go down unless another team made me. And if I did, I'd go down believing my team was still the best.

Midway through the year, the Lakers outbid Boston and Houston for Mychal Thompson, a former Portland Trail Blazer whose contract was up for grabs. Mychal added a lot of color to the team in many ways. He also added a lot of talent. He flew into town on the morning of the Laker-Celtic game and checked into the hotel across the street.

The week the Lakers play the Celtics is the biggest in the Laker year, with Laker fans unfurling their colors and some of the enemy's fans venturing out in green "suicide" shirts. A Laker slogan sums it up: "Just win two games a year. Beat the Celtics." The game at home is the players' favorite. The first thing we always checked when we got our schedule at the beginning of the season was when we played the Celtics at home.

The game was nationally televised, which added to the excitement, so I didn't sleep much the night before. I got to the Forum three hours early and saw thousands of fans tailgate partying already. When I went inside, there sat Mychal furiously studying plays with Bill Bertka. We had never even practiced together.

Boston's record matched ours when they arrived. The odds were even on who would win. When they came out of the locker room, the fans perfectly orchestrated a symphony of "boos" to greet them. When the Lakers hit the court, the fans stood, screamed, clapped and generally went crazy. I thought, This is what the NBA is all about. It was fun.

James Worthy, Mychal and I rotated during the game, matching up against Kevin McHale, a guy the *L.A. Times* had termed "unstoppable." We called him "the mechanic" because he had so many post moves near the basket. He had a turnaround jump shot, a jump hook, a running hook and all kinds of crazy shots that confused defenders. He led the league in field goals that year.

Then there was Robert Parish, Boston's center, who could occasionally outrun a small forward down the middle of the court to get a layup. He got a lot of easy buckets that way. He also was an exceptional rebounder and was famous for a high-arching turn-around jump shot. From seventeen feet in the air it dropped down, touching just the net as it swished through.

The Celtics also had Danny Ainge, the scrappy fighter with the deadly three-point shot. And, of course, they had the all-time great Larry Bird. Along with McHale, he was among the league's top ten scorers that year and could do just about anything on a court.

Boston quickly jumped to a ten-point lead. Earvin's free throws and James's and Mychal's assists helped, but we still trailed by eight at halftime. Mychal proved he was a quick study, adapting during that first half to our system and defending against both McHale and Parish. When we came back after the half, Larry Bird's game was on, and he took the Celtics to a seventeen-point lead.

Earvin wasn't going to be outdone by Larry, especially at home. Earvin and Mychal both had something to prove, so they picked up their game, scoring fourteen points in five minutes and bringing us within four by the end of the third quarter. In the fourth, Boston held the lead until the final two minutes. Once again it was Earvin and Mychal saying, "Not on our court you don't," and we edged them 106-103.

In the locker room Mychal said, "You thought that was something? You haven't seen nothing yet."

Byron argued back, "You've never played better."

"Yeah," said Maurice Lucas. "What else can you possibly do that you didn't do today?"

After big games like that the coaches always did a team MVP, which Mychal won easily. He had a great game, earning his keep in just one day.

We stayed at the top through the end of the season, then blew through Denver 3-0, Golden State 4-1 and Seattle 4-0 in the play-offs.

We started the finals in the Forum with another star-studded crowd. We smothered Boston in game 1. Even after Larry Bird hit his first eleven shots in a row, we won 126-113. Trying to stop us was like trying to stop a class of first-graders going to recess. Coop broke a record by shooting six three-pointers in game 2, and the newspapers called him "human flypaper" on defense. His game helped us rout the Celtics again, 141-122.

But when we got to Boston for game 3, we went flat, and they won 109-103. After the game Coach Riley was smoking mad.

"None of you has given 100 percent!" he yelled at us in the

locker room. "Who can tell me you've given 100 percent?"

No one said a word. He was right. After two big wins it was hard to stay mentally tough.

"We can't be full of pride," I told the team in our next meeting. God had spoken to me during my devotions, and I wanted them to know it. "If the team becomes full of pride, we could get ahead of ourselves and lose."

"He's right," Magic said. Everyone was sober. People had blamed our loss to Houston the previous year on overconfidence. We couldn't let it happen again.

Coach Riley's tirade that included me as a target was unusual for him. Byron and James have never let me live down the typical chewing out from Coach Riley. He'd rip everyone apart, sometimes showing guys films of how bad they were. Then he'd wrap it up.

"God bless A. C.," he'd say. Only he'd say it more like, "Gaaawd bless A.C."

"He's the only one," he'd continue, "the only out there who is really working. A.C., do you have something to say to us?"

Then I'd give some word of encouragement, a principle, a story — something that applied. Coach often called on Earvin and Kareem, too, but it was his comments to me that Byron and James never let me live down. In school you have teachers' pets. In the NBA you have coaches' sons. They called me Coach Riley's son.

With Coach's motivation ringing in our ears and the word I had from the Lord in my heart, the team showed up for game 4 ready to play ball. We tried hard, but the Celtics fought harder, and with two seconds left to play, they were ahead by one. Earvin would get this special look in his eye when he refused to accept defeat. We all knew that look. He wore it the entire second half of that game, and he never let up even when the game looked hopeless.

With two seconds on the clock Coop inbounded the ball with a pass to Earvin. Earvin got the ball, drove across the lane and threw a Kareem-style skyhook that none of us had ever seen him shoot before. We stood with our mouths hanging open as it arced toward the bucket. Earvin had his mouth open, too. The shot was good. We won 107-106, leaving us a game away from taking the whole show.

"A series to showcase great athletes at the top of their game," the press called the series.

Mychal Thompson proved during the series that he was strong

enough to play center and yet fast enough to play small forward when Coach needed him. Even though Mychal was backing up forty-year-old Kareem, Jerry West signed Kareem to another two-year contract before the final game.

We had a chance to repeat the victory of 1985 by beating the Celtics in Boston in game 5. But instead we came out stiff, and they came out fighting to win. Final score: 123-108. Earvin's winning look never left his eye when that game was over. He didn't accept defeat. None of us did.

We returned to the Forum for game 6. Boston led 56-51 at the half. Two minutes into the third quarter James made a play that is still considered one of the NBA's greatest moments. James swatted the ball away from Boston's Kevin McHale and chased it down the sidelines. He dove headlong to keep it in play, shoving it toward Earvin, who was already on the fast break. Earvin took it at a full gallop and dunked it. That gave us the lead, 57-56.

That quarter we played one of our greatest periods ever, outscoring the Celtics 30-12. Kareem had to sit out most of the third and fourth quarters with four fouls, but he still finished with thirty-two points in just twenty-nine minutes of play. James and Mychal took over for him, and we didn't skip a beat. The first-graders made it out to recess. We won 106-93. The series and the championship were ours.

"There's no question this is the best team I've played on," Earvin said when it was over. With his fourth professional ring that was quite a claim. It was also the Lakers' fourth title of the decade. It was my first professional championship.

The city of L.A. organized a parade in honor of our victory. I flew my dad down to ride on the float with me.

"Hey, A.C.!" people yelled to us. "Good going, A.C.!"

"Junior, they're cheering me!" he said. His face had the widest smile I'd ever seen, and his solemn eyes were lit up like he'd just been given a Cadillac. He waved at the fans and yelled back at them. A star was born.

"Junior, I'd better go on home tomorrow," he said, "before some Hollywood agents come around and try to put me in the movies."

I just laughed at him enjoying himself. The whole scene was funny. I was riding on a float with my dad, heralded as part of the greatest basketball team ever, rubbing elbows with the rich and famous — and I *still* didn't have any living room furniture.

Tom and Dave said they wanted to hang around with me that night. Even though I might have actually been invited to a party or two for the special occasion, I left with them. They drove me to the church, where a surprise party awaited me. Greg and his wife, Helen, and daughter Elizabeth were already hanging out with Pastor Phil and his wife, Karen, and their daughters, Amber and Kimberly, when I arrived. The whole church family and my best friends showed up to help me celebrate — James, Lawrence, Mercedes, Ali, Tom, Robert and Barbara. Their support and love gave even more meaning to my victory.

A few days later Dave and I left for a ministry outreach in the Philippines along with Darryl Flowers, Greg and some others. When we got back on July 15, someone gave us a living room set. And by the time I bought a house six months later, the entire apartment had been furnished, and we had never lacked a necessity. The lesson: Faith works.

10

MEET THE ENEMY

BYRON SCOTT, JAMES Worthy and I sat in the airport, away from the rest of the team, waiting to leave for training camp in Hawaii. "Ace, did you see the new guy?" James asked, referring to an eight-year veteran who was joining the Lakers.

"Yeah, what about him?" I asked.

"You should have seen him testing," he said with a glint in his eye.

Byron jumped in. "He didn't have any legs left with six minutes to go on the treadmill."

They burst into laughter.

"What?" I asked. They were talking about the standard fifteen-minute treadmill test that our trainer, Gary Vitti, put us through along with a series of other fitness tests, physical exams and routine blood tests about three days before we left for camp.

"We were in the room next to the treadmill," James said, "when we heard this wheezing and gasping, like someone was dying."

"He was choking," Byron said, "so we went to help and saw him on the treadmill. He was at nine minutes. I don't know how he did the last six."

"His legs were rubber," James said, and they started laughing again.

"Uh oh," I said. "This doesn't sound good for training camp. Well, we warned him."

In pickup games a month earlier we had told this veteran that Coach Riley's idea of training camp was more like Marine Corps boot camp, only without the frills.

Our first day in camp the team bus wound through Honolulu's gardens of colorful flowers and palms to Klum Gym on the University of Hawaii campus. We got off the bus and inhaled the warm sea air scented with the rich fragrance of island flowers. Then we walked inside, and the hot, stale air hit us in the face, stinking like an oven full of dirty gym socks.

Coach Riley chose that gym for its total absence of ventilation. He closed the doors to complete the sweat-box effect. The object was to make guys who came to camp looking like overweight NFL defensive linemen leave looking like lean, mean, fighting machines.

Islanders who normally created colorful leis for crisply dressed tourists came in to mop up our sweat. As the days progressed, the moppers couldn't keep up or else passed out, so Coach Riley hired more. I took two pairs of shoes to every session because I always sweat through one pair halfway into the three-hour practice. Needless to say, no one high-fived Coop at training camp.

The first day was half-court play with basic layups to loosen us up, then three sets of five-man teams to practice offensive plays.

The next day we started training for real.

"We're going full-court today," Coach said, "shooting layups on both ends."

Within a half hour, the would-be Laker was grasping his side like he had the world's largest sideache. Other guys hit the sidelines to regain their breath but came right back in. Not him. He tried to continue, but in less than an hour he hit the sidelines, then stumbled out the side door. We weren't allowed to stop running our drills, but James, Byron and I stole glances his way and nodded to each other. Gary Vitti followed him outside and told us later that he found him on the concrete lying face up, motionless, except for his chest heaving. No one was surprised when Coach announced the first cut.

The veteran wanted to join a championship team but tried to take shortcuts to achieve his goal. He found out that people reap what they sow. What we do in private, or don't do, will come to light in public. That's an unbreakable principle. He never wore a Laker uniform.

When young players lay their foundations, they may leave cracks. Skipping practice, late-night partying and not conditioning are fault lines that break when the shaking begins. Talent will get you somewhere, but when it comes to championship living, you must have a firm foundation.

PRINCIPLE #34
We reap what we sow. Whatever we do in private, or don't do, will come to light in public. Talent will get you somewhere, but to be a champion you need a firm foundation. Cracks will eventually show up.

The firm foundation we build in life — made of good character, good health and a good relationship with God — is the starting point to achieving victory. But it's only the start. No one lives in a house that has only a foundation. No one wins a championship just by practicing in the off-season. Once you build the foundation, you have to do something with it. You build the house, start the season, pursue your purpose. That's the fun part — accomplishing your goals. But be aware of what you're getting into. Once you set goals there's only one way to accomplish them: War!

Every victory is won by way of war. Victories aren't cheap. You win them by fighting. Like soldiers, champions have no discharge in times of war, only "charge." The Israeli fighter pilot kisses his family good-bye before leaving for battle. He lives by the creed "I fight to live and live to fight." That's a champion's creed.

Christians mainly fight spiritually against an unseen foe. The Bible calls it "powers of darkness," "the enemy," "the devil" and "Satan." He's the reason we can't leave cracks in the foundation. He tries to make us hang onto some little thing to get the advantage later when he jumps on it and torments us with it. It might be lust, jealousy, pride, a bad temper or something else. He uses anything as a foothold. He springs his attacks after something really great or in the midst of problems. Both can become opportunities to defeat us.

Once our foundation is built and our purpose is clear, defeating the works of the enemy becomes the name of the game.

Don't come running to me," Dad said when I ran in afraid of some bully. "I won't always be here. Learn to fight for yourself."

I went back outside.

"Lee, Steve," I yelled, "come help me fight a bully."

"Where is he, Junior?" they asked, and I pointed the way while I trotted along behind, thinking, Yeah, this is going to be good.

Spiritual warfare is similar. Our Father has given us the power and authority of His Son to fight and win battles. But the enemy is clever. He tries to make us feel alone or unworthy so we won't call on our elder Brother, Jesus. He knows that once we call, Jesus shows up. We have to learn to call for help.

"Jesus, help!" I say. "I've got this big, ugly, filthy bully trying to get me."

The power of humility enables us to call on Him, then to walk right behind Him, using His strength. We think, Yeah, this is going to be good!

We can't depend on our power, intellect and capabilities alone. We can't win a spiritual battle using only human power. There is one superpower in this world, the power of the Holy Spirit. His power is released when we admit we can't win the fight without Him. As soon as we do, the momentum swings in our favor.

PRINCIPLE #35
Don't do it yourself. Get out of your power,
intellect and capability, and see God's
power released. That will always swing
the momentum of the war in your favor.

Old Testament wars teach us spiritual things through physical examples. King David was one of the winningest kings in history. He prepared himself for battle by submitting himself to God, then putting on his battle gear one piece at a time.

Like David, who fought God's enemies, I am committed to kicking the devil's backside. To win our wars we have God's armor of salvation, righteousness, truth, faith and the Word of God. Our arsenal includes weapons like discipline, humility, friendships, faith, prayer and fasting. God's army cleans up on a battlefield.

Life has few simple solutions, but there are four keys for winning a spiritual war:

1. Know you have an enemy.
   No matter how you slice it, you're at war. Someone is out to kick your backside, and it's not the problems you see around you. It's the devil behind those problems. He doesn't like you, and he is actively trying to defeat you.

2. Understand your enemy.
   Every basketball player can be thrown off his game by opponents who learn his weakness. In a similar way, the enemy knows your weaknesses and he's prepared to exploit them. He even tempted Jesus, who had no weaknesses. The devil didn't want Jesus to accomplish His purpose, and he doesn't want you to accomplish yours.

3. Know your teammates.
   Who is on your side? Who's in your camp? Besides the people, know the Bible. You have to believe it by faith, confess it and meditate on it until it comes

alive inside you. The Bible is a weapon. But it's only
a lethal weapon when it's in your heart and spirit.
Get the words off the page and into your heart.

4. Use your arsenal.
    You have the power of the Word, prayer, humility,
    discipline and the gifts of the Holy Spirit: self-con-
    trol, wisdom and discernment. Discernment is spiri-
    tual understanding. In basketball we develop a nose
    for the ball, knowing which way it will come off the
    rim for a rebound. In spiritual warfare, discernment
    gives you that nose for the enemy, understanding in
    your spirit what he's up to before your mind can
    even grasp it.

PRINCIPLE #36
**The four keys to winning a spiritual war are:
Know you have an enemy. Understand your en-
emy. Know your teammates. Use your arsenal.**

Whether on the court or off, I stay geared up and ready for a
fight. Off court the fight is not physical but spiritual. On court it's
both physical and spiritual. I quote the Bible as Jesus did to defeat
the devil. When Satan tempted Jesus to turn stones into bread,
Jesus quoted, "Man does not live by bread alone" (Matthew 4:4).
God's Word shuts the devil up. On the court and off, I quote
Scripture to take authority over demons and evil powers.

When I play basketball, I play aggressively. I get hit. I get
thrown nine rows high in the stands. But that's part of the game. I
agree with my friend Orel Hershiser, who said, "Being a Christian
doesn't mean being a wimp." I aim to win, so I don't back down.

"What about turning the other cheek?" reporters ask me.

"In the middle of the day I turn the other cheek," I tell them.
"But not in the middle of a game. That would be stupid."

A third-year NBA player for Miami saw me in chapel service on
game day, so he assumed I'd be a wimp. He chided me when I
guarded him that night.

"Bring the ball over here," he said.

"You bring it here," I yelled back. "I'm ready for you."

The first time I got the ball, I slam-dunked it right over his head. "That's right, young fella," I said, "you'll have to keep up with me."

His whole team rallied, as teams do when a player gets stung. His young friends tried to get back at me.

"You kids," I said. "I'll hafta put you to bed. Play some more, get some more practice, before you come talk to me."

Young players talk a big game, but trash talk doesn't mean anything. You have to finish the job. Trash talk is part of basketball — the game and the mystique. I have my rules:

- No profanity

- Nothing derogatory about an opponent

- Nothing about mamas or sisters

When I was a teammate of Cedric Ceballos, he said I killed people with kindness. He's well known for not following my three rules, and he doesn't understand where I get my strength. I come into a game prayed up. I pray for my team, the opposing team, myself and my health, and I rebuke the enemy. My trash talk consists of "secret" lethal weapons, the weapons of spiritual warfare.

My first year after leaving the Lakers for the Suns, we went to the play-offs against Golden State. We played a see-saw, run-and-gun kind of game. With less than a minute left in the third quarter, we were down 86 to 85 when the Warriors' Latrell Sprewell fouled me in what he thought was a clean block as I drove to the hoop.

"No way. I didn't foul you," he said angrily. "You know that wasn't a foul."

I stepped up to the free-throw line, but he kept it up behind me. "You know that wasn't a foul," he said.

"He's talking," I told the referee. "Could you please tell him to be quiet?"

He kept at it, so I backed off the free-throw line and tucked the ball under my arm. I turned around to face him. "God bless you," I said.

That hit like a missile. He probably expected me to curse him. He was furious when I blessed him instead.

"Don't 'God' me," he said, thrashing his arms and stomping his feet. I just stood there as he got louder. "I don't believe all that God stuff.

Don't give me that junk. I believe the devil. I follow the devil."

I looked calmly at him and said, "Well, I guess that's why you look like him."

He shouted something, but immediately the referee whistled a technical foul against him. His teammates tried to calm him down, but they acted as though they wanted to fight me after that.

We won the game. The press reported that Latrell called me a "dirty player." I wonder if he told them that all I said was "God bless you."

About five times a year I manage to get myself in trouble. My rule about referees is: Speak with respect. Occasionally I'll let one know respectfully that he's missing a good game. And he'll let me know, respectfully, that I committed a technical foul. And if I tell him again, he'll respectfully ask me to leave the court.

Rarely does anything come my way that results in a physical fight, going beyond the usual guarding, pushing and elbowing. If someone pushes, I push back, but I won't make a fool of Jesus. I'll make dumb, not stupid, decisions. Stupid is when you lose your cool completely.

In my rookie year Byron and Earvin often coached me to stay calm no matter what came my way. When players were elbowing me, slugging, pinching, pulling and everything else that goes on in the paint, I automatically reacted as anyone would. The injustice of warfare grates against your sense of fair play until you toughen up and come to expect it. It's part of the game.

"Stay cool," Byron would say as he ran past me after I took a knee to the thigh.

"Easy, Junior," Earvin would say when I went to the free-throw line after an elbow caught me. He always sensed when I was about to erupt. "You're OK. Keep your cool."

I learned quickly that as soon as you think about retaliation, you start missing rebounds and free throws. The other player beats you when he gets your mind on him and off the game.

Pat Cummings of the New York Knicks made it his mission to stop my rebounding one night a few years back. He talked trash and pushed me, trying to make me either foul him or fight him. Finally he threw a fist at me, which is supposed to bring an automatic ejection. But the ref didn't see it. Michael Cooper did, however. Coop tackled Cummings, taking out two rows of chairs along the sidelines. They were swinging, and I saw Coop go down under Cummings. I jumped on top and pulled Cummings's jersey off trying to get Coop out of there. It looked pretty wild to the crowd, especially to Greg Ball who was there that night. The ref threw us all out — Cummings, Coop and me.

I went back to the locker room with Coop. The emptiness was eerie, surreal, with the muffled sounds of thousands of people cheering what should have been us. Ejections make guys feel stupid sitting there, watching monitors, seeing what's happening just yards away. It's like being confined to your bedroom, looking at four walls and hearing all the kids outside on their bikes.

I took a shower, but Coop stayed in uniform. We watched the end of the game in total silence. The minutes ticked off as our misery came to an end and our encounter with Coach Riley came closer. We wanted one to be over with, the other to wait longer.

"You looked like WWF wrestlers!" Mychal said when he came in.

"If trouble starts, you have to be there," Coach Riley said. He pulled us off to the side and spoke with great understanding. "You did what you had to do. Fortunately, we won even without you."

"You should have seen it!" Byron said when we left Coach. "Chairs flying, shirts ripping, guys jumping off tables ten feet in the air, the pile of bodies on the floor — what a fight!"

I left the locker room happy to be out of there. I thought the night was behind me. Greg and I got in the car to leave. He was quiet.

"That was different," I said to break the ice.

"Brother," he said, "you can't do that stuff and call yourself a Christian."

"Greg, I was defending my teammate."

"Ace, you've got to watch yourself. People depend on you."

"But you gotta defend yourself when someone attacks you," I insisted.

"You have to defend your witness, too," he said, refusing to back down.

He was partly right, and I shut my mouth. I am a witness for the kingdom of God. But I have to defend my family, too. Balancing the two is what makes a wise, mature warrior. Since then I've walked away from hundreds of potential fights, preferring spiritual weapons over physical ones. Probably far more sports writers have written about fights I walked away from than fights I got involved in.

The fight served a purpose, however. It topped the prostitute story as Greg's all-time favorite "A.C." sermon illustration. Lots of fans remember the fight, but the ones who will never let me live it down are my friends.

No team had won back-to-back championships since the Celtics of 1968-69. In 1987 Coach Riley promised that the Lakers would repeat in 1988. He couldn't have known that the league would be stronger in 1988 than in 1987. General managers made trades, picked up free agents and created good, solid teams. The Lakers were the reigning world champions and had the best record, but the other teams were vastly improved.

That season we got into a lot of dogfights. We burst into the season with eight straight wins, tapered off, burst forward with fifteen straight wins, then tapered off again. We went from city to city not so much like invaders, but more like desperate champions trying to retain our title. Still, by the time we hit the All-Star break, we had thirty-five wins and just eight losses. Then the physical demands and our aging stars brought us a string of injuries. Sports writers and fans complained that Kareem was too old. They tried to blame him for our struggles. Coach Riley and Jerry West stuck by Cap, and so did the team. We could barely win some games, but at least we won. We'd crawl into the bus afterward, wiping the sweat from our brows.

"Thank God we're out of there!" I heard often.

We got to the play-offs with sixty-two wins and twenty losses. That's when I became a mad dog. During the season, players have friends on opposing teams. But during the play-offs we're more apt to follow Coop's "no fraternizing with the enemy" rule. When the championship is at stake, we all become street fighters. That year we swept San Antonio in the opening series, but the rest of our opponents stretched us to the limit in three best-of-seven series. Utah fans couldn't stand us, so it was a pleasure meeting them in the next round.

We won in the Forum once, but then their enthusiasm and brilliant play, especially by point guard John Stockton, brought them back to win the next two.

"Beat L.A.! Beat L.A.!" Utah fans chanted when we entered their arena. It got our blood going.

We won two games, but then they tied the series 3-3, and we left for home. The morning of game 7 dawned clear, warm and beautiful in L.A. I rolled out of bed thinking, Yes! Today we're going to win game 7. We all got to the Forum early. The entire Laker team was thinking just one thing: Let's get ready to rumble!

In the third quarter we found the gear that got us over the hump. Utah had a big team, a strong team. Mark Eaton's 7'4", three-hundred-pound body hung all over us beneath the basket. He did his best King Kong impression, swatting shots and creating general chaos. John Stockton's quick feet, hands and eyes created quite a matchup for Earvin. John ended with records for the most steals and assists in a play-off series. Karl Malone scored over two hundred points in the series. Both teams were tough and gritty, but the Lakers were faster. Our speed and agility became the gear. We dropped it in and won in the last half of the last game.

We went to Dallas to put the young upstart Mavericks to bed, but instead they took us to seven games, too. We came away tired and aching. The Celtics struggled through their semifinal series, too, finally losing to Earvin's best friend, Isiah Thomas, and his Detroit team.

Next stop, the finals. We hosted Detroit at the Forum in game 1 because we had the best record. Earvin looked forward to that game the way I look forward to playing Lee. When our teams took the floor at the Forum, he acknowledged Isiah with their traditional kiss, which the media ate up. When the game started, they ran down the court once, and the friendship vanished. Isiah took the ball to Earvin like a schoolyard rival. They tried every playground move they had to beat each other. Theirs wasn't a contest for money or celebrity. It was for the ring, the championship, the pride. Their honor was at stake.

The Pistons were known as the NBA's dirty players. Their center, Bill Laimbeer, made former Celtic Danny Ainge look like a choirboy. Danny is booed everywhere he plays. I know because I play with him now on the Suns. He's certainly a lot better to play with than against. The Pistons didn't have just a bad reputation, though; they were bad boys in real life. They had power forward Rick Mahorn, Adrian Dantley, John Salley, rebounder Dennis Rodman, Isiah Thomas, Joe Dumars and mastermind coach Chuck Daly. Their team was solid, and we knew they could beat us. It was bound to be another dogfight.

I matched up against a veteran, 6'5" Adrian Dantley, a two-time

NBA scoring leader. In game 1 he scored thirty-four points, probably thirty-two of them against me. His senior moves and mind games took me apart.

We squared off. He did the same move he'd been making, but then he eye-faked. I stepped toward the basket, and he drove around me to score.

We squared off. Again he did the same move. I knew I could beat it. But now his head jerked and threw me off. He drove around me to score.

We squared off. I was hot, hyped and ready for him. He dribbled right, then stepped away from me. He started to shoot the ball, so I committed to block the shot, but he drove around me to score again.

"Your twin brother would fall for this stuff," I said.

"You can't hold me," he answered. "You can't hold water. You can't hold your own hand."

He was right. He was the teacher, and I was the pupil. He pump-faked. He backdoored me. He invented new variations on the same move, and each resulted in a score. Coach Daly's philosophy was "If you find a weakness, exploit it. As long as it works, don't change it." Soon they were calling Adrian's play every time, knowing that if they could get the ball to him, he could score on me.

I was humiliated in front of 17,505 fans, half of which were the most famous stars in Hollywood, a national television audience made up of maybe half the world, plus everyone I had ever met in my whole life. It was more than exposure. It was indecent exposure.

I was determined to get this guy. The next time we isolated one-on-one, we were about eighteen feet from the basket. Instead of dribbling, he took the ball, looked over me at the basket, crouched and began his spring to shoot right over my head. Pretty gutsy move to go right over the defender.

This ball is not going in, I thought. I'm going to get this one!

I sprang up to swat it down. All my lower muscles pushed me off the ground for the greatest, highest, strongest, longest jump of my life. All my upper muscles stretched as well until I was twenty feet high. There, from the rafters, I looked down and saw that Adrian's feet had never left the ground. As soon as I was airborne, he drove past the place where I had been standing and made the easy layup. Not even my teammates had time to come to my rescue.

I was skinned alive, totally embarrassed. I could hear my grade school teachers talking to their televisions and saying, "I always knew A.C. wouldn't amount to anything."

Fathers told their children, "Don't you grow up to be like A.C."

My friends at Nike unpacked the box of shoes they had just packed for me.

Ricky, Jeffrey, Darryl, Terrel and Lee sat on their couches, heads rolled back, sports pages laid over their faces, saying, "A.C., I taught you better than that!"

We lost by twelve points, and I went to the locker room with my head hanging.

You, A.C., are one of the main reasons we lost this game, I told myself. My coaches confirmed my thoughts.

"Junior, he was your assignment," Coach Riley said. "You have to find a way to stop him, or I'll find someone who can. Take the challenge. You can do it. Get out there and get it done."

"The only way we'll win the championship is if you stop him, A.C.," Coach Bertka said. "If it's not you, we'll have to find someone else."

It could have been worse. They could have tried negative reinforcement. The point was loud and clear. There was no miscommunication on our team about my performance.

I went home in total misery and defeat. That night I spent a long time in prayer. The next morning I got up ready to fight. I had lost one battle, but I wouldn't lose the war.

You have to know your enemy. Adrian Dantley is one of the greatest players I've ever gone up against. He made me respect him. Spiritually our enemy uses moves like Adrian Dantley's, but the enemy is not quite as smart.

The devil is a stupid yet wise foe. He's stupid because he uses the same things generation after generation to keep people in bondage to him. That makes him predictable. But he's wise because he keeps altering his approach to make people think that this time it's different. He disguises himself to fool people into believing the same old stinking lies. You have to learn to recognize him so you'll be ready for whatever he throws at you. It's the same in basketball. You have to study your enemy to figure out a way to stop him.

PRINCIPLE #37
Learn to recognize the enemy so that whatever he throws at you, you'll be ready.

Adrian Dantley was tearing me apart because he kept doing the same moves, but varying them just enough to fake me out, and then he'd score. That's a tough opponent. Some of the greatest opponents are unstoppable because players can't figure out a defense against them.

Larry Bird was a workhorse, a hard-nosed player with a deadly jump shot and high intelligence who could think through the game, then get the job done. Earvin loved to take him on. In the middle of team play they would practically play one-on-one because their rivalry was so intense. Most of our Laker-Celtic games were nationally televised, so the stakes were even higher, with their reputations on the line. In those games, instead of passing the ball the way Earvin normally did, he'd look to score more himself, not just assist. The two of them kidded around a lot, but Earvin was dead serious in not allowing Larry to get more of the spotlight.

Michael Jordan was the ultimate opponent, because we never knew what he might do. He came up in the league as we Lakers were winning our championships, and he became a force for the Chicago Bulls that eventually stopped us. He didn't change the game the way Kareem, Earvin and Larry did, but he embodied the best of what the game had become. He could jump, handle the ball, shoot, drive and rebound. Guarding him was exciting, challenging, fun and utterly frustrating, because he had so much ability packed into a single body. We watched game films and concentrated on matchups, but no matter how much you watched Michael, you'd just see more things he was capable of doing.

When we played the Bulls, I never worried about our guys on the bench not paying attention. The team watched and gawked as Michael flew through the air in front of them. They checked out Bulls films just to enjoy him, whether or not we were playing them.

In games against Michael, and only in games against him, no one complained about not getting enough playing time. Being benched was better than facing the humiliation of going up against

Michael Jordan. With his picture going around the world through endorsements, no one wanted to become the "other guy" in the next commercial or poster who Michael embarrassed as he scored. If you were the guy on the film, you would have to watch that clip or see that photo one thousand times and feel the embarrassment each time. One thing was certain: Players respected him.

Dr. J. was one of my most awe-inspiring opponents. The first time on the court with him was such an honor. I found myself wanting to cheer for him instead of play against him. I didn't want to play tough with him, hurt him or score against him. I had to shake myself to get into the game.

Charles Barkley was one of those players whose temper you had to watch. When we played against each other, we were one of the key matchups. When we became Phoenix Suns together, I learned to appreciate him. Off the court he's a genuinely nice guy. He goes out of his way for people. I wouldn't say he's all heart, but I would say his heart is as big as his mouth.

Knowing your opponent is the key. Players get to know other players and other teams' game plans. The Lakers were great offensively with the fast break, but we were also great defensively with knowing what another team would do. OK, play 5, with your big center posted up, I'd think, and they would run play 5. We were well prepared.

Spiritually you have to study the game films, which is the Word of God, to understand what you're up against. You fast and pray, because Jesus said some battles can only be won with those weapons. "The higher the level, the madder the devil," my friend Tom Sirotnak says. You stand your ground. You may lose some battles, but as you use your weapons, you eventually come out on top.

Adrian Dantley was an awesome opponent for me because of his veteran intellect and patented moves, but I had some weapons of my own to pull out. I prayed it through.

"Are you going to stop him today?" Coach Riley asked me before game 2.

"I'm going to get him before he gets me, Coach," I said. "I'm gonna stop him."

Now I had to get in the game and prove it.

11

USE YOUR STRENGTHS

I N GAME 2 I kept my word to Coach Riley. Adrian Dantley was a great offensive player, so I made him play defense. I used my size and quickness to beat him. I made him worry every time I got near the ball.

"Just get the rebound, Junior," Earvin said. "Get the rebound, pass it to me and run as fast as you can."

I fought for those rebounds, passed to Earvin and ran to the other end, where he passed and we scored. Earvin, who was fighting the flu in that game, helped me make it work. We held Dantley to nineteen points, and the Lakers won by twelve. The Laker fans started cheering again. My shoes got packed back in the Nike box. Everyone I ever knew was again saying, "Yeah, I know A.C." We were off to Detroit for game 3.

I got the knack, the smell, for Dantley's play. When you spend time praying and listening to God's voice, then when the devil speaks, you know it's not right. You might wonder for a day, but you're accustomed to the Father's voice, and you realize it's not His. When I went on family picnics as a kid, even with the kids screaming, I knew my parents' voices. Get in tune with God, and you'll know His voice. Then you can identify your enemy.

Detroit was close to Earvin's hometown so the hoopla was incredible when we moved there for game 3. We had to be focused, mentally tough. They had the second largest crowd in play-off history — 39,188 fans. Earvin was excited, but, as Mychal Thompson pointed out, he loved the game so much that he would be as pumped to play in Denmark as he was in Detroit. Coach Riley tried to ward off distractions so we would concentrate. He had one of his famous talks with us on Saturday, the day before game 3.

"Is there anybody in this room who has made his best effort yet in this series?" he asked. "Well, that's what we need to beat Detroit at home."

You don't have to be the most talented, but you have to play the best to win the championship. A positive attitude confirmed with positive words counts. The enemy throws doubts and sends doubters your way. You don't need to generate doubt yourself. Don't hand the enemy the tools to defeat you. If you act like you'll gladly give up victory to others, others will gladly take it.

"Whatever the Lord wills" can be false humility when you're really burning, yearning and churning for that sweet taste of victory.

"I'll be happy either way" just opens the door to defeat.

You can be happy for the winner, but if you try to make yourself not care, win or lose, you'll never win. You have to want it, live it,

VICTORY

breathe it, speak it, believe for it and not be satisfied until you see it happen.

"They just wanted it more than we did," losing basketball players say of winners. The winners believed for it, expected it, exercised faith for it (even if they didn't know they were) and got what they wanted.

Where the stakes are higher, the costs are higher.

Discipline yourself to a positive attitude confirmed with positive words such as:

"I'm going to win."

"The Lord has given me the victory."

"God has made me a champion."

I quote verses. I listen to my Ron Kenoly, Winans and Hosanna Praise tapes. I read my Christian books. I prepare mentally, emotionally and prayerfully for battle.

What are you going to do today, Junior?" Coach Riley asked me after his game-3 talk.

It was time to pull some cannons out of my arsenal. Coaches hate easy buckets. I'm sure Coach Riley had his hair parted on the side at one time. But when opposing teams scored easy baskets, the palm of his hand went to his forehead and rolled back over the top of his head, and soon his slicked-back hairstyle became a trademark. I thought I'd have fun giving Coach Daly some of the grief he gave me in game 1.

"I'm rebounding, and I'm getting easy baskets," I answered.

Kareem started game 3 hitting his first two shots. Everyone joined in, and we made our first six. Then we fell flat, going six and a half minutes with only two points.

"Just beat them on the boards," Coach Riley said during a time-out.

We started a war under the basket. I elbowed, pushed and pulled to intimidate people so they wouldn't come near me. I'm a cue stick, and I sharpen the tips. When I hit an opponent, he knows it. We came back and scored nine points in less than two minutes, taking a 32-27 lead. I scored easy baskets by rebounding, and I used my speed to beat my defenders. I knew now how I could beat Adrian Dantley.

"Just shoot," I told my teammates. "If you don't have a good

shoot," I told my teammates.

170

shot, shoot anyway, and I'll get the rebound."

My game was on. They fought back, but we led 47-46 at halftime. When we came out after the half, we all got involved in the fast break, running on seventeen of twenty-three possessions, producing twenty-two fast-break points, which helped bring us to a 78-64 lead in the third quarter. Earvin dished out no-look passes, hook passes and bullet passes. He had five assists in the third quarter, fourteen for the game.

Coach Riley had no more worries about Buck in his hometown. The Pistons had no more thoughts of shutting us down. Adrian had no more disrespect toward me. In fact, I earned more than just his respect. He began to fear me. When you've got the upper hand, guys start pulling themselves back, shielding their arms and legs, checking themselves from getting hurt. He was seriously concerned every time that ball went up. He never got the better of me again in that series.

Coach Daly came apart. Some Piston players complained about playing time, which was unusual in the finals, so he was unhappy with his team. He was also unhappy with the officials and their calls. He was really unhappy with the Lakers and my easy buckets. And he was particularly unhappy that he was losing, especially in front of 39,188 fans. In the fourth quarter the Pistons were flat, unable to make a run or score on back-to-back possessions. With 5:05 left to play, Coach Daly got in referee Earl Strom's face after a battle in the paint.

"Dantley was hacked on the arm!" he screamed. "This is the worst officiating ever! What are you — blind?"

He was ejected, leaving his team not only lost at sea, but also without a helmsman. We held Dantley to fourteen points. Isiah scored twenty-eight, but we won 99-86.

Christine Johnson, Earvin's mom, whom we affectionately called Mama Johnson, brought in mountains of homemade food for a buffet afterward in our locker room. We didn't have time for reporters when good home cooking was waiting for us. Nevertheless, even the Detroit press said we'd played brilliantly and that I had played spectacularly.

The next morning I felt the Lord impress me to read an encouraging psalm. I read it, then looked down and saw it was on page 777.

Hmm, I thought, I wonder if we're going to have to go to seven games again.

I called Dave and woke him up. He said it sounded as if it could be God telling me something. I was a little hesitant to accept it because that would mean we'd have to lose two games, but that's exactly what happened.

The Pistons' guards, Isiah Thomas and Joe Dumars, were not going to be denied in front of their own fans on their own court. Anything between me and Adrian was now history. They came out for games 4 and 5 like twin tornadoes and won the next two games by twenty-five and ten points. We headed back to the Forum for game 6. We trailed 3-2 in the series. They only had to win one more.

Each game in the play-offs is like a moment of truth. Once again you have the gut check. Can I defeat this opponent? Am I ready? It's too late to add more weapons or bolster your foundation. You only have the faith that you have at that time. Regardless of how intimidated you feel, you have to take out your weapons and start firing.

Your moment of truth might not be a life-or-death situation. It might not be a won-lost contest like a ball game. It might be simple.

"Will I catch the ball when it's thrown to me?"

"Will I actually study if I go to college?"

"Will I go to the job interview even though I might not make it?"

You need courage to step up to the line when you feel like running and hiding. You can get nervous, have a beer, call a friend and watch some television, or you can get on your knees and thrust yourself into the presence of God. Pray to get an answer. Ask God for courage. I've prayed for courage for years. I don't get pregame jitters going into the big games now. I fret a little about whether my muscles are properly warmed up. I'll run down the hall to get them more limber. But I release my pressures to Jesus.

Having courage doesn't mean you won't experience fear, but that fear won't control you. Courage enables you to encounter hatred, disapproval and contempt without leaving what's right. Cowardice causes you to shrink from duty, danger and pain and yield to fear. Fear is a natural emotion. How you deal with it makes the difference. A hero is just a person who's willing to stay in the battle zone a little longer than the average guy.

172

PRINCIPLE #38
Pray for courage. Have a positive attitude. Speak positively. Prepare yourself in prayer.

I came out pumped for game 6. We led 53-46 at halftime. Then the Pistons came out swinging again. Isiah scored twenty-five points in the third period, a record for one quarter, bringing them to an 81-79 lead. We hammered away in the fourth quarter. With a minute left to play, Isiah made a seventeen-foot jumper, and Joe Dumars sank two free throws to bring them to a 102-99 lead. We called a time-out. While we strategized, the Pistons celebrated. It was like the ushers coming out at Benson High School all over again.

When we returned from the time-out, Byron dropped a twelve-foot jumper to cut their lead to 102-101. Isiah went for a bucket, but Coop defended it. We called another time-out with less than thirty seconds left. We took the ball straight to Buck, but he couldn't shoot. He passed to Byron, who couldn't get a shot. Byron passed to Kareem. Cap pulled up and was about to score when he was fouled. He stood on the free-throw line with 17,505 fans watching, many who had criticized him for being too old. He scored the 7,608th and 7,609th free throws of his career, taking us to a 103-102 victory. We were one game away from history.

Game 7 in L.A. was the same old dogfight, played exactly twelve months and one week after Coach Riley's promise to re-peat. Isiah had sprained his ankle in game 6, and he was listed as doubtful for game 7. But he still came out like a wounded warrior and fought valiantly for his team.

James Worthy started game 7 with sixteen points in sixteen minutes, taking us to a 34-28 lead. The Pistons quickly answered with a 16-7 run that put them ahead 42-41. Kareem made a bad pass over Earvin's head. Isiah, grimacing with pain, got the easy layup. We went into the locker room at halftime trailing and feeling pretty bad about eleven turnovers in the first half.

"This is it," we told each other.

"This is what you worked hard for in training camp," Coach

Riley told us. "This is what the regular season was all about — getting a chance to win another championship. I never said it would be easy or painless. This game is going to the men who want it most. They're fighting for a championship, but you're fighting for a place in history."

Submitting to your authorities is a powerful weapon. David didn't throw stones every single day. He submitted to his father. That's the main reason Coach Riley has always remained "Coach Riley" to me instead of Riles or Pat, as other players called him. I wanted to show him respect as my authority in the game.

David was also where he was supposed to be every day, in the middle of what he was supposed to be doing. He wasn't doing what his older brothers were doing, trying to be big like them. He was in his own position, right where he needed to be. I had to get into my position and win my part of the game. I could influence others, but I couldn't win for the whole team. I came out knowing I could only do my part, and God would have to do the rest.

The Pistons held their lead for three minutes in the third quarter. Then we made ten shots in a row. James scored seven of the first eight points. Byron scored eight straight points in the quarter. We led 83-73 at the start of the fourth.

Coop took his turn next, scoring one of two three-pointers that brought us to a fifteen-point lead. With 7:30 left to play, out came the "Lakers 1988 NBA Champions" T-shirts. We remembered 1986. This was too close. Kareem and Earvin kept working like mechanics, keeping the team machine running, tuning up, adjusting the timing. They were both playing with five fouls each. One more and the machine would break.

The Pistons were unrelenting, especially on defense. John Salley had seventeen points and ten rebounds in the game, and Dennis Rodman scored fifteen points and five rebounds. They were not going to lose easily. With a minute and eighteen seconds to play, our fifteen-point lead was cut to two. Earvin made one of two free throws. The Pistons' Bill Laimbeer missed a three-pointer. Dennis Rodman missed a jumper. Byron was fouled and made his free throws. Tension rose on the sidelines. A four-point lead is nothing in the NBA. Bill Laimbeer hit a three-pointer to bring them within one point. With seconds left to play, we led 106-105. They could still win. I'll never forget those last six seconds.

Earvin got the ball. The Pistons' defense went to work, and so did I, taking off downcourt like a wide receiver. I was the Steelers' Lynn Swann, the Niners' Jerry Rice, the Raiders' Cliff Branch, out on a pass pattern, looking for an opening. Earvin was mauled as he tried to control the ball. He saw me run downcourt the way I'd done a thousand times, and he faked a lunge, then stopped, pulled back and passed a seventy-foot lob over midcourt to me. As the ball came my way, I was sure to score, but suddenly I was confused. I wondered, Are we up by one, or do we trail by one? I drove to the basket with Bill Laimbeer breathing down my back. I didn't want to shoot that ball. I could either be the hero or the goat. Is everyone depending on me, or can I just run out the clock? I thought in a panic.

I felt like I was in one of those blooper films, like the Vikings' Jim Marshall running the ball the wrong way for a touchdown while the fans yelled at him to go back. In a split second all this went through my mind. Then I got a surge of courage. "It never hurts to score," Dad always said. I went up awkwardly. In summer camps I drill kids to jump off their left legs and shoot with their right hands, but I jumped with my right leg and shot a layup with both hands. Nothing seemed real. No one tried to stop me. It seemed like I was alone at the basket. I scored. We won by three points.

Twenty years earlier the Celtics claimed their second straight championship in the Forum, winning 108-106. Now we had done it 108-105. Only three professional sports teams had ever won five championships in a single decade — the NHL's Montreal Canadians in the 1950s, 1960s and 1970s; baseball's New York Yankees in the 1930s and 1950s; and the Celtics in the 1960s. Now historians added the Lakers in the 1980s.

I felt that God redeemed me, after getting butchered in game 1, by letting me score that last bucket.

We walked down the ramp into blinding camera flashes and television lights. As we ran into the locker room, a bottle of champagne was thrust into each player's hands. The TV cameras caught me as I set mine back on the same table it came from and kept walking. I was pumped and thrilled, but that was no reason to start drinking. Reporters pressed against Buck, Cap, Coop and especially James, who got a triple-double and was named MVP of the series. Then they crowded Mychal, Wes Matthews, Byron and me. They thrust a TV camera in my face and stuck a microphone to my mouth.

My adrenaline was pumping. Fiery excitement coursed through me. I waited for the question, expecting to say the usual stuff:

"It was a team effort. Everyone worked real hard."

"Yeah, it's exciting to make history."

"That last bucket felt real good."

Instead they asked me a question that to my mind wasn't about basketball. The television reporter, with a voice full of enthusiasm and an ear-to-ear smile, asked me what he was sure he knew the answer to: "A.C., is this the greatest moment of your life?"

His question stopped me cold. This was my job, not my life. I was on an adrenaline high, but what drug was he on?

"No," I said. "Getting saved was."

I was excited and eager to go on talking about the game, but instead I felt the wind on my face as they whisked away that camera and mike. A few reporters stayed to see what else I might say, but others moved on swiftly.

I wasn't the first one who talked to the press that way. Dr. J. talked about the Lord toward the end of his career and left them just as baffled. My friend NFL All-Pro Reggie White got the better of them when a mike was thrust in his face after losing a game.

"How do you feel about the game?" the reporter asked.

"Jesus is still Lord," he answered.

They pulled back and were on the run when he called after them.

"Isn't that just like the devil," he said. "You say the name of Jesus, and he runs away."

They felt challenged and obligated to return.

If you can't remember anything else when a crisis comes or you face your enemy, remember that the name of Jesus is the strongest word you can use. When you speak that name, every filthy, demonic, satanic thing comes to attention.

Guys can get crazy on the court. Some players are so insecure that winning defines them. They base their security on what the statisticians tell them after the games when they run over and ask for their numbers. They have no identity apart from their game. It's the same sometimes with kids at school who excel at something or people who reach the top of their professions. I go out of my way to speak to those players about Jesus. When they don't receive it, I drill them with it, just as I did with Lee years ago in college.

One Dream Team member, whose name I won't mention, is a great winner on the court, but he's consumed by insecurites. Our teams played a close game one time, with the lead going back and forth. We led by one, then fell behind by two, then took the lead again. My game was on. So was his. We teased each other with trash talk in the first half, nothing serious, and left for halftime with a tie score.

In the third quarter he started sweating it when we held the lead. He couldn't face not winning. Big ego veins started popping out on the sides of his head. He struggled, talked trash and became agitated.

"Why are you so full of pride?" I asked him while guarding him.

"My game is on, man," he said.

"Look at the scoreboard," I said. "If your game is so 'on,' why am I winning?"

"Look at my stats, man," he said. "My stats are better than yours."

"Why are you so insecure?" I said. "You've got that old pride problem."

"Who are you to tell me about my problems? Let's just play," he said.

Through the whole quarter I'd score a bucket and run past him saying, "Your game is old, man — your game is old."

Later one of his teammates was at the free-throw line, and he was at the top of the key, outside the three-point line. I walked over and stood next to him.

"We'll see who's on the real team one day," I said. "What are you going to tell God on judgment day? Are you going to tell Him your game was 'on,' that you scored thirty points every night?"

"That's all right," he said, "I'm not worried about that right now."

"He's going to ask you what you did with His Son," I said. "This game doesn't matter, but what you do with Jesus does matter."

"Don't bring that stuff into the game," he said.

"You can't even talk about it — you're so insecure," I said. "Matter of fact, I'm going to call you Mr. Insecurity from now on."

Through the rest of the game I'd get the ball and look at him and say, "You want this, Mr. Insecurity?"

I had the better of him, and we won.

Humility does not mean acting as though you're less than who you are. Humility is losing your identity in Christ. The power of humility is unleashed when you surrender your reputation, your agenda, and pick up the cross of Christ. The devil doesn't recognize who you are, but he recognizes who Jesus is.

One All-Star forward and I always battle each other. I remember one game in particular when he tried to intimidate me.

"Do you think I'm afraid of you?" I said.

"You should be," he answered.

"Man, I'm not afraid of any demon in hell, so why should I be afraid of you?" I said.

"I'm tougher than you think."

"Yeah? Well, so what. My big Brother Jesus watches out for me."

"Come on — let's just play ball," he said.

"Now you want to play ball," I said. "A few minutes ago you wanted to fight me, but I mention the name of Jesus, and you just want to play ball."

Players don't expect to hear "God" or "Jesus" in a positive way. I totally disturb them by bringing up the most important warfare in the universe.

When someone uses God's name to cuss, often they will stop just when I look their way. Other times I get more demonstrative. Once when the Lakers were playing the Knicks, one of their stars said "G. D." in anger. I turned around to him.

"Don't take the Lord's name in vain," I said.

That really got him off his game, but I was serious. Players say junk about mamas and sisters to get other players off their game. I cherish God's name just as much as my mother's or sister's, so I'm offended when they use it. I say all kinds of things to shut people up.

"God's last name isn't Dammit."

"You actually eat out of the same mouth that just came out of?"

"Why don't you wash your mouth out with soap?"

If they persist, I rebuke the spirit, just as I do before the game when no one is around.

"I rebuke that spirit in the name of Jesus," I say.

That generally gets a guy's attention.

Spiritual warfare isn't for mowing down other Christians, of course. When I play fellow believers, I have to resort to talent or tricks. Playing the San Antonio Spurs recently, I felt exposed next to my seven-foot friend David Robinson. He was about to win the NBA scoring title for the season, and I was assigned to guard him.

"The Holy Ghost is in the house!" I said when he went up for a shot. He made it anyway.

He was shooting like a machine. I kept trying to break his concentration.

"What's Valerie cooking for dinner?"

He was smiling, nodding, laughing and shooting. He had thirty points by halftime.

I couldn't find anything that worked to get him off his game, so I started tugging at his shorts and kneeing him a little, but he was unstoppable. I got twenty points, ten rebounds and stole the ball three times, but they still won 107-88.

That just proves that Christians are hard to beat.

12

KNOW YOUR TEAMMATES

M Y FRIEND BARRY Sanders of the NFL's Detroit Lions was ten yards away from the individual rushing title his first year in the NFL. With seconds left in the last game, his coach called him to the sidelines. "I'm calling a different play," the coach said.

"Whatever will win, Coach," Barry said.

Barry didn't run the play and get the title, but his team won. Christian Okoye won the title. The next year when Barry won the rushing title, everyone knew he won for the team, not for himself.

When David Robinson was within reach of the NBA individual scoring title in 1994, his San Antonio team forced it on him. In their last regular-season game his teammates kept passing to him, and his coach ordered him to shoot. He scored seventy-one points to capture the title for them as much as for himself.

Bill Russell could easily have taken the credit for being the Celtic dynasty of the sixties. Instead he took Boston to eleven titles by passing the ball. He could shoot as well as anyone, but instead he dished it out.

Piston coach Chuck Daly once blamed his 1988 championship loss on players who complained about their individual playing time instead of concentrating on the win.

The lesson in all of this is: You can't play for yourself. You have to play to win. Some players watch their stats because they get paid for their numbers. But ultimately they get paid to win, not to rack up stats. Some guys "cherry pick," waiting near the basket for a pass they can use to score. That selfish attitude destroys team spirit and diminishes morale. Numbers don't win. Teams win. The team comes first.

To win the war you have to be prepared, engage the opposition, know your teammates and become a team player.

PRINCIPLE #39
**Play to win. You can't play for yourself.
Numbers don't win. Teams win.**

With the schedule players keep, we spend most of our time together. My season schedule is: Devotions at 5:00 A.M.. Breakfast at 7:00. Practice or travel at 9:00. Eat at noon. Sleep from 2:00 to 4:00. Leave at 4:45. Dress for play at 5:15. Shoot from 5:45 to 6:45. Team meeting from 6:50 to 7:20. Play from 7:30 to 9:30. Go to the locker room for a brief meeting. Shower. Talk to reporters. Go home at 10:30 or 11:00. Get up at 5:00 and start again. Time zones make it interesting.

The team lives, eats, breathes and even sleeps together — in the bus, plane or airport. Fortunately we don't have to share hotel rooms. We spend so much time together that we probably qualify as exemptions on each other's tax return.

When I join any team, my primary goal is to glorify God, and my primary mission field is that team. I serve my teammates, minister Jesus to them and make myself available to them. They're my extended family. We live under conditions where almost everything any one person does affects the others. My goal is to make a positive impact.

When the Lakers played the Seattle SuperSonics one year, I was able to live out my convictions in a game none of us will ever forget. With no fight left, we seemed destined to lose. By the third quarter we were down by twenty points. Seattle fans are well known for their thunderous cheering, and they were making themselves heard — on national television, no less. Something rose within me, and I decided not to let this one get away.

"One man can affect the many," I told the guys. They didn't catch on.

"Jesus was one Man who affected the many and still affects us today," I said. "It's a principle, a law, so it's true for us tonight."

I got myself pumped up to win, as one man and I kept after the others, determined to affect the many. Revival is like that. It always begins within, then spreads outward.

"One man!" I said to Byron, nudging and slapping him. He stepped up his shooting.

"One man!" I yelled to James, and he picked up his speed.

Soon the Sonics were only fifteen points up. Kareem, Earvin and Coop started hustling. Earvin caught on to what I was saying and got his determined look. Now he was in agreement. We weren't going to lose this baby.

"Come on — play up to your potential," I told the guys during a time-out. Coach Bertka looked at me in amazement because of my sudden burst of intensity.

"One man," I said to him and held up one finger in his face. He smiled.

We scored six more points, and the crowd quieted down.

"Come on — come on, man," I shouted to my teammates as I ran on the fast break.

We brought their lead to five, then two. We tied. I held up one finger to my teammates as we ran down the court together. With a burst of renewed strength we blew past Seattle, and they never caught us. To this day Bill Bertka will hold up one finger when he sees me and say, "One man."

People may not always respond immediately, but if you determine to affect them, eventually you will.

PRINCIPLE #40
One man can affect the many. Make it an individual goal to be a positive impact on others.

The team is the team, just as the family is the family, for better or for worse. I've played with some of the all-time greats and not one of them was perfect. We learned how to appreciate each other, to hold each other accountable and to improve each other. Earvin was one of my best friends on the team. He was the kind of team player who earned the right to be called Magic. On the court he was a naturally talented, intelligent and unselfish player. Off court he was outgoing, the life of the party, the captain of every ship. He loved being part of a team. No matter what happened outside the Laker organization, when he joined the team wherever we were, his eyes lit up. We were his guys, his friends, his homeboys. On the road he loved people, and he never tired of signing autographs.

"You go over there and sit," we told him at airports before they started chartering flights for us. "The crowd wants your autograph, Buck, so get them away from us."

"You're just jealous," he said, laughing.

People talk about me and my work ethic. Buck's was just as strong. I constantly prepare for the whole game. If a game is forty-eight minutes long, I prepare to play forty-eight minutes. He was the same. He was always the first to practice, always ready to give his all.

We were both highly excitable. On old game films I laugh to see how we jumped around together, slapped, bumped and elbowed each other. But he was more consistently excitable. When the team did something great, he just about broke our wrists slapping high fives. If we did little jive moves during our celebrations, it was probably just because our hands were stinging from Buck.

Cookie, who became his wife, was a strong woman, and the

team knew her for years. She and I had shared long conversations at official team parties while Buck was out being the center of attention. She possessed a deep, inner strength and always appreciated the small things people did. She was a gem for Earvin, whether he always knew it or not.

The party would be over, though, when Buck got the look. That's when we had to work, and work well, because he held us accountable for it.

"It's time," he said, and he owned the court.

He didn't demean, deride or derail anyone, but he let us know if our game wasn't up to what it should be.

"You'll have to shut him down," he said sternly as he dribbled past someone.

"We're going to win this," he said to anyone acting like giving up.

He used peer pressure in the way God intended it to be used — positively. The way he held us accountable made him not only a great player, but also a great leader. He put on just enough pressure to keep us in check.

Kareem was another team player who became a good friend. He is still considered by many to be the greatest basketball player ever because he transcended the generations, becoming the greatest of one era and one of the greatest in the next. His size certainly helped. Cap dwarfed people, towering over them like a hang glider. He had dangling arms that could make him look like he should be uncoordinated, but he was ultimately coordinated, never out of control, never uncertain. He was the closest you could get to a basketball machine.

Kareem was usually a gentle giant. He was gracious and generally soft-spoken. But when he got riled, that giant would awaken, and he would yell long and loud. I loved bringing out that side of him. He was usually so cool, so nonchalantly perfect in his play that I loved upsetting him.

At practice we got away with a lot of fouls. Coaches called fouls on us, but we would never be benched for them, so we fouled a lot. Our practices were so rough that games seemed easy by comparison. In my rookie year, when I was still trying to figure Kareem out, I elbowed him or pushed him at practice.

"Sorry," I said.

"OK," he said the first time or two.

I kept pestering him. I stepped on his foot, tripped him, pushed him off balance. When he finally got upset, his face didn't express anger — his whole body did. His famous goggles would start to cloud. He did deep neck bends, and his ropey arms would swing. He ran down the court, head bobbing, arms cutting huge arcs, goggles steamed, and we knew the next person who defended him was going to get smashed.

"Get the ball to me," he told Earvin. "Throw me the ball!"

We weren't allowed to leave the court during practice, but we didn't want to be near him when he got like that, either.

"Your turn to guard him," I told some unsuspecting teammate. Usually Mitch Kupchak became his target.

Cap would catch Buck's pass and stand in the paint with the ball between his hands, elbows extended on each side, swinging wildly from the waist up, elbowing anything within reach. Mitch was a seasoned veteran, so he wouldn't back down. Instead they'd start talking trash.

"You did that on purpose," Mitch said.

"You shouldn't have gotten in my way," Cap insisted.

Cap wasn't easy or open, but he was so set in his eccentric ways that we could practically read his mind. Even better than practices was watching Cap with autograph hounds. That was the highlight of every trip. He sat away from us in airports, usually reading a newspaper he spread out double-wide. If we were close to home, he always wore his favorite old pair of blue jeans left over from the hippie era.

People are funny. They would recognize him, then stand back. They fumbled for a paper and pen, then mustered their courage to approach him. They made this slow arc, angling in and ending with a burst of resolve. We could almost hear the theme from *Jaws* as they approached.

Ta dum. Ta dum, ta dum.

"Excuse me, Mr. Jabbar," they said. "May I have your autograph?"

He signed wordlessly, then folded his paper across in half and pulled his legs in. The next one came up. Ta dum. Ta dum, ta dum....

"Excuse me, Mr. Jabbar. But could I please get your autograph?"

He breathed deeply and signed. Sometimes the person would revert to a second childhood and fantasy would overtake them, like some neighborhood kids were going to see them talking to Kareem Abdul-Jabbar.

"You know...," they started in.

"No, no," we said under our breath as we watched. "Get in and get out. Get in and get out!"

"I'm your greatest fan...."

"Get outta there," we whispered. "Come on — get outta there!"

He shoved their paper back at them, and usually they dropped what they were going to say and left. He folded his paper down in quarters, crossed his legs and concentrated until the next one. Ta dum. Ta dum, ta dum....

"Excuse me, Mr. Jabbar. Could I please have your autograph?"

He signed, folded the paper, signed, folded the paper, until finally the newspaper was about the size of a letter envelope. Each time he pulled in his arms and legs, making himself as small as he could.

"Twenty bucks says it will be the next one," one of the players would say.

"My twenty dollars says it's going to be a lady."

"Cap's in a good mood. I'll bet twenty dollars that he'll do three more."

It seemed as though he always blew up on some nice, gentle, Sunday school teacher who wanted an autograph for her pastor.

"Excuse me — "

"No!" he snapped. "I'm not going to sign!"

He would stand up, stretch to his full, overwhelming height, grab his bag and storm over to another seat, head bobbing, arm swinging. She'd be left standing there, shocked.

"Whooo, I got you!" the guys said.

"No, you owe me. I said it would be a lady."

"Come on. Pay up — pay up."

Buck tried to get Cap to enjoy his public and the media a little. And Cap finally seemed to mellow toward the end of his career. He scared only men away then.

Cap claims I was the team's practical joker because of the thumb wrestling and lip burning I brought to the team, but really he was. I always brushed my hand across a player's lip that drooped when he fell asleep. Cap thought that was pretty funny. He was quiet and serious but always ready to pull a prank.

On one game morning after the usual shoot-around, I was still on the court practicing free throws when Kareem went in to change. He was usually the first in the showers. Something took hold of him that day, and he got a surgical knife from the training room, went to my locker and got my street shoes. I had a brand new pair of soft rubber-soled sandals that I'd only worn about three times. With a size fifteen foot, they obviously didn't come from Shoes-R-Us. He carved out a three-inch-wide hole in the bottom of one, replaced them on my shelf, then sat in front of his locker waiting for me.

I heard this sinister "Hee, hee, hee" when I walked in. I turned to see Kareem's eyes sparkling while he watched me.

"What did he do?" I asked the other guys. No one had seen him. I went into Gary Vitti's room.

"What did Cap do to me?"

"I don't know," he said.

I looked through my stuff, but it looked OK, so I went to the showers. I knew I'd been had. I dressed without incident, then grabbed my shoes and saw the bottom.

"Hee, hee, hee." I heard Cap's laugh fading down the hall as he left. I decided right then that I wouldn't get mad; I'd get even. I kept the shoes as a reminder.

Sometimes you get thrown together with people you don't think you'll get along with, especially in a small church, small school, small office or twelve-member basketball team. But if you chip away at the surface, you may find a diamond in there. The Laker team had a good, solid core, but Jerry West was always on the lookout for talent to keep us going into the next decade. In the summer of 1988, Orlando Woolridge came to us after struggling with a personal problem.

"Perfect," I could almost hear Coach Riley saying. "Let's seat him next to A.C."

We always sat in a particular order on buses and planes. That season I sat next to Orlando and talked to him about the Lord the whole season. He was a funny guy who practically lived on a fishing boat during the off-season. He and Coop would compete for who could get the blackest before training camp. He was eventually traded to Philadelphia, but not until we had become good friends. The Laker experience was good for him, a stepping stone. We still stay in touch, going out of our way to have dinner together at least once a year.

187

Vlade Divac joined the Lakers during the 1989 season, a 7'1" center from Yugoslavia. I knew he joined but hadn't met him officially. Then one day I was in Marina del Rey with my friend Kerry Jones, getting a frozen yogurt. I came out of the store just as Vlade came out of a store across a broad parking lot.

"Look at that seven-footer," I told Kerry.

"Wow, he's tall," Kerry said.

"Hey," I said, "that's Vlade! Let's go meet him."

When we got to him, he was walking around, looking inside a car.

"Hey," I called out.

He looked up, and his eyes brightened like a kid's.

"A.C.," he said with his thick, funny accent, and he thrust out his hand to shake mine. "A.C.!"

"How are you doing?" I asked.

"How you do, how you do," he answered.

Then I saw the bent coat hanger in his hand and realized he had locked his keys in the car. I went to the store he had just come out of, but they hadn't understood him. He'd been stuck there for about an hour. Although he was intelligent and bilingual, he probably spoke only about ten words of English at the time.

"I'll call a locksmith," I told him.

"Yah," he said as he kept wiggling the coat hanger in the window. Kerry and I bailed him out, but that wasn't the first time Vlade needed bailing. I ended up becoming his American big brother.

"What is wrong with you?" James asked him one day as he strolled in ten minutes late for practice. "Why are you always late?"

Vlade just smiled, his eyes crinkling with sleep in them, his hair sticking out in every direction. "Sorry I late," he said. "I oversleep."

Vlade overslept a lot. It seemed he never got up in time to catch the team bus or get to practice. He was incredibly talented, though, and very funny. I always asked him to translate things for me into Croatian or Spanish.

"How do I say that rookie is a big moonhead in Croatian?" I asked him.

"Neblo Glavenya," he said, or something like that.

He taught me my name in Spanish, "A. Che. Verde."

I learned my jersey number. Soon we could carry on a conversation for about ten seconds in his language. He had me talk to his friends on the telephone back home.

"Yaso, atsum, zelanee," I said, I think.

When fighting broke out between the Croates and Serbs, he was terribly upset. His entire family was within miles of the heaviest fighting. When he called home, he could hear guns and bombs in the background. For a while he brought them to America, but they returned when the worst was over. Certain players from other teams wouldn't speak to him because of their ethnic differences.

"I hate to see this happen," he told me once in a quiet, somber moment. He remained impartial, in the middle, which made some even more angry.

Vlade was a great addition to the team and an interesting character, but no one was as big a cultural experience as our center from the Bahamas. When Mychal Thompson came during the 1987 season, he quickly took the prize as the biggest mouth in L.A., if not in the universe.

"I've done everything" was his attitude, "and not only have I done it, but I've excelled at it."

On typical days he insulted, taunted and bragged to excess to every member on the team.

"The only team you couldn't beat back in college was mine," he told Earvin in his thick Bahamian accent. Then he went off on something else.

"I only shot in the seventies yesterday in golf," he said. "I shot a couple over par, a seventy-two, with three or four birdies."

"Mychal," someone said, "that doesn't even add up."

"Come to Nassau," he said. He always invited us to his home. "Everybody knows me there. I'll show you the sharks, real sharks, baby sharks, killer sharks."

"Mychal," we asked, "how do you know where to find these sharks?"

"I fight them," he said. "I jump off my surfboard, I go down, and I start kicking at this thing. It's a shark, at least sixteen feet long."

"Mychal, do you really expect us to believe you fight sharks?"

"All of you guys are chickens," he said. "Me, I'm not scared of anything."

He always laughed while he talked, but he was serious. His brother, Andy, lives in New York and is a good friend of mine. They have wonderful parents. Once when I was with the family, I tried to get to the bottom of his stories.

"Mrs. Thompson," I said, "your son says he snorkels with piranhas and fights sharks."

"Oh, that Mychal," she said, laughing. "He's always had such an imagination."

Coach Riley and Earvin took him up on the invitation to Nassau one summer, and one thing was true — everyone there really did know him.

Of the relationships I build on a team, one of the most important is with the coaching staff. The Bible says to honor those who are given charge over you and respect people in places of authority. Coaches don't always make the best decisions; but as long as I don't flat-out rebel, I can pray for grace, and God will honor that.

When Byron Scott was injured during the 1992-93 season, Coach Riley was gone, and Mike Dunleavy had taken over. He pulled me into his office before practice one day. "A.C.," he said, "we need you to cover for Byron."

"But I haven't played guard since college."

"We know, but we think you're our best choice."

I rubbed my face and shook my head. I was willing to do anything to produce consistent, quality play, but I wanted to talk about it a little more. As Yogi Berra would say, it was like déjà vu all over again. When Kareem retired and Mychal Thompson was injured, I started as the center. It wasn't my choice, but I managed to score twenty-five points and grab eleven rebounds. The phrase "I can do all things through Christ who strengthens me" (Philippians 4:13) ran through my mind.

"Whatever it takes," I answered.

"Good. Then we'll change practice to start on the new rotation."

I ended up averaging 12.7 points and 10.9 rebounds in Byron's place. Not bad, but I was sure happy when he got back into the game.

As I put my trust in leadership, they can put their trust in me. I don't murmur or gossip behind their backs, so they listen to me. They know I'm praying even before I come to work. The mutual respect and trust that grew between me and Coach Riley for the five years we were with the Lakers together inspired his team chats.

"You call yourself winners?" he'd say. "You're not winners. You are nothing. Nothing! Only one guy, one guy, showed up today. Gawd bless...."

Hey, Coach, I said to myself, you could just call me at home and tell me that.

When we parted, Coach said he always appreciated the fact that I came to work. Coaches and players have always said that I give 100 percent whether for practice or games. For the most part I try to deserve that kind of praise. I don't always agree with leadership, however. When you believe a decision is not just questionable but wrong, you have to pray for grace.

"Oh, Lord, cover this bad decision."

One year a certain college player was being considered for a Laker draft pick. I wasn't making the decisions, but I didn't feel right in my spirit, so I called Jerry West. "Mr. West, what are you thinking about with this player?" I asked.

"We'd like to draft him," he said.

"I don't feel comfortable about it, Mr. West. I don't believe he has the kind of character it takes to work with our team."

"We've heard rumors, but he's got the talent."

"He's talented, but is his lack of character going to be a problem for this team?"

"We won't know that unless we try."

"Well, I hope he turns out to be a diamond in the rough for us."

"So do I," Mr. West said. "Thanks for calling about it."

I kept praying about it. I hoped I was wrong and that it would work out after all. At least I knew God's grace would cover me. But the player turned out to be a problem child. He wasn't totally bad; just his attitude was. I had a difficult time committing myself to a teammate who wasn't committed to the same cause I was — winning.

If you're given leadership — in the NBA, church, school, business or anything else — evaluate character first, talent second. Talent without character won't win ball games or lost souls. It doesn't matter how many hoops someone scores, how many seats fill the stadium or how many members join the church. The leadership will pay for it eventually in embarrassment, regret and loss of morale.

PRINCIPLE #41
Honor those who are given charge over you. Respect people in places of authority. When you know your leader has made a bad decision, pray for grace.

You can't always choose your leaders and teammates, but you can choose those you draw closest to, your covenant partners. In the spiritual battle you have to know which people you can depend on. Johnny-Be-Good who doesn't want to get his hands dirty isn't a good backup in a fight. I don't want someone clean-faced as a covenant partner. I want someone with the marks of a warrior; someone who knows how to combat the darkness with the light; someone who knows how to get inside a situation and pray until it changes.

I have Greg, Dave, Tom, Lee, Pastor Phil, Pastor Irving, Dennis Peacock and Rice Brooks among my covenant men. I can call on them to stand with me, pray for me, toss ideas around and give me spiritual counsel. The Bible says a multitude of counselors will help you make wise decisions. When I'm faced with a major decision, I pray and submit it to those I trust until I believe I've found a wise answer.

People may not be all you want them to be, but they are all you have. We have to work together as a team, as the body of Christ. "We are desperate men at a desperate time, and we desperately need each other," Greg likes to say.

From my brothers I get the antidote I need to counteract the enemy's lies. Satan is the biggest trash talker there is. If I start to believe him, my brothers will correct me. When I feel down, low on faith, my brothers pick me up or just give me a kick in the backside. They know me and know what I need. The devil wants me to lose my effectiveness, to lose sight of my purpose. I use the weapon of God-given friendships to thwart his attacks.

Any good, solid basketball team is going to have the mental attitude that each player holds the others accountable. You've got to leave all your niceties back in the hotel room and come out speaking the truth. In the same way, with my covenant friends, we speak the truth in love. It's part of a warrior's armor, the belt of truth.

Accountability is just positive peer pressure, like what Earvin dished out on the court.

My inner circle helps keep me on track even during the good times. When my team is winning five or ten games in a row, it's easy to slack off in prayer, to get arrogant and fall into pride. Victories are one of Satan's open doors of opportunity. He loves to distract us when we feel we're so cool, so together, so on top.

"You've accomplished something," my brothers say, "but don't start thinking you're greater than you really are."

PRINCIPLE #42

Become accountable to others. Accountability is just peer pressure used the way God intended — positively. Put just enough pressure on to keep your teammates in check.

You can just do things, or you can do effective things. I don't want to spend my life and spin my wheels doing things that are not effective. My brothers know my heart, and they're not afraid to tell me when I do something wrong. That's true love.

The other side of the equation is that you need to seek out wise counsel and listen when it's offered. Dave Soto and I know a professional baseball player who failed to do this. We had been praying for him specifically, and then we heard he had become a Christian. One morning a few months later, Dave came running into my room.

"Ace," he said, "we have to believe God to talk to this guy. I woke up this morning, and he was the only thing I could think about. Something is going on!"

"OK," I said, "later on."

"Come on, man," he said. "Let's pray now."

So we prayed for the guy and went on about our business. Then, for some reason, his team's public relations office called my office a few days later, so Dave and I arranged to get tickets to a game. When we arrived, a team employee called me down to the dugout to talk to him.

"It's really great that you want to find out more about Jesus," I told the player. "You need someone who can teach you, mentor you, help you along."

"Yeah, I have friends who want to help," he said.

"Well, I don't know everything you're going through, but being in the sports world, I'm available to help you out in any way I can."

"Thanks. I'm fine."

I talked to one of the two solid Christian brothers I knew on the team. "You've got to help him along," I told him.

"He won't let me get close," he said.

Within months we saw the player's face smeared all over the newspapers because of a drug problem. He underwent therapy and has gone back and forth ever since, year after year, with various problems. I ran into him again recently.

"If there's anything I can do, let me know," I said.

"Yeah, thanks," he said, but nothing has come of it.

God gave us relationships so we'd have help. But what the mind will rationalize, the heart will justify. That guy rationalized not plunging into new, solid friendships, and it's still costing him.

At the end of the 1988-89 season, Kareem retired and left a huge, gaping hole in what used to be the image of basketball. People loved him. Regardless of how he'd treated fans for twenty years, huge crowds came out to see him to the end, especially to witness his last performances.

After a 57-25 season we blew through the play-offs. We broke records by winning eleven straight postseason games, three to get past Portland, four to stop Seattle and four to rout Phoenix. People started saying "three-peat" about us. We were certain we'd send Cap off with another championship ring. But just before we started the finals against the Detroit Pistons, Byron tore a hamstring.

Detroit led the league that year with a 63-19 won-lost record. We met them on their court for game 1 and lost 109-97. Things went from bad to worse. In game 2 Earvin tore a hamstring. We lost by just three points. In game 3 Cap scored twenty-three points and brought us to within four points of a win. In game 4 James Worthy put down a career-high forty points, but that still wasn't enough to bring us out on top without our two starters. They swept us. We lost game 4 105-97 in front of the Forum crowd on the last day Kareem wore a Laker uniform.

I ended that season the fourth highest scorer on my team, averaging 13.3 points, and was easily the leader in rebounds with 739. I also got ninety-four steals and was named to the All-Defensive second team along with Kevin McHale, Patrick Ewing, Alvin Robertson and John Stockton. It was a great individual season, but that only shows that individual scores don't win championships.

We didn't win the finals, but I found great joy that year in finally

194

getting even with Cap. We all went in together to buy him a white Rolls Royce for his retirement — quite a gift for quite a player. We seated him on the court in a rocking chair before we brought it out, then surprised him. A lot of the old Laker players from previous years came. Cap's son, Amir, sang the national anthem. The ceremony was touching, but the best part came later that night.

While Cap did interviews, Buck, Byron, Coop, James and I snuck back to the locker room.

"Come on," Buck said. "Someone get the scissors."

"Where're the jeans?" Byron said.

We took scissors from the training room and started cutting out pieces of Cap's precious pair of jeans. "This is for old times' sake, fella," I said as I cut out a big part.

Other players and former players came in and got a piece of the action. We folded what was left and put the jeans back on the shelf.

Amir had come in at some point and stood horror-stricken next to the door.

"Dad!" he said as Cap came in the door after his last interview. "They cut your pants! They cut your pants!"

"Who cut them, son?" Kareem asked.

"They all did," Amir said, "and so did A.C. I saw him."

I was right around the corner, so I let out my very best Cap impression: "Hee, hee, hee."

Kareem picked up the jeans and saw them cut to shreds. At first I could see he was mad. After all, this wasn't just a possession he guarded but a prized possession he cherished. Then he laughed. We were already laughing with the sweet satisfaction of getting even, especially to see the ridiculous sight of Cap holding those jeans up in front of him, trying to figure out a way to wear them home. He settled for wearing a pair of sweatpants and carrying the jeans.

You have to know your teammates. When I left the Lakers to join the Phoenix Suns, I had to get to know a whole new team. Charles Barkley, as a Dream Team member, was the Suns' biggest star, next to Kevin Johnson. One person described him as someone who "doesn't own an unexpressed thought." He's a loud, small, but bulky package of natural talent, and he uses his ego as his biggest weapon.

"You better double-team me," he tells opposing coaches.

"You doubled, but you better triple-team me," he says after he scores.

Charles occasionally rips into a guy, but not in excess or when it's undeserved. He doesn't mind telling the truth as he sees it. His hyperactive mouth is definitely obnoxious, but he's consistent, so he's consistently obnoxious. After Mychal Thompson he seems tame.

Coach Paul Westphal and Kevin Johnson are Christians. I already knew Kevin and enjoyed having his great ability on my side for a change. Coach Westphal and I hit it right off. At the end of my first season he told reporters I was his choice for MVP because I showed up for every practice, every game, and gave it my all.

Joe Kleine, our center my first year, said I was looked to for leadership by the end of the season for the same reasons. Danny Ainge was one of my primary recruiters. After our intense rivalry from his time with the Celtics, he was as eager to get me on his side as I was to get him on mine. He said I made the Suns a better team. Team owner Jerry Colangelo called me in for the traditional postseason talk and said I was a warrior. He said that if he went to the trenches for hand-to-hand combat, he'd definitely want me in his platoon. I felt honored that he thought that much of me.

But not all my new teammates appreciated my drive and enthusiasm for the game. Once again I took some getting used to. At one practice Oliver Miller became livid with anger. "I'm sick and tired of it!" he yelled. "I'm not going to take it anymore!"

None of us knew what he was talking about. He stayed hot right through practice and carried it into the locker room. I was just around the corner when he exploded.

"That wild A.C.! He's always hitting me in the face. I'm on his team, but every time I go for a rebound, he's hitting me in the face."

I came around the corner and smiled at him. "I just go after the ball," I said, "but sometimes people get in my way."

Oliver's outburst reminded me of Tyrone Miller, an OSU forward I played with for three years. He used to get upset with me back in college. "You beat me up in practice," he said, "throw me to the floor, then help me back up and ask if I'm OK."

I wasn't the Suns' superstar, but they couldn't complain too much. I led the team in rebounds, posting double figures for thirty-four games my first season with them, and I offered a three-point threat if opponents double-teamed Charles or Kevin. Plus I averaged 14.7 points per game, fifth highest on the team.

The Suns team overall knew how to have fun, and they enjoyed the competitive nature of the game. That makes for a healthy playing environment, even if we didn't quite gel yet my first year. When a team gels and becomes more like a family, the playing level usually intensifies.

In our Laker team we accepted each other's family as our own. James Worthy's parents, Earvin and Gladys, were wonderful people from Gastonia, North Carolina. Mama Worthy, who passed away last summer, would make us a spread of food when we played the Charlotte Hornets. Mama Johnson, Earvin's mother, would make us a buffet when we played Detroit. And Mama Green would make a feast when we played Portland.

Whenever there was food to be had, guys did anything to get near it as quickly as possible. "You give me two tickets for the Portland game, and I'll give you two for Seattle," players usually said. But when food was involved they said, "I'll give you my tickets in Portland if you'll let me be one of the first three in line."

Guys ran for the bus, dragging others along. "Let's go! Let's go!"

"Come on — no more interviews."

Faye and her friends — Chris, Rosetta and others — helped Mom cook enough for eighty to feed the twenty of us. It was the best of Christmas, Thanksgiving, Easter and our birthdays rolled into one meal. The coaches, security and some reporters joined us, but the players always elbowed to the front of the line. They wanted to be sure to get the favorites — Mom's barbequed ribs and macaroni and cheese, and Faye's hot rice and collard greens. Earvin was up front and filled his plate, then headed for the table with my dad. "You can drive my Rolls Royce anytime," he told Dad, between bites of Mom's incredible biscuits and cornbread.

"You mean it?" Dad asked.

"The next time you come to L.A.," Earvin said, "you call me."

After the players and coaches made their first pass, reporters and security still found plenty of turkey with the trimmings, fried and barbequed chicken, vegetables, potatoes and every kind of salad. Smart players went back for seconds, then stood around the tables, talking and eating while waiting for the desserts to come out.

Mom's pound cake and carrot cakes were the first to go. Once those were gone, Faye could hardly cut the pies fast enough. Byron just stood there helping himself to Lee's mom's banana pudding.

"What about that haircut?" James would say, then scoop another piece of sweet potato pie into his mouth.

"What kind of car are you getting next?" Mychal would say, then inhale some apple or pecan pie.

"Let's get something for the driver," someone called out. "Mama, can we make the bus driver a plate?"

Only scraps were left of what had been mountains of food.

"Mama, can we have this again the next time?" Coach Riley asked the first year. From then on, Mom was his mama, and every time we had a Portland game, he'd ask, "Is Mama cooking, Junior?"

I never worried again about getting tickets for the whole family to see our games in Portland. I had plenty of tickets to give the nieces and nephews and, I think, a few family pets.

13

SETBACKS IN
THE WAR

I'M NO ANGEL. I'm a trash-talking, chest-bumping, elbow-hitting, head-thumping basketball player. But I'm a Christian. Sometimes people sin against me, and sometimes I sin. I get angry when I should stay cool, listen and wait. I say things I regret. I let my friends down sometimes.

Every day I repent for some dumb thing I've done, but every day

I come closer to not making the same dumb mistakes again.

The devil is a fierce opponent. Sin brings consequences whether the sin is our own or others'. The devil uses sin and its consequences as leverage against us. When he can't destroy us by circumstances from without, he tries to destroy us by guilt from within. We have power over him, but we have to learn how to use it.

PRINCIPLE #43
The devil uses sin and its consequences as leverage against us. When he can't destroy us by circumstances from without, he tries to destroy us by guilt from within.

One summer I was working on a television project with a lot of my friends. We were really excited about it. The production crews I hired had my complete trust. In a meeting with them I gave them my blessings, and then I left for Austin, Texas, and the Champions for Christ conference. They went home to the East Coast.

Texas was my last stop before going home to Portland for a month. I was looking forward to spending the Fourth of July with my family. Ashley, Nicholas and my other nieces and nephews were eager for Uncle Junior to come home. I left Austin pumped up, geared up, on a superspiritual mountaintop high. Greg, Rice Brooks and the rest of us had enjoyed a great time ministering to a small army of professional and amateur athletes there. I flew into L.A., packed a month's worth of clothes and caught a flight home on July 1.

My brother Steve picked me up at the airport in one of the classic autos he collects, the 1967 convertible Lincoln Continental with the suicide doors. He took me to Mom and Dad's in Gresham. *What a great life You've given me, Lord,* I thought as my head hit the pillow that night.

The next morning the phone rang as I sat at the kitchen table with a glass of fruit juice. "Junior," Mom said, "it's for you."

"Hello," I answered softly, still waking up.

"A.C.," said a friend's voice from the East Coast.

"Hi, what's happening?"

"We need to talk with you about something," said another friend.

"You guys are together?" I asked. "Listen — we've got stuff planned here. Can I call you back?"

God showed me the person to give the project to after a few days of prayer. The project ended up tying into my campaign for abstinence that has reached people nationally and even internationally. No wonder the enemy fought so hard against it.

PRINCIPLE #46
Perseverance is a machine gun because it's an attitude of the heart that says, I won't give up. Something can be a permanent defeat or a temporary setback. Let God finish what He starts. Refuse to quit.

Other setbacks in my life have been more serious. In the 1989-90 season the Lakers were hot again. The joke about evangelists is that they blow in, blow up and blow out. The Lakers did the same, only we were more like a wrecking crew. We arrived in a city one day, practiced if it was early enough, went to a shoot-around the next morning, destroyed the home team that night, then left the following day to destroy the next team on our list. Kareem was gone, but the rest of the team was intact, and we had added some good talent, including Vlade.

"I've got the board," I would yell to Earvin. "Just shoot it!"

Earvin would shoot, and if he missed, I would get the rebound against the opponent I had worn down. When the opponents changed their defensive strategy, we just read it and adjusted.

"He's mine," Coop would say, racing past Earvin. Earvin would get the ball to him.

"Face!" Coop would say as he dunked it, short for "in your face."

"You can't make them both," an opponent would taunt when Byron took the free-throw line.

"Well?" Byron would answer, running past the guy after sinking both free shots.

We were hot, winning sixty-three games and ending up at the top of the league. I went after the ball like a kid after chocolate chip cookies, ending the season tops on my team in rebounds with 712 and fourth in scoring with a 12.9 average. A few years earlier I easily beat Dennis Rodman in rebounding, and for the previous two years he narrowly edged me out. This was the year he broke away, and by the following year he led the league. I didn't have the spike upward as he did. I just kept even in rebounding year after year.

"No rebounds, no rings," Coach Riley said more than once during that season. We were headed for another ring.

James Worthy, Earvin Johnson, Coach Riley and I went to the All-Star game in February. I had won the spot Karl Malone expected since he had won the All-Star MVP the year before. I think he's still mad about it. No one could believe I was there, so some friends, Darryl Span and R.P., interviewed the players for a home video they titled "A.C. Who?" They pulled Michael Jordan, Kevin Johnson, my teammates and a lot of other superstars into their show. Each one of them played along, saying, "A.C. who?"

My teammates and I played for fun as much as for pride, which is what you say when you lose. We had a great time together with our families. The weekend ended with Earvin winning the All-Star MVP after scoring twenty-two points against the East.

When we got back from the All-Star break, we rode the wave until we hit the play-offs. Then we were stopped dead in our tracks during the second round by the Phoenix Suns. The Suns beat us by two points on our own court in game 1, and that seemed to give them the confidence to get past us. We had to play on all cylinders, which is the nature of the play-offs. But they were young and energetic — and desperate. We got caught flat-footed and lost.

The team was stunned by the loss. Even though we didn't advance, Earvin was named the league MVP that year for the third time. We heard that Michael Jordan was mad that he didn't win the award. Larry Bird's back was beginning to bother him, so the rivalry between Earvin and Larry was gradually shifting to Earvin and Michael. I thought Earvin deserved the award as much as anyone. He was the complete player, individually great and also team-oriented. I was proud of him and, of course, a little biased.

That summer Coach Riley announced his retirement. He went down in NBA history for winning the highest percentage of regular-season games, at .733, and the most play-off victories, at 102. He even surpassed Red Auerbach, the Celtics' coaching legend. In August, Coop announced his plans to retire from the NBA and play in Italy. I rolled through the upheaval, knowing that part of the original team was still intact with Earvin as our leader.

Mike Dunleavy became the new coach. Vlade Divac was now in his second year. Like Mychal Thompson he had skill as both a forward and center, so we had versatility as well as depth. James Worthy, Byron Scott and I were still the "three amigos" on the team. Two more additions, forward Sam Perkins and guard Terry Teagle, rounded out the team. Rookies Tony Smith from Marquette and Elden Campbell from Clemson came on board and ended up on the ride of their lives. I determined to do my best, believing God had made me a winner and that I'd remain a champion as long as I followed Him.

At training camp in that fall of 1990, Earvin and I got together for breakfast, which we typically tried to do. We played pickup games during the summer, so training camp just signalled the beginning of the more intense play and friendship we were so accustomed to after five years together.

"Man, my dad is still trying to run the whole plant all by himself," Earvin said one morning. "I can't buy him out."

"That sounds just like my dad," I said, and we laughed together. Our dads, with their incredible work ethic and old-world values were our strongest points of pride, which we cloaked with humor.

"My parents won't move," he said, "even though I keep offering to move them. 'No, Junior,' they say. 'This home was fine for us before, and it's fine now.' "

We didn't usually talk basketball, except maybe to laugh at what had happened the day before at practice.

When the season started, we slugged our way through another year of dogfights. In November we were shaky, but by midseason, when we went out of town, opposing teams' fans cheered us. The same thing was happening to the Chicago Bulls and Michael Jordan, who really came into his own that year. We finished the season in fairly good shape, behind Portland and Chicago, then started blowing through the opposition in the play-offs. We beat Houston 3-0 and Golden State 4-1. Then we outlasted the top-ranked Trail Blazers in the Western Conference Finals, winning 4-2. The series was great for me because I had fans in both cities cheering me.

We went to Chicago to play the Bulls in the finals. What a shock to discover it wasn't just the finals! It wasn't just a quest for a championship. It was actually media heaven, the one-on-one fight of Johnson versus Jordan. It was the old, battle-worn veteran who changed the game challenged by the youngster who embodied all that the elder had created. Two huddles of reporters swamped the two players. None of the rest of us existed.

Even though we didn't have home-court advantage because their record was better, we knew we could beat them. It would be tough, but we could do it. They were a young, energetic team with crazy fans, and we respected them. We didn't fall to overconfidence. This was our first year with Coach Dunleavy, who wasn't General Schwarzkopf leading us into war, but he was a good coach. Our first goal was to beat them at home. We had to do that to win the series.

In the first quarter of game 1, Michael Jordan scored fifteen points, but his teammates missed shots, rebounds and passes. They were nervous. That was good. We took it to them, with James and Sam each scoring fourteen points in the first half. James was nursing an injured ankle, but he didn't show it in his play. We led 41-34 in the second quarter; then they led 53-51 at the half. We bounced back, and at the start of the fourth quarter we led 75-68. Jordan came out gunning for us, quickly racking up ten unanswered points and running up the score to 75-78, their favor.

He was almost unstoppable. Every move was different. Every stutter step, block, fake, leap or rebound was like playing a different person, a specialist in that field. We had to do something to stop him. We used an umbrella defense to keep him away from the bucket. Offensively we passed quickly out of the post to open spot-up shooters. Our strategies worked. The fourth quarter was a see-saw fight between battle-weary soldiers. The Bulls led 89-91 with twenty-four seconds to play when Jordan missed a shot. We called a time-out.

When play resumed, Earvin threw the ball in to Sam Perkins, who squared up behind the three-point line and shot a beautiful arc. The ball dropped neatly into the basket and gave us a one-point lead. Jordan brought the ball back to midcourt, but our umbrella defense stopped him, and the ball went out of bounds. Jordan missed again. We rebounded, got fouled and scored a free throw to win 93-91. One goal was reached: We beat them at home. Now for the rest.

Game 2 became a nightmare. They were mad and came out gunning for us. By halftime they led 48-43 on their way to a 107-86 rout over us.

The highlight of the entire series came in the fourth quarter. After I missed a routine shot, Jordan got the ball, drove to the basket and leaped to shoot with his right hand. While airborne, he saw Sam Perkins on his right about to block the shot, so he dumped the ball into his left hand, twisted in the air and scooped the ball into the bucket. It became one of his most famous plays. I've seen that highlight tape a thousand times and still wish I'd made my shot.

Back in the Forum for game 3, the fans surprised us by keeping up their enthusiasm even though the Bulls led 48-47 at the half. The rest of the world thought it was "The Magic and Michael Show," but our fans cheered for the entire Laker team. Vlade scored five times on Jordan and brought us to a 67-54 lead in the second half, but the Bulls roared back. With just over a minute left, Sam scored to bring us within one point. Jordan missed, then Vlade hit an awkward three-pointer that gave us a 92-90 lead.

With only ten seconds in the game, we called a time-out. We had a good opportunity to win. Our whole assignment was to keep Jordan from getting the ball. If he got it, we were supposed to double-team him to make him pass it. Sure enough, Jordan got the rebound. We hustled downcourt, but instead of double-teaming him, we allowed him to get a wide-open shot. He pulled up and hit a seventeen-foot jumper to tie the game. We went into overtime injured and tired. The Bulls won 104-96.

I felt as if we'd totally blown it. We lost our concentration. For the first time we choked. Maybe some guys respected Michael a little bit too much.

"He's not going to make a highlight film off me," some guys said to themselves. "I'm not going to be on his next poster."

It's hard to remember that you can't stop a person by yourself. It takes the whole team. You can't feel that you're going to get embarrassed. You have to take chances and do the best you can. We needed to pull together and stop him together. Instead we fell apart.

In game 4 we led 28-27 at the end of the first quarter, but we went into halftime trailing 52-44. We were headed for a 1-3 deficit. At our team meeting on the day before the game, Coach Dunleavy likened it to falling in a ditch. We left the locker room at halftime ready to get control of the game. We wanted our crowd back, making the chaotic noise that would boost our play. We were pumped up. Earvin had his look that told us he was going to win and we'd better cooperate. We pulled together, then fell behind by fourteen. We geared back up, scoring seven straight points. They came back. We scored five straight points.

It was chess, not basketball. We moved; they matched. We moved; check. They never let up. We lost 97-82, the lowest finals score by a Laker team in forty years. We were honed, conditioned and well prepared for that game, but everything we did, they matched. Checkmate.

James was out for the rest of the series, so I started game 5 for him. Byron Scott was also injured, so Terry Teagle started in his place. With two starters injured, no one thought we had a chance. Elden Campbell and Tony Smith came in, their first year, their first finals, and they were up against the Bulls. We had preschoolers in diapers up against assassins, toddlers playing a virtual reality scoring machine named Air Jordan.

"It was a good try, but you guys aren't going to get it this year" was the feeling we got from Forum staff and management.

But there's not a quitting bone in my body. I felt like David against Goliath. I wasn't having any of that giving-up stuff. No one had ever recovered from a 1-3 deficit, but I refused to let an opponent win a championship on my court. No one comes to my place to celebrate.

"It isn't over yet," I told the team at practice the day before game 6. "Let's just take it one game at a time. We have to step up, play strong and show ourselves to be men."

I was prayed up and pumped up, yet I slept well at night. I got to the Forum early to shoot the next day. There was no way we were going to lose. We came out of the locker room to a cheering, star-studded crowd. I was excited, energetic and scored first. I wanted to get the game rolling from the beginning.

Young Tony Smith hit five of six shots. Earvin's game was on, and he racked up a triple double. Elden Campbell scored twenty-one points total. He and I hit our stride in the third quarter and brought the Lakers to a 91-90 lead. With six minutes to play, the Bulls called time. The Laker fans stood and screamed through the entire time-out. We came off the bench, and our rookie Campbell scored again. The Forum erupted as if we'd just won the series. We felt good, up by three.

The Bulls' Scottie Pippen quickly shot a three-pointer to tie the score at 93. Two more Bull buckets. One more. With three minutes left, they led 99-93. We rushed back with Sam scoring, getting fouled, scoring and getting fouled again. We trailed just 103-101 with a minute left. We were still in it. Jordan drove for the basket and lured us to him, but he dished the ball out, and they scored. They got the ball and scored again. And suddenly it was over. The Bulls won the game 108-101 and the finals 4-1.

I hate losing.

In retrospect Michael Jordan was starting to make his bid to be one of the best. Jordan and Earvin had become friends. I'm sure they enjoyed starting the Jordan-Johnson rivalry, but they never got to play it out. Losing to the Bulls was Earvin's last finals. That makes me wish all the more that we'd won.

Coach Riley came out of retirement in the summer of 1991 when the New York Knicks offered him a 300-percent raise over his Lakers' salary and what he probably saw as an opportunity to win another championship. Earvin and Cookie finally married in a hastily planned wedding in September. After the summer break we came to camp ready to go the distance again. The Lakers hadn't won a championship since 1988, even though we were always considered the team to beat.

Training camp was a little easier under Coach Dunleavy, but I prepared myself as if Coach Riley were there shouting at us. We fine-tuned our machines, preparing mentally and physically for the long haul. We were ready to lick some opponents when we left for Utah to play a preseason game on October 25.

On the road it was business as usual, with people flocking to Earvin like an assembly line. He was shaking hands, signing autographs and posing for pictures.

"OK," we said, "this is it. You gotta go."

We kicked him out of every place we went. He moved to another area with his entourage, meaning everyone within five miles.

The rest of us went about our usual stuff, laughing at rookies and having fun. At the hotel a man walked through the lobby with three suitcases while trying to eat an ice cream.

"Come on — put something down," we yelled to him. "Do yourself a favor." He laughed and tried to wave.

The next day Earvin didn't show up for practice because the team doctor called him back home. It wasn't unusual for him to miss practices, but he usually came at least to watch. Since this was his twelfth season of professional ball, having the doctors take extra precautions didn't surprise us, either. Kareem had always amazed us with his warm-up routines. I understood the need to take care of stiff joints and less-than-limber muscles as the years progressed. I don't know if other teammates asked about Earvin, but I was concentrating on my game and didn't think about him.

We flew back to L.A. and played some more exhibition games, then started the regular season on November 1 in Houston. Earvin had the flu and couldn't join us, so we faced the slugfest without him. James scored thirty-seven points, yet they edged us out, winning by just five. At our home opener against the notoriously bad L.A. Clippers on November 5, they beat us by five, too. None of us was on his game. I began to wonder what was happening. Without our leader, our team was falling apart. I hoped Buck would be strong enough to play soon.

On November 7 we practiced at Loyola at 9:30 as usual. Again Buck wasn't there. When we finished about three hours later, one of the coaches came in and said, "Let's go over to the Forum locker room for a meeting — now."

It was an unusual request, but nothing to raise suspicion. Later I found out that of the whole Laker team, only Sam Perkins and I didn't have a clue about what was going on. Others had been hearing rumors on news broadcasts. I don't read the sports pages, and I hadn't turned on a car radio or watched the news that week, so I was completely in the dark.

We went to the locker room and sat in our stalls. Instead of the usual joking and horseplay, people were basically quiet, almost somber.

"What's going on?" I asked Byron.

He shook his head and sat there quietly. No one was crying, no one appeared upset, so I didn't think anything too bad had happened. We sat there for almost a half hour before Coach Dunleavy walked in.

"Earvin is retiring," he told us.

I was shocked. Buck? Why? But before I could begin to mull it over, he answered my questions.

"Earvin has the HIV virus that causes AIDS."

This was the first time I had heard those words about anyone, anytime, anywhere. The players sat there, stunned. I would have thought it was a joke, but no one laughed. I looked around the locker room. Players dropped their heads, then covered their eyes with their hands. I didn't believe the words, but I believed the players' reactions. This is real, I thought. If I hadn't been sitting, I would have fallen over. My stomach felt hollow, like the center of my body had just been cut out.

"Buck will be here in a few minutes after he talks to management," Coach said. Then he stepped into his office.

No, Lord, no. I started crying. Everyone did. No one hugged. No one talked. No one looked at each other. We were each an island, suffering alone in our pain. I got up and began pacing the floor, crying and praying silently.

God, please help me. Help my friend. Where is he? Oh, Lord, I need to see him. I need to talk to him. I need to hug him. I need to pray for him. He needs me, Lord. Please, God, help him.

The locker-room door opened while I was standing next to it. Lon Rosen, Earvin's manager and one of his best friends, swung the door wide. Buck walked in. We caught each other's eyes immediately. He was wearing his look. I'm going to get the job done, his eyes said. I hugged him. He hugged me back as though he needed it. We stood there clenching each other tightly for a minute.

He wasn't crying, wasn't broken, wasn't defeated. But he didn't know what he would be walking into, either. It was a roomful of puddles, grown men in tears. We were like crestfallen boys whose older brother was going off to war and certain death. Each player took turns hugging him, one by one, stifling sobs on his shoulder. His tough defensive posture crumbled, and he cried along with us. It was the first time he had cried since learning the news. After everyone hugged him, he finally collected himself and told us to sit down.

"This is what's happened," he said. Then he explained how he found out about the virus through a routine insurance blood test.

"It's probably best that I don't play the rest of the season with you guys. I have to deal with my health situation now. I'm going to fight it. I'm going to take care of myself. I'll be strong and overcome it, and then I'll be back. I need you guys to be strong with me. At the same time, you need to go out and kick some backside on the courts."

He walked out of the locker room and went upstairs for the press conference. We followed him, unwilling to leave his side. He finally drove home with Cookie. We were left behind with a cloud over us. We just looked at each other, still stunned. Slowly we got our things together. I hugged Byron and got ready to leave. I saw James leaving and hugged him. I went out to the parking lot and crawled into my car.

For hours I drove aimlessly around L.A., crying and praying. I went to our church staff house on the USC campus and sat out front in my car, trying to get some understanding. I couldn't grasp what had happened. The old replay machine was wearing itself out. I kept hearing those words: "Earvin has the HIV virus that causes AIDS." I kept seeing Buck's eyes with the fight and determination in them, but I knew all the fight of thousands of other people hadn't saved them from the consequences of that disease.

I couldn't pray enough. It was an endless day, an endless prayer, an endless searching for what was going on, why God would allow such a thing. For five years I'd spent almost every day with Buck. For five years I had prayed every day for God to work in Buck's life. Now this.

I needed to call my parents and let them know. Probably everyone had seen the press conference, but I called anyway. My parents tried to console me, but they were also in shock. I couldn't eat, couldn't think of anything I wanted to do. I just cried and prayed and wandered around alone.

That night I drove home and finally dropped into a fitful sleep. The next morning I woke up for my devotions and started praying immediately for Buck. The consequences of the way he had lived on the road seemed too harsh, too cruel, yet they were the consequences. I couldn't change that. Now that my mind was more clear, I thought about how I should pray. I pulled out God's love, the most powerful spiritual weapon of all. Love can demolish, transform or resurrect. God's love covers sin completely, obliterating it. Love is as strong as God because God is love. The only thing I could do in this situation was to love my friend, to blanket him with love.

PRINCIPLE #47
Love is bigger than anything else on earth.
God's love covers sin. God says He is love.
When nothing else is possible, God's love prevails.

I got together with Earvin as soon as I could. He had been on Arsenio Hall's show saying that condoms could have saved him from catching the disease. I knew through my abstinence work that this wasn't true. Abstinence is the only 100-percent sure way to keep from catching diseases, including AIDS.

I talked with Earvin just to love him, but I ended up explaining to him the harm his message could bring. Young people could end up in the same situation as he had if they counted on condoms to save them. In his next interview he modified his message. He started telling people that they should not have extramarital sex, but if they did, to use a condom. It isn't the exact message I give, but it was an improvement.

Sin and its consequences don't care about someone's image, position or talent. On the night of Earvin's announcement, Coach Riley's Knicks were playing the Orlando Magic. He brought the teams together for a moment of prayer, then recited the Lord's prayer. It was a nice gesture, and I appreciated his sentiment. Most NBA players got blood tests after hearing the news, but there wasn't a big movement to change their behavior.

The real tragedy in Earvin's announcement is that something like this happens, yet people don't learn the lesson. A great man is down. But they continue in the same behavior. That hurts me as much as anything.

I cannot imagine the horror of what Earvin is living through. It's unfathomable to me. But I don't concentrate on the things that could have been. I just love him. I think about how I can support him. When nothing else is possible, God's love prevails.

As close as I was to Earvin, there was an even worse setback in my life when my brother Steve's life was almost snuffed out in an instant. Only God could save him. It became a moment of truth for me, and I learned how to use another great weapon — intercession.

Steve was the stallion that no one could break, the wild one in the family. He was the life of our home as well as every party, the friendly one who brought others into our tight circle of friends. He could probably run for mayor of Portland and win on his first try.

On August 1, 1987, a Friday night, Steve came with some of my cousins and friends to cheer me on at one of my Portland summer league games. The next day I was to check in for the 1987 Laker summer league in Southern California. Two days later would be my six-year anniversary of becoming born again. God was building my level of faith, but this was the ultimate test.

Steve had become my biggest supporter. Always looking for a reason to celebrate, he was the natural to become my number-one fan. That night in Portland he screamed himself hoarse. The game finished at about 9:00.

"Junior!" he called to me after the game.

People were milling around, including friends who were trying to see me. I looked up.

"We're leaving, but we'll see you later," he said.

"OK," I hollered back to him over the din. "Remember — I leave tomorrow morning, so let's go out for pizza tonight."

"All right," he yelled back. "I'll meet you at home at about 10:30."

I said a slow good-bye to my friends and went to the showers, then said good-bye to my teammates. I looked at the dashboard clock as I was driving home. It was 10:00. I drove through the neighborhood in pitch darkness, easily navigating the familiar turns. As I zigzagged through the grid of city blocks, I passed a street that I often drove down and saw the lights of emergency vehicles at the bottom of the hill. I was getting home early, and since I was just five blocks away, my curiosity got the better of me.

I parked in front of a neighbor's house and walked down the block toward the accident. From the corner I saw my parents' car in a driveway with the doors open like someone had jumped out in a hurry.

That worried me, so I quickened my pace. I could see a crowd of about fifty people at the bottom of the hill, but I still couldn't see the vehicles involved. Over the heads of the crowd, I finally spotted Faye and Mom standing near an ambulance, arms around each other, looking worried. I passed some people to try to get to them, but no one attempted to say anything to me. Suddenly I heard an unfamiliar voice.

"There goes his brother," the voice said.

I heard the words and ran, pushing people aside, sprinting the last few yards toward that ambulance. Dad came into view on the opposite side, so I headed his way. Emergency workers were scattered around inside the wad of people, working feverishly. Paramedics who had been bent over now stood and started sliding a stretcher into the back of the ambulance. That's when I saw Steve. It wasn't really him, though. It was a grotesque, bloody, swollen mask that resembled Steve's face on a mangled body dressed with bandages, tubes and wires, belted to a cot.

No, Lord! I thought.

Dad and I didn't say a word. He looked at me and shook his head in disbelief. I peered through the ambulance window and saw that it really was my brother on that stretcher. Through the window on the other side I could see that Faye was holding Mom up.

I crossed my hands behind my head to try to alleviate the sudden throbbing in my head, then walked over to the car where medical personnel were still trying to extricate my cousin from the wreckage. He and Steve had hit a tree, which demolished the car and pinned my cousin behind the steering wheel.

I walked back to the ambulance, where workers were fastening Steve in for the ride to the hospital. I couldn't even get to him. A feeling of utter helplessness shuddered through me. I put my palms on the window, spread my hands out and began to pray out loud. Within a minute the ambulance sped off.

Dad took the other side of Mom and helped her and Faye toward the car. Dad, Mom, Faye, Lee and the rest of the family followed the ambulance.

I walked back to the rescuers' efforts to get my cousin out of the car, praying while they worked. A police officer approached me. "Are these your relatives?" he asked.

"Yes, that was my brother, and this is my cousin," I answered.

"We need some information," he said. "It would help if you could stay around for a while."

"What happened?"

"Your brother went through the windshield, flew about thirty feet, landed on his head and skidded."

"And my cousin?"

"It looks like he'll be OK once we get him out."

I watched them cut the car to take my cousin out. The second ambulance sped off. The crowd thinned out as I talked to the police officers, and then they were gone.

I sat on the cold, hard curb, my hands crossed behind my head, my head cradled in my elbows. I stared at the ground, not knowing if I'd ever see my brother again, and I prayed weakly, faintly at first. My prayers became deep groans and sobs, like my whole inner man was crying out to God. I didn't know how or what to pray, so I released myself to the Holy Spirit to pray through me. I was praying in intercession, where I stood in the gap between life and death.

After about forty-five minutes I got up, walked back to my car and drove to the hospital. All the way there I prayed loud, fervently and hard, but I kept hearing horrible thoughts, terrible voices that tried to torment me.

"Why pray? He's already dead."

"That's the last time you'll see him alive."

"He's crippled."

"They're cutting him up right now."

I kept praying regardless of the thoughts. I crossed the parking lot and entered the hospital. Friends had heard about the accident already and were gathered there. They tried to speak to me as I walked through the waiting room and into the elevator, but I didn't hear anyone. I was focused on praying silently. I reached the door to the wing where they had Steve. It dawned on me that the voices I was hearing were the same ones I'd heard on the day I was saved. The devil and his evil demon spirits were trying to stop me from intervening in the death they planned for my brother. They wanted to strip him away from me, to rob me of seeing him come to know Christ, to stop Steve from spending eternity with God.

I was worn out from the intensity. This was a much greater workout spiritually than the game that night had been physically. This was a fight for life. All I need, I thought, is a good report of any kind. I just need to know that God is working — anything to boost my faith.

I swung open the door and saw my family. They were huddled in twos and threes with Pastor Irving and my cousin's family. The atmosphere was heavy with gloom and despondency. I knew Steve wasn't dead. The devil is a liar. I could have asked if he was alive, but I didn't.

"How is he?" I asked instead.

"They're working on him right now," Pastor Irving said. "He's in surgery, and we're waiting for the doctor."

"That's all we know?"

"That's all," he answered.

It wasn't much, but for me it was a victory signal. I knew my enemy now. I had that nose for him and knew what he was up to. If I could get to my arsenal, I could stop him. Prayer can affect any situation. Satan had my brother standing at the gates of hell. But the Bible says that even the gates of hell can't prevail against God's children — and that includes me.

I looked in the faces of my family, drawn with worry and fear. They were praying, but fear was attacking their faith. I felt compassion for them and knew I was on my own. I turned around and left as quietly as I could. It was a chilly summer night in the Northwest, but I had no senses, no feelings in my body. I set off on foot, praying hard. As death and fear tried to overtake me, faith and hope welled up inside. I rebuked the devil for trying to kill Steve. I rebuked death. I rebuked permanent injury, disability and everything that came to mind that could result from such a serious accident. I shouted victory over death. I quoted Scripture verses of victory with Steve's name inserted into them.

I walked around the hospital and the next block, stepping off curbs without seeing them, walking past friends who were arriving without acknowledging them. Then I walked that circuit again. I didn't want anyone to interrupt me, talk to me or even pray with me. I was fighting a war.

Finally I felt as though I had broken through. The devil's forces were on the run. An invisible barrier that I could only sense had collapsed. I felt a tug in my spirit to get back to the hospital.

"Still waiting for the doctor," Pastor Irving said as I walked into the ward.

I stood against a wall. Again I was moved by seeing my family, especially my parents, with such helpless looks on their faces.

In minutes the doctor walked in. "He's going to make it," he said.

I slugged my palm with my fist. Yes!

The doctor went on to explain the kind of surgery they had done to his skull. "We don't know how permanent the injury may be," he said, "but the good thing is, he's going to be OK."

A sense of relief flooded the room. For me a sense of confirmation settled into my spirit. I have a right to pray, I thought. I have a right to speak the Word of God and see it accomplished. This is my family, and Your will, Father, can be done. I don't have to settle for defeat.

Prayer wasn't something I was making up. It wasn't a useless psychological trick to help cope with life. It was powerful. Intercession worked! I know that God won't always miraculously save a person in response to prayer. But I also know that sometimes He will and that sometimes His Spirit will give us the inner assurance I felt that night.

PRINCIPLE #48
**Intercession works. You have a right to intercede.
You have a right to speak the Word of God. Life
and death obey the will of Christ.**

I have never had such a feeling of helplessness as I did that night, knowing that all I could do was pray. Once I prayed, however, I had never had such a feeling of power. The final result would be left in God's hands, but I just knew God would intervene in this case.

When my faith was tested, everything I'd ever learned or read in the Word came true. We can say we believe a lot of things, but until we're put to the test, we don't know what we really believe.

I still had my commitment to the summer league. I called Jerry West the day after the accident and explained the situation.

"That's all right, son," he said. "Do what you have to do. I understand, and I'm sorry for what happened. Just come down when you can."

When I finally got to the summer league a few days later, I averaged thirty points and seventeen rebounds — incredible stats, my best ever. It was crazy, because my thoughts were on home the whole time. I was voted the MVP. All that happened without my mind on the game but with the power of prayer coursing through me daily.

I went home as often as I could. My cousin regained his health fairly quickly after a severe neck injury. Steve's progress was slower. First I pushed him around in a wheelchair, and then I helped him take walks and finally jogs. I helped him learn his coordination again by dribbling a basketball around the block using his left hand, his weak hand. I cheered each new step in Steve's progress. I had new respect for life.

People get caught up wondering things like, Was it the will of God or the prayers of saints that caused this or caused it to end the way it did? I'll take both. The prayers of God's people, prayed after God's will, move the arm of God to act on our behalf.

Just a few months before winning the battle for Steve's life, I had fought another battle. It was like David who had to kill the small enemies to prepare him for the big ones. I fought this battle outside my immediate family and won — but in a different way.

Mr. Johnson, a dear friend who lived across the street in Portland for ten years, contracted lung cancer and went into a coma. I went to the hospital to see him as often as I could, praying not just for his health, but also for his salvation. He rallied from the coma and went home, and while he was home, he got saved. His body was never healed completely, but his spirit was. Six months later he died. But Mr. Johnson is in heaven today because God answered prayer.

Now I wait for Steve to make the same commitment to God. It's a person's whole life that needs healing, not just a body. As long as they're breathing, God can keep working.

The Lakers won the 1988 championship ten months after Steve's accident. He and Dave Soto rode in the parade with me. They may as well have kicked me off the float, because they hogged the whole show, screaming and squirting the crowds with champagne, 7 Up and Coke.

"Yeah, we're the champs," Dave shouted.

"We did it. Did you see my shot?" Steve yelled. People squinted, trying to recognize him.

I gave my first championship ring to Mom and Dad. When we got our rings in 1988, I gave mine to Steve.

14

BEYOND VICTORY

LOSING TO THE Bulls in the 1991 finals was tough. Once again that year, I had the faith to win, the confidence and the belief that we would win. When we didn't, I had to accept it. Sometimes doing your best is all the satisfaction you'll receive. God doesn't want us striving to be better than others. He just wants us to become all He created us to be.

When the series was over, I sought out my family and friends. My brother Lee and sister Faye were sad, too, and not just because they were next in line to get championship rings from me. Once I got some of their great comfort and solace, I was ready to get a little crazy. Some people get drunk when they want to cut loose. I've proved that I can embarrass myself just as well without a drop of alcohol. This time I called Pastor Phil.

"I don't care what anyone says," I said. "Tonight it's over. This is it."

"What's it, Ace?" he asked.

"I'm taking all of us to watch wrestling at the Forum."

"Are you kidding? Let's go!"

Pastor Phil is a wrestling fanatic. He's slightly built, about 5'4". Physically he's completely opposite to any wrestler you would ever see, but he loves the sport. The only thing that could be better for him as a pastor was if God had made me a wrestler instead of a basketball player. I called the Forum ticket office and got fifteen tickets. Ringside. This was going to be fun.

When I'm out and about, people can see that I'm a basketball player, but they don't usually talk to me or make a big deal over me. Compared to some of my friends, I'm able to stay pretty low key. That night, though, I didn't care if I attracted attention. I just wanted to have fun. I put on a black hooded sweater and a pair of dark sunglasses with a row of blinking red lights across the top. I checked myself in the mirror. Yes!

I had put up with fans' harassment for six years. This was my night to dish it out. Some basketball fans become famous just for being fans. Leon the barber in Detroit was one of the most vulgar, obnoxious fans in the league. All the players knew him. We always knew what to expect in Washington, too, where loud-mouth Robert, a guy with an irritating voice, always took on anyone from the Atlantic Coast Conference. On our team it was James Worthy, a University of North Carolina alumnus.

"We used to spank you and send you home to your mommies," he yelled to James. They went up and down the court on it.

"It's the Laker show tonight!" a fan we called Dr. Zeke always screamed in the Forum, with a voice that God must have intended for open-air preaching. "The Lakers are in the house!" he yelled. Then he went down the roster, telling us each what to do. When he followed us on the road, he really warmed up the opponent's house.

Tom, Phil, Dave, Greg Brennes, Sweet Lou, Super Jack, J.P., Jim Burton, Sergeant Stephan, Gino and some others headed for the Forum. We were pumped even before the program began.

"Bring on the wrestlers," I shouted.

I jostled Tom next to me, and he pushed back like we were fighting. We became the ringside attraction.

"Down in front," a fan yelled playfully.

"Quiet in back," I yelled back.

Our row set the tone for the whole arena. Little kids were tugging at their fathers' sleeves saying, "Isn't that...?"

The wrestlers came out. My friends chose bad guys and good guys, and we split the cheering. I cheered the bad guy. When the good guy came out, I booed him. "You're gonna lose," I yelled. "You'd better bring your little sister out here to help you."

A three-hundred-pound blond guy named Oz came out midway through the program. He was definitely the bad guy. He walked around the ring, looking menacing. When he came close, I could see we were the same height, but he was about a thousand times bigger. He had muscles in places where I never knew they could grow, like popping out his ears. I decided to root for the good guy this time, against him.

"You're gonna lose, man," I shouted as he walked by.

"Yeah, right," he said. That's about what I would have said to a fan as obnoxious as I was.

The match started while I kept up the verbal barrage. Little kids screamed out, "You're gonna lose," then looked at me to see if I noticed. I gave them the thumbs up, then started hollering again.

Oz won. Then he walked over to us and leaned over the ropes. "Now what are you going to say?" he demanded.

I booed him.

"Just shut up!" he said, snarling.

He strolled around the ring slowly with the fans cheering wildly. We kept shouting as he deliberately made his way back to us. He looked right at me, and the place began to quiet down.

"Get him, Ace," Phil said, laughing. I was beginning to wonder if it was funny or not. Is this a rumble? I wondered. Doesn't this guy want to play anymore?

"I told you you'd lose," I yelled. "What happened?"

The crowd hushed, waiting to see some action they hadn't paid for.

"Yeah, well, what happened to you against Chicago?" he bellowed.

The place went wild, laughing, cheering him. He strolled up the ramp laughing. My friends, who had been in my corner, suddenly turned on me, punching me, laughing at me.

"Yeah, what happened to you, Ace?"

"He got you, Ace. He got you good."

"We're with him now."

The next guy out was named Elegante. He was about 7'7" and 350 pounds. We all looked at each other.

"You might lose," we called out weakly. We didn't want to mess with this guy.

An usher handed me a note. Oz had written that he hoped he hadn't offended me. He invited us to the locker room at intermission. We laughed and whooped it up, the fifteen of us, in the locker room. For all the abuse that wrestlers take, they were nice guys. When I was introduced to Elegante, I had to crane my neck back to look up at him. So this is what people feel like when they meet me, I thought. Phil was all eyes. This was his night.

The muffled sound of the announcer filtered into the locker room. "Ladies and gentlemen, take your seats. The wrestlers are ready to come back out."

The other guys ran back to their seats. Phil and I lingered just a little longer. When we left, we paused at the top of the ramp leading down to the ring. People were looking up, waiting for the wrestlers. Phil looked up at me and nudged me. "Champ!" It was the closest he'd ever come to being a professional athlete.

"Let's do it," I said.

We walked down the ramp stabbing at the air, punching our fists high, yelling to the fans. The crowd went along with the gag. "Yeah, yeah," they cheered, raising their fists.

Security tried to usher us to our seats, but since we were ringside, we went the whole distance to the bottom. We circled the ring, taking the long way to our seats. People cheered us all the way. It was one of Phil's greatest moments.

After a great summer of ministry, family and friends, I returned to a team I barely knew. The fabric of the Lakers was unraveling. First Kareem retired, then Coop and Riley left, and then came

Earvin's announcement. We stumbled through the 1991-92 season like wounded men groping in the dark. Not only did we suffer from the drain of talent, but we also suffered from cracks in our foundation. Some of the guys were so spoiled by playing in the "big time" that they stopped playing to their potential and concerning themselves with the game. They became like the actors who watched us, playing to the crowd, playing their role, but not playing the game in reality.

The only bright spot was our trip to Chicago in December. We had a lot of hurt feelings. They were talking trash about us, saying we were nothing without Magic, so we had a lot of reasons to want to kick their backsides. The game was endless trash talking. The lead went back and forth. In the end we avenged our loss in the Finals by beating them on their own court, without Earvin. I love to win.

Earvin retired in February, a week after he played in his last All-Star game. His ceremony was a good excuse for a Laker reunion, for being together again. After retiring, Earvin often came to shoot with us before games, to be one of the guys again. At games we'd see him and Coop in the stands together. They were the best fans we could have, empathizing and encouraging us. I missed them. I missed Mama Johnson along with Coach Riley's asking me, "Is Mama cooking?" I missed Cookie at our parties and Coop's sweaty hands. And I missed watching Cap in airports, wearing his old jeans, eating nachos and hot dogs at 7:00 in the morning. I had been a part of history, witnessing the end of an era.

We made it to the play-offs, but we lost in the first round in a rematch with the Portland Trail Blazers. For them it was a grudge match, and we didn't have the spirit or concentration to topple them. Michael Jordan took his Bulls to their second straight Finals, powering past the Miami Heat, then defeating the Knicks team that Coach Riley had built. Chicago met Portland in the Finals, where the Bulls repeated their world championship, matching our feat of the eighties. My numbers at the end of the year were the same as usual, leading the team in rebounds with 762 and fifth in scoring with a 13.6 average. But numbers don't win championships. No one's individual effort could get us over the top.

The 1992-93 season didn't look to be any better. Earvin tried to come back for five weeks at the start of the season. I was glad to be playing with him again, but many players were apprehensive about his health. I had guarded him during pick-up games in the summer, so I didn't worry about it. I knew Earvin wouldn't put anyone at risk. He was too big of a person to take chances with another individual's health. But when he cut his arm in a game and it wouldn't stop bleeding, he felt the pressure and made the decision to retire again, this time for good.

By December we really weren't playing up to our potential. We had hungry young players and talented, wise veterans. We should at least have been competitive. But we were careless and lost the games we should have won. I felt like a stranger on the team. I found myself reflecting to when we played so well together with tremendous continuity. No matter which five were on the court, we knew what we would do, how we would get the job done. We knew all the combinations, and they all equalled victory.

I appreciated those days more than ever now that we battled for every win. I respected teams enough not to feel humiliated just because they beat us. But at the same time I had a reality check. Where once the Lakers walked on the court and the opponents would look at us with awe and fear, now that was gone. Although they had never rolled over and let us win, they used to have a tremendous amount of respect.

Rumors flew. People talked about my going back home to Portland. I didn't think about that. I had enough in my face every day to occupy my mind.

Around New Year's, when people generally reflect on their lives, I prayed in earnest. I didn't want a resolution. I wanted a solution. Blessings naturally follow the righteous, so how could my team be condemned? In my devotions I read Psalms 63 and 58 repeatedly about God's avenging the righteous man after he goes through a tough time. I wanted to be stable and unshakable. I fought off the oppression that was trying to settle down on me. When I'm down, and my prayers aren't answered quickly, I hook myself up to the rope of the Holy Spirit and hang on. As my team sank, I clung to the Lord.

After a week of almost constant prayer, fasting and study, the Word released my spirit. I checked out with my covenant brothers what I thought I heard from God. They agreed that my team wasn't under God's blessing, although we were under His grace. Some of my teammates were frustrating the grace by not acknowledging Him. We weren't perfect when we won the championships, but at least we respected God, willingly prayed for His guidance and acknowledged that He was the One who gave us the talent and strength.

Once I prayed it through, I stopped banging my head against the wall. I just played my best, but without the anxiety of unmet expectations. We barely made it to the play-offs, but we still almost beat Phoenix. We won the first two games on their court, then lost the next three. Our season was over.

Everyone was saying "three-peat" about the Bulls as they did about the Lakers in 1989. This time a team was able to pull it off. Chicago met Phoenix in the Finals and won. In game 3 they went into triple overtime, a first for the Finals in almost twenty years. My friend Kevin Johnson made the record books for most minutes played in a Finals game — sixty-two backbreaking, heart-racing, hard-fought minutes that ended in defeat.

A season of life had passed. I felt peace. I ended the season with about my usual numbers, but again, no ring.

I always believed I was in L.A. to stay. I had purposely dug deep roots in the community and felt tremendous loyalty to the fans, my team and the area's young people. Friends like Rocky, Kevin, Daren, Bob and Gary were helping me reach my goals through the A.C. Green Foundation for Youth, and it seemed that God turned everything we attempted into a slam-dunk success. But during the summer I started feeling unsettled. God seemed to be urging me to move on. My second four-year contract had expired, so other teams were contacting me. The Phoenix Suns were a natural enemy of the Lakers by then. Rumors were that they were going to trade Richard Dumas and another player to Detroit in exchange for rebounder Dennis Rodman. When Dumas had personal problems, the rumors stopped. Suddenly the Suns were looking at me.

At one time, players would come to the Lakers for less money than other teams offered, just to become part of "Showtime." Now the Lakers offered me more money than other teams offered, a multimillion-dollar contract for five years, but I didn't feel right about staying. I didn't want to play a whole season and not go for the title. I love pursuing championships. I had been to the play-offs eight years and to the finals four times and had won twice. I expected to win, so the competitive spirit of the Suns appealed to me. They were hungry.

"We want a championship," team president Jerry Colangelo told me. "We want it now."

Daily decisions determine your destiny. One poor decision can ruin a lifetime of effort. I've blown some big decisions. This was one I couldn't mess up.

I once could have accepted an endorsement opportunity to earn twice the average person's annual salary. But because I hesitated I ended up losing 90 percent of what I could have had. I had felt that moving slowly was the right thing to do even if I risked the contract. But when I lost the contract, it tasted like putting two spoonfuls of castor oil in my mouth and holding it there. The opportunity slipped through my hands. I looked in the mirror every morning for a few days and said, "You big dummy!" Then I got out that weapon of perseverance, dusted myself off from the loss and kept going.

It's always safe to follow godly principles in making a decision. Then you won't worry about the outcome. Base your decision on a pure heart and truth — the facts, not the potential. Seek out truth, or else your heart will justify your desires and your mind will rationalize following them.

PRINCIPLE #49
Follow godly principles in making a decision. Then you won't worry about the outcome. Base your decision on a pure heart and truth — the facts, not the potential.

I almost always take the same steps in decision making. First I pray privately. Then I look for professional advice. Then I look for godly counsel, that "multitude of counselors" the Bible says will establish plans. I watch for the red lights when I'm not sure of the green lights. That helps me discern what's from the Holy Spirit and what's a distraction. Then I ask myself, Is this a decision I can live with? When I have peace, I know I'm all right.

I talked with James and Vlade about my contract. I contacted Byron, who had already left to join the Indiana Pacers. The players understood my mixed feelings. I didn't get any red lights from them. Danny Ainge became the chief recruiter for the Suns, talking to me about the club. People say he complains a lot, but he's a fierce competitor, and I knew I'd enjoy playing with him. He's got a warrior mentality and wants to get the job done, whatever it takes. He was straight with me. Danny told me about Portland, too, because he had played for them, and they had also contacted me. It was a good opportunity to go home, and he didn't try to talk me out of it. The Knicks contacted me, too. Playing again for Coach Riley had appeal.

PRINCIPLE #50

Steps for decision making:
- **Pray privately.**
- **Look for professional advice.**
- **Look for godly counsel.**
- **Watch for the red lights when you're not sure of the green lights.**
- **Ask yourself, Is this a decision I can live with?**
- **You'll know it's right when you have peace.**

The idea of leaving L.A. became more painful as the decision grew nearer. Jerry West dealt with me directly as always. He had trained me and helped mold me. I wouldn't be leaving a team. I'd be leaving friends. L.A. wanted me. Other teams wanted me. But Phoenix needed me, and in the end that outweighed the other considerations. I signed with the Phoenix Suns on September 28, 1993.

As I walked across the parking lot to their office, my agent questioned me. "Are you sure you want to do this?" he asked.

"I hope I know what I'm doing," I answered.

I had crossed the line into the enemy's camp, but the L.A. community was kind to me. One reporter said that I never brought disrespect to the team, never mis-spoke, was never lazy. Coach Randy Pfund called me "the heart and soul of the Lakers."

Charles Barkley and I were now on the same team. The press joked that we were as different as AC and DC. I sometimes agree with Charles professionally, politically and personally, but in general we don't see eye-to-eye.

"I am not a role model," he said in the television commercials that helped boost his popularity.

While I understand what he means — that the parents, teachers, coaches and neighbors who are with the kids every day are the real role models — still I can't agree with his statement. Leaders have followers, or else they're not leaders. When you make it to the front of the pack, you are a leader and therefore a role model to your followers.

Everyone has influence, and everyone is responsible for how he uses it. Those of us who have more influence just have more responsibility. God has given me an honor to play professional basketball, but with that honor comes a duty to myself, to God and to others.

"Maturity doesn't come with age, but with the acceptance of responsibility," my friend Ed Cole says. People who won't accept responsibility for their influence stay immature.

PRINCIPLE #51
Everyone has influence, and everyone is responsible for how he uses it. If you're a champion, you are a role model. With that honor comes responsibility to self, to God and to others.

We are responsible first to God.

The apostle Paul said, "Follow me as I follow Christ." Most of us don't want to say the same thing because we're afraid we'll mess up. Like a basketball player guarding Michael Jordan, we don't want to put ourselves in a position where people will see us at our worst. It's scary to invite attention to ourselves, to think all eyes are checking us out. We can worry about hiding something, or we can be honored that someone looks at us for more than a split second. We can adopt a "do your own thing" attitude to avoid responsibility, or we can learn to say as Paul said, "Come hang out with me if you want to know what Jesus is like."

I make my share of mistakes, but I'm not afraid to let others see how I live my life. I can influence people more by admitting and overcoming mistakes than by trying to appear perfect, superhuman, an untouchable role model. I'm just a guy. I accept my limitations, but I still hold high standards. I try to measure up to the perfection of Christ. There's nothing wrong with missing that mark sometimes, but there's everything wrong with not even trying.

We're also responsible to ourselves.

When God brings us to the top, it challenges our insecurities and fears. We have to get hold of ourselves and move to the front of the battle line. It's a great feeling to lead troops into battle, letting them follow every move, every decision. It's like getting your hands on the steering wheel of a car. Jerk the wheel, and the passengers in back fall over. Make good decisions, and everyone rides smoothly.

God expects us to step up to the line and reproduce in others what we have learned. When Jesus and His disciples were walking one day, Jesus cursed a tree that didn't bear fruit. He didn't curse it because He was hungry or mad. He cursed it because it was a fruit tree, and fruit trees should bear fruit. It didn't do what it was supposed to do. God expects your life to influence others who become like fruit to you, who are influenced by how you live.

When Jesus prayed for His disciples, He didn't pray that the Father would take them out of the world. Otherwise, the best thing that could happen to us when we give our lives to Christ would be to die right then — you're saved; you're dead; it's over.

Instead Jesus prayed that we'd have the courage, strength and power we need to live this life. He empowers us to fulfill our purpose and bring others along with us.

We're also responsible to ourselves not to let our successes change us. Accolades will eventually come our way if we're living the life of a champion. Victories, accolades and respect confirm what we're doing. If we believe God and honor Him, honor is going to come our way, whether from a small crowd or large. Recognition doesn't make us any better or worse than we already are. It only confirms our beliefs.

We're responsible to others, too.

Sometimes you may be in a position to help someone, perhaps someone you don't know. You can do something good, something positive. You can be the person who puts a hand on a young man's shoulder and says, "Keep trying. You have potential."

In 1989 I formed the A.C. Green Foundation for Youth to help build hope, confidence and self-esteem in young people. That idea of a river flowing through me spawned the concept for the foundation. There are things I can do and get that the average person can't, especially a needy young person. I want to become the one who reaches out and helps others to reach out, such as corporations and small businesses.

The foundation staff and the army of volunteers who help me want to see young people have more ambition and opportunities than to hang around the park after school. I love to see young minds challenged. I want to see young people mature into people of value. Jesus has done so much for me. I want to show Him my appreciation and love for Him through spending time with Him and doing what He asks me to do.

I invest as much time as I can in kids. In 1985 I went back to Portland to start a summer basketball camp with Coach Gray. After the first year his other camp schedule interfered, so Joel Schuldheisz, the head coach at Concordia College, stepped in. For almost a decade Joel and I have trained young people in fundamental basketball skills. But, more important, we've tried to increase their skills for living.

Kids come to camp with T-shirts that say things like "He who dies with the most toys win." They leave with a little enlightenment that life isn't that simple or material. They learn about attitude by having turns in the "Bad Attitude" chair if they mess up. I teach them health and diet. I instill in them the desire not to do anything halfway. They need to start young to do the right things, to be honest, not cheat, do their chores and not fight. My whole family comes out to run our summer camps, along with my old neighborhood friends.

In Los Angeles my camps include job mentoring in the afternoons, where we take them on field trips to learn how the world works outside their small view of life. It's a crazy week with those kids, but we get as many as we can straightened out as much as we can. We consider it a success if only one or two don't make it through the program.

It's a leader's job to encourage others. I give basketball tickets to kids who do well in school. I sponsored a contest last year to take some Phoenix Suns fans to the Finals as a fund-raiser for our foundation. They decorated the chartered airplane with a sign that said, "Flying to the Finals: Turn up the A.C." Everyone on board got a mask with my face on it. I never heard the end of that from Kevin Johnson and the rest of the team.

I was the unofficial sponsor of the Special Olympics in L.A. for three years. I saw champions in every event there, not just those who won but all who showed up. It's true what people say: 90 percent of success is just showing up.

I invest in total strangers. When the L.A. basin was rocked by an earthquake, the foundation used our good name to bridge the gap between businesses and victims. We acquired several trailers for businesses that were shut down and radios for the shelters of the homeless, particularly the Spanish-speaking community, to keep them in touch with the Spanish station that was broadcasting updates for them. After that huge success Circuit City went above and beyond the call of duty and threw in some wide-screen televisions so people could watch the Superbowl at the shelters. A health clinic for low-income families was one of the businesses we helped keep open.

When my basketball season was over, I went to the cities of Piru and Fillmore to see how they were doing. They were so shocked I came. They named it "A.C. Green Foundation for Youth Day" in their cities. It was an honor. They tried to make me out as an example of what one man could do. It reminded me of my "one man" game against Seattle.

The foundation was just a conduit between the needs and the people who were able to meet those needs. It's a team effort, a group effort. Every minute of volunteered time helps, and every cent counts. Because it's a foundation, I can only give a third of the total budget legally. The other two-thirds have to come from grants or individual and business sponsorship. As far as I can see down the road right now, I see myself continuing this work.

PRINCIPLE #52

Help someone, perhaps someone you don't know. You can do something good. You can do something positive. You can put a hand on a young man's shoulder and say, "Keep trying — you have potential."

I tithe not just my money, but also my time, to God's people. I work closely with Greg Ball and Rice Brooks in Champions for Christ. We want to train and develop other athletes to be mighty men and women of God. These athletes have been called from within their generation to become separated, to take a stand for the right and not just talk about it. We help develop them in body, soul and spirit. I want to continue that as long as I can, too, becoming even more involved once my professional basketball days are over.

On our outreach to the Philippines in 1987, Greg, Dave, Eric Knox, Darryl, Tom and the rest of us preached open-air style at a downtown Manila shopping mall. One of the girls who listened was President Aquino's daughter. She was definitely challenged. What a great thing to influence the next generation of a nation's leaders. We helped local ministers led by Pastor Steve Merrill start churches there that now run just over a thousand in attendance between them.

I help my friends with their causes, just as they help me with mine. Not long ago, Kareem made a video for a fashion show and dinner and entertainment benefit for my foundation. Each celebrity signed his or her jacket, and we auctioned them all off.

"A.C., I know you're going to get more for my jacket than for any others," Kareem said on the video. I cracked up. He's still got that competitive, winning edge.

I played in David Robinson's Celebrity Golf Tournament as a favor. It was the first time I had ever golfed. I borrowed clubs that seemed to be made for a midget. Every time I bent down to swing, my knees started talking to me.

"You can get up now," they said. "Quick! Hit the ball and straighten up!"

I used a calculator to keep my score.

"You're getting the hack of it now," guys in my foursome told me.

"Thank you," I said until someone told me it wasn't a compliment.

Finally I did something right. On a hole where a family of quail was trotting around, I smacked the ball a good one.

"You got a birdie!" one of my partners called out.

I grinned from ear to ear, so relieved and happy that I finally did something right. We walked out to take our next shots, and one of my foursome came over to me.

"Here's your birdie," he said, and he laid a dead quail in my hand. They all cheered and got a picture of me with the bird.

VICTORY

Of course, my first and primary responsibility will always be to my own family. I take care of my parents as much as they will allow me, and I teach kids to honor their parents, too.

People today seem happy to blame their own decisions on their upbringing. Immature people don't accept responsibility for themselves, but mature people accept responsibility for every decision, regardless of their background. Forgiveness and love are two of your biggest weapons, even if your parents let you down. Exercise those weapons on your past, and get on with living in the present. Use love actively, not just in words alone.

I told Mom one year that I'd buy her a car for her birthday if she'd pick one out. For weeks, every time I called her, she gave me excuses for not choosing one. Finally she said she just couldn't decide.

Yeah, I thought, she just can't find a car that she can get into when she's wearing her church hats.

"Mom, I'm sending you a ticket to fly down to L.A.," I said. "I'm going to solve that problem."

Sure enough, Mercedes Benz makes a car for women who wear church hats. She flew home, and I shipped one up to her on a train after we made sure it fit. She has driven it proudly ever since.

My father was easier to please. He was getting a little anxious driving his old, perfectly kept cars when Mom had her new, shiny Mercedes parked in the garage. I knew the car he'd always wanted. It was a no-brainer once I got God's green light to buy it for him.

The Suns were playing the Trailblazers in Portland. Since I was going to be in town, my alma mater, Benson High planned a ceremony to retire my high school jersey. Before I got to town, I contacted the Cadillac dealer that my family had driven past for twenty years, right across the street from the high school.

My family and a lot of our friends turned out for the assembly at Benson. The news media, Cadillac management and school officials gladly helped me with my surprise. After I gave the kids a speech about self-esteem, I encouraged them to honor their parents.

"Dad, would you join me up here?" I said at the end.

Dad walked slowly up to the front. He and Steve are so much alike; they soak up attention.

"Dad," I said, "I want to teach these kids a lesson about respect.

Tell me — what kind of car have you always wanted to have?"

After wishing for a Cadillac his whole life, especially one that didn't require monthly payments, Dad suddenly drew a blank. "Well, I don't know, Junior," he said.

The situation was hopeless, so I just shoved the keys into his hand. "Dad, you know what you want," I said. "So just look out those doors at your new car."

Right then the Cadillac people and school officials swung open the huge double doors leading to the parking lot at the back of the gym. Dad turned and smiled, shocked, not knowing what to do. He was as emotional as I'd ever seen him, which wasn't much, but I knew he was either jumping or crying for joy inside. Before he could make it out the doors, the kids swarmed all over the car.

To me that was a metaphor of life. All his life Dad accepted what he had and cherished it. After washing, waxing, tuning up and polishing Buicks, Fords and Chevys his whole life, he was rewarded with the car of his dreams, a fully paid-for Cadillac. It was a great moment for my whole family.

The metaphor stops there. Dad treats that car like the biggest baby. He won't take it out too early in the morning or keep it out too late. And he'll never, ever, skid his tires.

15

RAT IN
THE HOUSE

O K, HERE'S MY last point: What does a champion do with
a rat?

When I bought my home in L.A., my new neighbor-
hood was beautiful, with gardeners working daily on meticulously
manicured lawns and flower beds.

Coming out of an apartment that we decorated to compete in

"Worst Homes and Gardens," I wasn't too concerned that the house was still unfurnished when it came time for Dave and me to move in, so we moved in anyway. From the apartment we took the best seat in the house with us, the recliner. We gave away a lot of things, so I bought almost everything new for the house. Trucks drove up daily to make deliveries of furniture and appliances that Anita Scott had helped me select.

One day I got home and noticed some dirt in the kitchen that at first I thought a delivery man had tracked in. But it looked just like what a giant rat would leave. "Dave, what does this look like?" I said.

"Naw, it can't be," Dave said.

The next day I saw it again.

"Dave, I think we've got a roommate."

"No, please, no," he said.

Drawing on childhood memories, we set traps to catch her. (We assumed it was a her for some reason.) Every night we tried a new food in the trap, and every morning it was gone. The crawly creature enjoyed our games with her — hide and seek, tag and peekaboo.

"What do you want next, ma'am?" we said as we laid out her steak, cheese or New-York-style deli sandwich each night.

We figured she was coming in through the plumbing in the laundry room, where the washer and dryer hadn't yet been delivered. Dave and I piled boxes of soda pop over the holes, but this was a rat on steroids, a real bodybuilder. She ate a hole through the bottom of the cardboard case and made a trail for herself to get in and out.

After a week we took more drastic measures. We set the trap, then stayed up waiting for the rat. We still couldn't catch her. One night Dave went out late with some guys and left me home with her. I know she's got to be around here somewhere, I thought. I was determined to get her. I perched myself on a barstool in the kitchen, turned on a single light and armed myself with one of my size-fifteen shoes and a stick. Nothing could happen in the pantry and laundry room areas without my seeing it.

Midnight passed. 1:00. A shuffle. False alarm, just the ice dropping in the freezer. 2:00. Noise. False alarm again — just a neighbor's sprinkler system turning on. At 2:30 I thought I heard something, but I dismissed it as another false alarm. I went to the back of the house for a few minutes, then started walking toward the kitchen.

Coming around the corner from the living room to get to my stool, I made a right turn into the kitchen. At the same moment, my crawling friend made a left from the pantry, heading toward the laundry room. We met face-to-face and stopped, frozen. I wanted to run.

A rat! I thought.

A giant! she thought.

I'm getting out of here! we both thought at the same time.

I spun around to take off. Wait a minute! I thought. I'm the only one home, and I want this thing out of my house. I spun back around to face her, but she was gone. A little commotion in the laundry room got me back on her trail. I moved the boxes and looked down the hole where the washer would hook up. All I heard was the pattering of her giant feet. Hmm. Sounds like she wears Nikes, too. Once again I blocked the hole, and the next day my washer and dryer came. I never saw her again.

Eventually a real champion draws the line, faces that moment of truth, has a reality check and says enough is enough. I challenge you to live on the championship level of life, to face the rats in your life, the ones eating your lunch and keeping you from reaching victory.

Years ago, before my light came on, I thought I was a good guy. I sat in church, did good things and made fresh resolutions every New Year's Day. But until that switch turned on, I was not in the kingdom of light but in the kingdom of darkness. I needed help.

It's not the do-betters or Mr. Feel Goods who get to heaven. I had to realize I was desperately wicked, sick and evil apart from God. I needed a Savior, but I also needed a Lord. I was looking over a free-throw line with 20-20 vision, but I couldn't see anything important because I was spiritually blind. That blindness had to come to an end. Once I asked Jesus Christ into my life, I could see. I went to the same free-throw line, but I could see from a totally changed perspective.

When it comes to finding our Savior and our Lord, champions are not mediocre. We don't try just to make it into heaven by the seat of our pants. We want to make our lives count for something.

We face the reality that we're going to give an account for our lives.

You may go through some chaos the way I did when I faced that rat. I challenge you to endure the chaos, pull yourself up to the line and muster the courage to take the shot. Draw a line with sin, with weakness, compromise and procrastination. Don't settle for being free from sin. Go beyond that and get cleansed. Don't be satisfied because you've got some ticket to heaven that's non-changeable and nonrefundable. Get on track with what God has for your life. Doing His will, and His alone, will give you the most fulfillment of all. It's never too late and never too early to go the whole distance. It starts when you draw the line and say, "No more of the old. I want to live the life of a champion." Then you're on your road to victory.

If you have never asked Jesus Christ to be your Savior and Lord, you're not even in the game yet. You can read what the Bible says about why and how to do this in John 3:3 and 16 and in Romans 10:9 and 10. To get started, pray this prayer:

God, I realize my spiritual house is overrun with rats. I'm a sinner. I don't want any more rat parties at my expense. I want to become a champion, to fulfill my purpose in life. I admit that Jesus Christ is Your Son and that He promised to forgive me if I just asked. Please forgive me today for everything I've ever thought, done or wanted to do that was wrong and selfish. Forgive me for sinning, for compromising, for not pursuing a championship level in life. Wipe it out with your super weapon of forgiveness. Please clean my house and move in as Lord. I humble myself and admit that I need Your help to become a true champion in life. Please take me, change my life and bring me into total victory. Thank You, Lord. Amen.

STUDY QUESTIONS

PRINCIPLES
FOR
CHAMPIONSHIP
LIVING

Chapter 1

Steps for Champions

1. See how God's grace protects you. Realize that God's grace has kept you for a purpose that only you can accomplish.

2. Discipline will preserve you. Accept discipline from others and develop self-discipline. Start your arsenal of championship weaponry with discipline.

3. Don't settle for anything less than victory. Admit that you desire to win, to be a champion. That's the first, small step toward achieving victory. If your desire has been trampled down, ask God to revive it and make it strong again.

Questions for Thought

1. What was your worst accident ever? How has God's grace kept you from disaster?

2. Have you ever pushed your luck because you didn't get caught at first? How does that attitude stop you from having a championship attitude?

3. Parents aren't the only ones who bring discipline. Who has ever disciplined you? Who disciplines you now? How does self-discipline help make you a champion?

4.   The Bible says a person becomes what he thinks. What do you think about yourself? Do you have a dream of winning? How can you get your dream back if you've lost it? What's the first step you can take toward your dream?

Read: Proverbs 23:7; Romans 5:20; 1 Corinthians 15:10; 2 Timothy 2:15

Chapter 2

Steps for Champions

4.   Get the big picture of life. Spend time in prayer, talking with someone you respect or just getting away from it all to look at the possibilities God has for you.

5.   Find a leader; then follow that leader. Look for someone who is reaching some goals. Remember: peers don't make good leaders.

6.   Never quit, *especially* when you're ahead. Never stop playing until you're past the finish line. If you don't quit, you won't lose.

7.   Learn to live unselfishly. Realize that you can't do it all by yourself. You need the team.

8.   Admit you don't know everything. Open yourself up to learn from others. Develop a teachable spirit.

Questions for Thought

1.   Who was your favorite teacher in school? Why?

2.   Does someone you know act as if they know everything? What don't they know? What about you? What don't you know?

3.   What is the big picture of your life? Who can help you see the big picture? Will you let someone help you?

4.   Do you follow a good leader, a bad leader or no leader? Whom do you think God wants you to follow? Why don't peers make good leaders?

5.   Have you ever quit too soon? What can you do to stop giving up?

Read: Proverbs 4:13; Ecclesiastes 12:1; Jeremiah 24:6-7; Matthew 15:14; John 14:26; Ephesians 4; Philippians 4:13

Chapters 3-4

Steps for Champions

9. Lay a foundation. Only the strongest, best foundation can support the gifts, talents and abilities of a champion.

10. Add courage to your faith. There are no "gimme" victories in life. You must have courage to work for the victory.

11. Have an attitude of respect. Respect life. Respect your opponent. Respect yourself. Victories are not cheap.

12. Purify your motives and your heart. Don't settle for being free from sin. Get a pure desire for victory that wants victory for the Lord's sake, not just for your own.

13. Set goals. Take practical steps to reach each goal — little steps of faith, courage and boldness.

Questions for Thought

1. What was your worst grade or subject to study in school?

2. Do you have a guess, a strong idea or no idea of what your mission is in life? How will you find out for sure?

3. Have you built a strong foundation? What weaknessess do you have? How could Satan use them against you? What can you do today to fix them?

4. If you join a team, do you want to play the game or just be on the team? Do you want to be serious about God, or do you just want to make it to heaven?

5. The Bible says to do your best as if you were doing it for God Himself. Are you doing your best?

Read: Ecclesiastes 9:10; Philippians 3:14; Colossians 3:23; 2 Peter 1:5

Chapters 5-6

Steps for Champions

14. Make true friends. Show yourself friendly to quality people who are working toward finding and fulfilling their destiny. Pray for God to cement your friendship together.

15. You have a destiny to fulfill. You're the only one who can do it. Nothing is more fulfilling personally. And nothing makes a greater impact on the world around you.

16. Accept that you're different from everyone else. Your qualities, talents and gifts enable you to fill perfectly the position God has for you on His team. You're unique. Ttake joy in that.

17. Develop integrity. Integrity is essential in championship-level living. Value your name. Value your reputation.

Questions for Thought

1. Who was your best friend as a child? Who is your best friend (or friends) today?

2. Which of your friends try to help you reach your goals? Which ones stop you? Name some people who would be good, quality friends for you. How can you befriend them?

3. The mission God has for you is just as important as anyone else's mission. How does it make you feel to know that no one else can fulfill *your* mission if you don't do it?

4. What is unique about you? Have people ever tried to make you feel ashamed of it? How could God use your unique qualities to make you a champion?

5. How do lies keep people from achieving victory? Is your word trustworthy to others?

Read: Psalm 25:21; 139; Proverbs 3:5-6; 11:3; 18:24; 22:1, 24; 1 Corinthians 12; James 4:4

Chapter 7

Steps for Champions

18. Admire the talent, but don't copy the character. Don't substitute performance for substance.

19. Find new heroes. Heroes can be dangerous. Find people whose lives match up with how you want to live your own.

20. Make Jesus your biggest hero. He intends for us to look up to Him and copy His works.

21. Identify with something bigger and greater than yourself.

22. Admire the character; don't copy the personality.

Questions for Thought

1. Who were your childhood heroes? Who is your hero today?

2. What is the difference between performance and substance? Whose talent do you admire, but not their character?

3. Do you know someone who copies someone else's personality? If you wanted to copy anyone, whom would you copy?

4. Who or what is bigger than you that you can relate to? How will that make you more of a champion this week?

Read: Luke 17:33; 1 Corinthians 4:2; 2 Corinthians 5:17, 10:7; Galatians 6:15; Hebrews 11:4-40

Chapter 8

Steps for Champions

23. Good health is essential to championship living. Modify your diet. Learn to exercise; find out what your body can handle. Get enough rest. Take vitamins and antioxidants. Get regular checkups. Pray daily for supernatural health.

24. Control your mind and body. Make yourself do what you know to be right, what you know to be the habits of a champion.

25. Will to win. If it's not your desire to fulfill your destiny, your destiny won't be thrown on you.

26. We all have the power of choice, but once used, our choice has power over us. Weigh the consequences of your choices.

27. Practice self-control. Keep your body pure morally. Tolerate others, but don't compromise.

Questions for Thought

1. Who do you think has a "zeal to win"? What motivates them? Do they use their drive for good or bad purposes?

2. Did you ever make a choice that you regretted? What have you allowed to control you? Do you have trustworthy friends or counselors who can help you with your choices? Who are they?

3. Does your diet need changing? What about what you are feeding your eyes and ears? What can you do this week to change it?

4. How do you think self-control over your mind and body helps you become a champion? What steps from this chapter can you apply to control your body? your mind?

Read: Proverbs 4:23; 1 Corinthians 3:16-17; 6:9-20; 9:27; 10:8, 13; 1 Peter 1:13-15; 2:21-24

Chapter 9

Steps for Champions

28. No matter who you are, you have to live by faith. It's hard to trust and believe God in a crisis when you haven't exercised your faith regularly.

29. Look beyond God's provision to the Provider Himself. Remember that the resources ultimately come from Him.

30. Cover yourself in daily prayer. It doesn't matter when you have devotions. Don't be legalistic about it. It's quality, not quantity, that counts. Let the Holy Spirit guide you.

31. Fast for deliverance, direction and decisions. Spend time in prayer when you would normally eat. I try to hear from God. Just about anyone can fast.

32. If you don't work, you don't eat; if you work, you work hard and give God His tithes.

33. Freely give; freely receive. When we don't do either part, we get in God's way. Ask for help. Receive help that's offered.

Questions for Thought

1. What would you do if you became a professional athlete and suddenly had a lot of money? Can you understand why someone would not spend money on himself?

2. In the Bible, Abraham was willing to sacrifice everything for God. What are you willing to sacrifice for Him? Do you have a limit?

3. Can you believe that God wants to provide you with food, clothing and shelter? Is it hard or easy to trust Him to do that? Why?

4. Are you a "river" or a "reservoir"?

Read: Genesis 22:1-14; Psalm 112; Isaiah 55:11; Malachi 3:8-12; Matthew 6:33; 2 Corinthians 8:9; 9:9; Hebrews 4:1-3

Chapter 10

Steps for Champions

34. We reap what we sow. Whatever we do in private, or don't do, will come to light in public. Talent will get you somewhere, but to be a champion you need a firm foundation. Cracks will eventually show up.

35. Don't do it yourself. Get out of your power, intellect and capability and see God's power released. That will always swing the momentum of the war in your favor.

36. The four keys to winning a spiritual war are: Know you have an enemy. Understand your enemy. Know your teammates. Use your arsenal.

37. Learn to recognize the enemy so that whatever he throws at you, you'll be ready.

Questions for Thought

1. Have you ever accomplished something great as an individual or with a team?

2. Do you believe you have an unseen enemy? If so, in what ways does he attack you personally? How can you fight those attacks?

3.	There are no "Lone Ranger Christians." When was the last time you asked God for help and saw Him answer prayer?

4.	How can words fight Satan? What Scripture verses can you use against him? What positive words can you use to boost your faith?

5.	Are you ready for your next unexpected battle? What can you do to get ready?

Read:	Psalm 44:5-8; 34:1; Proverbs 18:20-21; Isaiah 14:12-17; 54:17; Matthew 4:1-11; 10:1; Galatians 6:7-8; Ephesians 4:32; James 4:7

Chapters 11-12

Steps for Champions

38. Pray for courage. Have a positive attitude. Speak positively. Prepare yourself in prayer.

39. Play to win. You can't play for yourself. Numbers don't win. Teams win.

40. One man can affect the many. Make it an individual goal to be a positive impact on others.

41. Honor those who are given charge over you. Respect people in places of authority. When you know your leader has made a bad decision, pray for grace.

42. Become accountable to others. Accountability is just peer pressure used the way God intended — positively. Put just enough pressure on to keep your teammates in check.

Questions for Thought

1. Did you ever play on a team as "we" instead of "I"?

2. What team are you on today? Is it a small church team or a large school or office team? How well do you know your teammates? What can you do to work better together?

3. What one person has affected you most? Was it for good or bad? How can you work today to have a positive impact on others? How does that make you a champion?

4. How do you expect to be treated when you are in a place of leadership? How do you treat authority figures?

5. Have you experienced "peer pressure" in a positive way? How does it help a team effort?

Read: Ecclesiastes 11:9-10; Romans 5:15; 6:16; Hebrews 13:17; 1 Peter 2:13

Chapter 13

Steps for Champions

43.   The devil uses sin and its consequences as leverage against us. When he can't destroy us by circumstances from without, he tries to destroy us by guilt from within.

44.   Repentance is spiritual dynamite. Repenting explodes and disintegrates sin and keeps sin from setting in. Use the power of repentance instead of wallowing around in guilt.

45.   Forgiveness destroys other people's sins. You don't have to suffer bitterness, low self-esteem, feelings of failure and violation. Apply forgiveness, and God will restore what you lost.

46.   Perseverance is a machine gun that doesn't run out of ammo. Something can be a permanent setback or a temporary setback. Let God finish what He starts. Refuse to quit.

47.   Love is bigger than anything else on earth. God's love covers sin. God says He *is* love. When nothing else is possible, God's love prevails.

48.   Intercession works. You have a right to speak the Word of God. Life and death obey the authority of Christ.

Questions for Thought

1. What is the worst thing that has ever happened to you? How did the Lord help you through it? How could He have helped?

2. Are you holding a grudge? How does that keep you from becoming a champion? How can you gain power over that?

3. If something terrible happened to someone you loved today, would you be prepared to pray seriously for them? What can you do today to prepare yourself for setback?

4. Have setbacks taken you further from God or toward Him? Have they been permanent or temporary? Do they still keep you from victory? Has Satan used circumstances or guilt to keep you from God? How can you become guilt-free today?

Read: Psalm 91; Matthew 6:14-15; 10:22; John 11:22; 14:12-14; 20:23; Hebrews 12:15; 1 John 4:7-12

Chapters 14-15

Steps for Champions

49. Follow godly principles in making a decision. Then you won't worry about the outcome. You base your decision on a pure heart and truth — the facts, not the potential.

50. Steps for decision making: Pray privately. Look for professional advice. Look for godly counsel. Watch for the red lights when you're not sure of the green lights. Ask yourself, Is this a decision I can live with? You'll know it's right when you have peace.

51. Everyone has influence, and everyone is responsible for how they use it. If you are a champion, then you are a role model. With that honor comes responsibility to self, to God and to others.

52. Help someone, perhaps someone you don't know. You can do something good. You can do something positive. You can put a hand on a young man's shoulder and say, "Keep trying — you have potential."

Questions for Thought

1. Do you like wrestling? What would you do for a fun night on the town?

2.   What was the last big decision you made? What was the result? What would you do differently if you could? Which of the steps above will you begin using for decision making?

3.   How could you help or influence others? How do you generally use your influence? Does it lead people toward or away from victory?

4.   The Bible says that your words can either build people up or tear them down. Which do you usually do? Is it right or wrong?

5.   What is the greatest lesson you learned from this book?

Read: Proverbs 13:10; 15:22; 20:18; Colossians 3:15; James 1:26-27; 3:1-13

For information about

The A.C. Green Foundation

Programs for Youth

Athletes for Abstinence

contact

575 South Figueroa Street
Suite 2000
Los Angeles, CA 90071

1 800 A C YOUTH
213-622-8326

For information about

Champions for Christ

contact

4505 Spicewood Springs Road
Suite 307
Austin, TX 78759

512-338-0433